William Henry Davenport Adams

St. Paul

his life, his work, and his writings

William Henry Davenport Adams

St. Paul
his life, his work, and his writings

ISBN/EAN: 9783741175824

Manufactured in Europe, USA, Canada, Australia, Japa

Cover: Foto ©Lupo / pixelio.de

Manufactured and distributed by brebook publishing software (www.brebook.com)

William Henry Davenport Adams

St. Paul

ST. PAUL THE APOSTLE.

ST. PAUL:

HIS LIFE, HIS WORK, AND HIS WRITINGS.

By

W. H. DAVENPORT ADAMS,

Author of "*Earth and Sea,*" "*Buried Cities of Campania,*" "*The Queen of the Adriatic,*" *&c.*

"Tum bene de Paulo sensit Deus, ut non solum gentibus hunc magistrum daret, verum etiam ut per eum veritas Christi innotescat spiritualibus in cœlestibus qui sunt principatus et potestates."—ST. AMBROSE, *Epist. ad Ephes.*, iii.

LONDON:
T. NELSON AND SONS, PATERNOSTER ROW;
EDINBURGH; AND NEW YORK.

1875.

TO THE

RIGHT HON. THE EARL OF GLASGOW,

&c. &c. &c.,

THIS VOLUME

IS

(*By Permission*)

MOST RESPECTFULLY INSCRIBED

BY

HIS FAITHFUL, OBLIGED, AND OBEDIENT SERVANT,

𝕿𝖍𝖊 𝕬𝖚𝖙𝖍𝖔𝖗.

Preface.

THE life and character of the Apostle Paul present a singularly interesting subject of study, from the vast influence which they have exercised on modern thought and belief. It is to St. Paul, in fact, that we owe the science of Christian theology. Specially commissioned to undertake the task, and carefully prepared for it by conditions which it is impossible to regard as fortuitous, he filled up, as it were, the grand and complete system whose outlines his Divine Master had sketched, and supplied the comments necessary for a right understanding of our Lord's teaching.* It was St. Paul whom God charged with the enterprise of revealing to the heathen world the perfect beauty of the Divine Life. It was St. Paul who broke down the barrier between the Law and the Faith; who showed that the former was absorbed in, so far as it was not abolished by, the latter. It was St. Paul whose indefatigable enthusiasm raised the fabric of a spiritual society on the foundations of the death and resurrec-

* Consult Reuss, "Histoire de la Théologie Chrétienne au Siècle Apostolique."

tion of Jesus Christ. The career of a man so marvellously gifted, and set apart for the execution of so colossal a work, may well attract, then, the attention of the philosopher, the moralist, the historian, the humble believer, since for each it possesses a peculiar value. Such we find to have been the case from the days when St. Augustine called him the "Master of the World," and St. Chrysostom the "Teacher of the Universe," * down to our own time, when his intellectual development, his life, and the nature of his teaching, have stimulated the inquiries of critics so opposite as M. Renan and Mr. Matthew Arnold. The former, indeed, asserts that "the reign of the Apostle is nearly at an end," † and the latter seeks to prove that his scheme of doctrine has been absolutely misunderstood. ‡ However this may be, their own labours, and the reception accorded to them by the reading public, demonstrate that, in a certain sense, we are all *Paulicians*,— that the world is still under the power of his enthusiasm and his genius.

In the following pages, however, I have not attempted any examination of the Pauline system of theology, or any analysis of the various methods, direct and indirect, by which it has succeeded in permeating Christianity

---

* The Fathers are very copious in their expressions of admiration. For instance: St. Jerome distinguishes four ranks, or classes, of apostles. The first includes those chosen neither by men, nor the man, but by God the Father and Jesus Christ. The second, those who come from God, but through the man (as Joshua through Moses). The third, those who come from the man, and not from God; and the fourth, those who come neither from God, nor the man, nor men, but from themselves. In the first category he places Paul along with the prophet Isaiah.

† Renan, "St. Paul."

‡ Matthew Arnold, "St. Paul and Protestantism," p. 9.

and colouring religious thought. This book has a more modest aim—namely, to set forth in a continuous form the principal incidents of the Apostle's career; to trace his missionary wanderings from land to land; to demonstrate the magnitude and indicate the difficulties of his enterprise; and to furnish a concise introduction to the study of his writings. I know how largely the field has been occupied by the industry and scholarship of Conybeare and Howson;* but it seemed possible, and, at all events, I felt it to be desirable, to undertake, on a small scale and in an unpretending fashion, for the benefit of the general reader or young student, what has been accomplished so elaborately for the advantage of the critic and the divine.

In the present volume, then, I have sought to compile an exact summary of the results of the latest research in connection with the biography of St. Paul.

The original sources of that biography are as follows:—The Acts of the Apostles, attributed to St. Luke, and whose authenticity has never been disputed; the Pauline Epistles, containing several valuable details omitted by the writer of the Acts; the numerous traditions, more or less probable, handed down from the earliest times; the profane history of the stirring age which witnessed the building up of the Christian Church; and the works of geographers and travellers devoted to the cities and countries visited by the Apostle in the course of his journeyings.

These sources have been examined and collated with

* I must not forget another writer of great merit—Mr. Lewin—to whose "Life and Epistles of St. Paul" I have been much indebted.

so much diligence by a host of commentators, that not a stray fact is left to reward the toil of any later gleaner. Of the information thus collected I have made, however, what use I could; and I venture to hope that the following pages will tend to the reader's entertainment and edification. The labour bestowed upon them will not have been in vain, if they should encourage any youthful student to study the character and imitate the example of the great Apostle of the Gentiles; should induce him to follow in the path which he so gloriously trod, to run the race in which he gained so lofty a triumph,—looking, indeed, not to Paul alone, but to Paul's Lord and Master—to "*Jesus* the author and finisher of our faith; who," says the Apostle, "for the joy that was set before him endured the cross, despising the shame, and is set down at the right hand of the throne of God" (Heb. xii. 2). "*So run, that ye may obtain*" (1 Cor. ix. 24).

I have to acknowldge, with many thanks, the valuable suggestions made by the Bishop of St. Andrews, who has kindly favoured me by reading these pages.

W. H. D. A.

Contents.

I.—FROM TARSUS TO DAMASCUS.
THE APOSTLE'S BIRTH—EARLY TIMES—OCCUPATION—TARSUS—JOURNEY TO DAMASCUS—CONVERSION 9

II.—OPENING YEARS OF THE APOSTLE'S MINISTRY.
IN DAMASCUS—RETIREMENT INTO ARABIA—AT ANTIOCH 32

III.—PAUL'S FIRST MISSIONARY JOURNEY.
SALAMIS—PAPHOS—PERGA—ANTIOCH—ICONIUM—DERBE—LYSTRA—JERUSALEM 45

IV.—THE APOSTLE'S SECOND MISSIONARY JOURNEY.
LYSTRA—TROAS—SAMOTHRACE—NICOPOLIS—PHILIPPI—THESSALONICA—BEREA—ATHENS—CORINTH—CENCHREA—ANTIOCH 68

V.—PAUL'S THIRD MISSIONARY JOURNEY.
GALATIA—EPHESUS—TROAS—ILLYRICUM—CORINTH—TROAS—MITYLENE—CHIOS—SAMOS—MILETUS—COS—RHODES—TYRE—PTOLEMAIS—CÆSAREA—JERUSALEM 111

VI.—PAUL'S IMPRISONMENT AT CÆSAREA, AND VOYAGE TO ROME.
CÆSAREA—MYRA OF LYCIA—CNIDUS—THE FAIR HAVENS—PHŒNIX—CLAUDA—MELITA—SYRACUSE—RHEGIUM—PUTEOLI—APPII FORUM—TRES TABERNAS—ROME 175

VII.—LAST YEARS OF THE APOSTLE'S LIFE.

HIS FIRST IMPRISONMENT AT ROME — HIS EPISTLES — HIS TRIAL AND ACQUITTAL—FURTHER APOSTOLIC LABOURS—THE PASTORAL EPISTLES—SECOND IMPRISONMENT—MARTYRDOM... 236

VIII.—THE CHARACTER OF ST. PAUL.

HIS EARNESTNESS—HIS FAITH—HIS TOLERANT AND CHARITABLE SPIRIT—HIS ZEAL TEMPERED BY PRUDENCE—HIS CONTEMPT OF EARTH—HIS YEARNING AFTER HEAVEN... 277

APPENDIX.

I. WRITINGS ATTRIBUTED TO ST. PAUL................................. 307
II. CHRONOLOGY OF THE LIFE OF ST. PAUL............................. 314
III. THE CREED OF ST. PAUL.. 316
IV. AUTHORITIES.. 319

ST. PAUL THE APOSTLE:

HIS LIFE, WORK, AND WRITINGS.

CHAPTER I.

FROM TARSUS TO DAMASCUS.

The Apostle's Birth—Early Times—Occupation—Tarsus—Journey to Damascus—Conversion.

THE great Apostle of the Gentiles,—who, whether we look at the extraordinary success and extent of his missionary labours, or the marvellous energy and logical force of his writings, must be regarded as one of the most illustrious of the world's heroes,—whose name, in the history of Christianity, stands second only to that of his Divine Master, and who was specially chosen by that Master to develop the doctrines he had laid down,—Paul, the great Apostle of the Gentiles, was born at Tarsus, a considerable city in Cilicia (Acts xxi. 30 ; xxii. 3). A legend, recorded by St. Jerome, and seemingly adopted by him, affirms that his birth-place was Gischala in Galilee, and that his parents migrated thence to Tarsus, on its capture by the Romans. But we have the Apostle's express testimony in opposition to this curious fable. His parents were Jews, of the tribe of Benjamin, who had gained, by some unknown means,* the privilege of Roman citizenship; an important circumstance for their illustrious son, as we shall hereafter discover. In fact, the conditions of his birth eminently fitted him for the work he had to do: he was at once a Jew and a Roman; he came of the "chosen people," and yet belonged to the great conquering nation which was rapidly welding the heterogeneous parts of the known world into one vast empire; he possessed all the qualifications of the strictest Hebrew, and enjoyed all the rights and immunities of a Roman citizen. Had he been other than what he was, he would not have successfully fulfilled the important mission entrusted to his burning enthusiasm and powerful intellect.

Why or when the Jewish name of SAUL† was exchanged for the Roman one of PAUL‡ is unknown. We may dismiss, without hesitation, the conjectures of St. Jerome and St. Chrysostom: the former, that it was in honour of Sergius Paulus, the convert of Cyprus (Acts xiii.); the latter, that the Holy Spirit imposed a new name upon the Apostle to signify his entrance upon the service of a

---

* Perhaps by purchase; or Paul's father may have rendered some important service, during the civil war, to a Roman of rank and influence. *See* Lewin, "Life of St. Paul," i. 4.

† That is, *Shaul,* "asked for" (שָׁאוּל),—Greek, Σαούλ.

‡ From *Paulus* comes the diminutive *Paululus,* and thence the double diminutive, *Pauxillus.* Two of his kith and kin bore Roman names, *Junia* and *Lucius.* (Rom. xvi. 7, 11, 21.)

new Master, as was the Roman custom on purchasing a slave. The more probable reason is, that Paul was the name he bore as a Roman citizen, and that he preferred it to his Jewish designation * when he began his missionary labours among the Gentiles.

TARSUS, where he was born, and where he spent his early years, was a considerable and opulent town, very pleasantly situated in a wide, rich plain on the river Cydnus, within sight of the rugged mountain ranges of Cappadocia and Lycaonia. By steep, romantic defiles through this great barrier of peaks and summits, it communicated, in one direction, with Iconium and Lystra; in another, with Antioch. The more famous of these passes were the so-called "Cilician Gates," the "Amanian" and "Syrian Gates." The river Cydnus was celebrated far and wide for ,the icy coldness of its waters, which were fed by the tribute of the perpetual mountain-snows. From bathing in these waters, Alexander the Great on one occasion contracted a dangerous illness. It was at Tarsus Antony met Cleopatra, the voluptuous Egyptian queen, who entertained him with luxurious devices and magnificent pageants. Both history and poetry have immortalized one of her "shows" on the "river of Cydnus":—

> "The barge she sat in, like a burnished throne,
> Burned on the water; the poop was beaten gold;
> Purple the sails, and so perfumèd that
> The winds were love-sick with them; the oars were silver,
> Which to the tune of flutes kept stroke, and made
> The water which they beat to follow faster,
> As amorous of their strokes. For her own person,
> It beggared all description: she did lie
> In her pavilion—cloth-of-gold of tissue—
> O'er-picturing that Venus where we see
> The fancy outwork Nature: on each side her
> Stood pretty dimpled boys, like smiling Cupids,
> With divers-coloured fans, whose wind did seem
> To glow the delicate cheeks which they did cool,
> And what they undid did...."

* As it means "small," he may have used it out of humility.

> "Her gentlewomen, like the Nereides,
> So many mermaids, tended her i' the eyes,*
> And made their bends adornings: at the helm
> A seeming mermaid steers; the silken tackle
> Swells with the touches of those flower-soft hands,
> That yarely frame the office.† From the barge
> A strange invisible perfume hits the sense
> Of the adjacent wharfs. The city cast
> Her people out upon her."‡

The founder of Tarsus was Sardanapalus, King of Assyria, and it seems always to have preserved something of its founder's splendid and luxurious character. But its population was chiefly Greek. As a reward for its fidelity to him, Julius Cæsar bestowed many privileges upon Tarsus; and Augustus made it a "free city" (*urbs libera*), thus preserving to it its own laws and magistrates. It was celebrated for its polite culture and devotion to letters; and Strabo places it above even Athens and Alexandria, as an asylum for, and a patron of, learned men. Here flourished Diodorus and Artemidorus, the grammarians; the Stoics, Athenodorus, the tutor of Augustus, and Nestor, the tutor of Marcellus—he whom Virgil has immortalized in a well-known passage.

Thus Paul spent his early years in a very atmosphere of refined and elegant civilization; and it is impossible but that his strong, eager, and inquiring mind must early have obtained an acquaintance with the Greek philosophy and literature.§ There is no need to suppose that this was very profound; the allusions to Greek poets and writers which occur in his speeches and epistles are not indicative

---

* That is, in the bow of the boat.

† That is, nimbly do their duty.

‡ Shakespeare, "Antony and Cleopatra," ii. 2. The description is borrowed from Plutarch.

§ It is noticeable that Paul's knowledge of the Old Testament seems to have been derived from the Greek version, called the Septuagint (from the seventy writers engaged in the work of translation); since it is from the Septuagint that all his quotations are made.

of any very deep and extensive reading :* probably his knowledge of Greek was—like Shakespeare's knowledge of Latin—not the knowledge of a scholar, but of a quick and discriminative intellect, searching for and acquiring information in every direction.

According to the Hebrew custom, he was brought up to a trade,† as had been the case with Him Whom, in due time, he was to acknowledge as his Lord and Master. He became a maker of tents; tents of a cloth (called *Cilicium*) woven from the hair of a large species of goat indigenous to Asia Minor. Hence, in after-life, when his confession of Christianity had necessarily separated him from his family, and cut him off from his inheritance, he was enabled to support himself and his companions without having recourse to the offerings of the Church. "I have coveted no man's silver, or gold, or apparel," he said to the Ephesians; "these hands have ministered unto my necessities, and to them that were with me" (Acts xx. 33, 34). Not the less was he a firm supporter

---

* The principal allusions occur as follows:—In the address to the Athenians (Acts xvii. 28) is a quotation from the Cilician poet Aratus:—

Τοῦ γὰρ καὶ γένος ἐσμέν.
"For we are also his offspring."

In the argument for the resurrection of the dead (1 Cor. xv. 33), a quotation from the "Thais" of the Greek dramatist Menander:—

Φθείρουσιν ἤθη χρήσθ' ὁμιλίαι κακαί.
"Evil communications corrupt good manners."

And his rebuke to the Cretans is borrowed from the poet Epimenides:—

Κρῆτες ἀεὶ ψεῦσται, κακὰ θηρία, γαστέρες ἀργαί.
"The Cretans are always liars, evil beasts, slow bellies."

† It was a Jewish saying that "He who taught not his son a trade, taught him to be a thief." For allusions to Paul's tent-making, see Acts xviii. 3; xx. 34; 1 Cor. iv. 12; 1 Thess. ii. 9; 2 Thess. iii. 8.

of the righteous law, that the labourer in Christ's vineyard is worthy of his hire (1 Cor. ix. 13, 14; Gal. vi. 6; 1 Tim. v. 17).

Intended by his parents for the honourable position of a Jewish rabbi, he was sent, while still young, to Gamaliel,* one of the most famous of the doctors of the law, and an influential member in the Sanhedrim † (Acts xxii. 3). Thus he acquired an intimate familiarity with the minutest details of the Jewish ritual (Gal. i. 14); ‡ a familiarity which has left abundant traces in his writings.§ There, too, he must first have heard of that new body of innovators,—a small, obscure, and ignorant body,—who professed belief in the supernatural claims of one Jesus of Nazareth, and denied, in many points, the authority of the law, proclaiming its insufficiency to meet the wants and desires of the soul. Paul was fortunate in his master, for none among the "doctors of Israel" were more revered. Gamaliel was one of the seven who alone have been honoured with the title of "Rabban." ‖ Since Rabban Gamaliel died, says the Talmud,

---

* He is supposed to have been the son of Simon, and grandson of Hillel. The Jewish authorities state that he died a Pharisee, about eighteen years before the fall of Jerusalem; the Christians assert that he was baptized by SS. Peter and Paul.—Conybeare and Howson, i. 56.

† This was the highest council of the Jews, composed of chief priests, elders, and scribes, seventy in number, presided over by the high priest, or *nāsī*. As the supreme judicial court, it took cognizance of all offences against the law.

‡ "St. Paul seems to have belonged to the extreme party of the Pharisees, whose pride it was to call themselves 'zealots of the law, zealots of God.' To this party also had belonged Simon, one of the twelve, thence surnamed *the Zealot*."—Lightfoot, "On the Galatians," i. 14.

§ Conybeare and Howson, "Life and Epistles of St. Paul," i. 62.

‖ Paul is supposed to have been sent to the Holy City before he was thirteen. According to a letter of St. Chrysostom's, of which the authenticity is doubtful, he was born in the year 2 A.D.

the glory of the law has ceased. He was fortunate in the place of his training; for upon a mind so enthusiastic and imaginative, JERUSALEM, with its glorious memories, its superb edifices, its striking scenery, could not but have produced a very powerful impression. We can easily imagine with what emotions the young Hebrew, bred up in the very "strictest sect" of Pharisees, gazed upon the noble Temple, which was to the Jew all, and more than all, that the Capitol was to the Roman, or the Acropolis to the Athenian. Emotions partly of pride, partly of sorrow; for if he were proud of the ancient glories of his race, he must have felt saddened when he saw the glitter of Roman spears on the battlements of the city of Zion, and the pomp of Roman governors in its palace-courts.

Sitting at the feet of his renowned teacher, Paul became—who will doubt it?—an earnest and unresting student. He tells us himself that "he made progress in the Jews' religion above many his contemporaries in his own nation, being more exceedingly zealous* of the traditions of his fathers" (Gal. i. 14). He threw himself with all the energy of his fiery nature into the study and defence of these traditions; and, as a natural consequence, grew inflamed with a persecuting zeal against all who presumed to hold them of small account. Nor was he disregardful of the praise of men (Gal. i. 10); which he undoubtedly earned by a conscientious life, by extraordinary learning, by unusual vigour of character.

---

* In the original, περισσοτέρως ζηλωτὴς ὑπάρχων τῶν πατρικῶν μου παραδόσεων, —a zealous assertor or defender of my ancestral traditions; that is, of those of the Pharisees.

We have no means of ascertaining how many years Paul remained at Jerusalem; but it is certain that he had returned to Tarsus, or, at all events, left the holy city, before our Lord's crucifixion. Otherwise, he would assuredly have made some direct reference in his writings to an event so momentous, and in which he would probably have taken part as one of the persecutors of Jesus. There is no reason to believe that he ever saw the Saviour in the flesh; when he remarks, in his First Epistle to the Corinthians, "Have I not seen the Lord?" (ix. 1), he alludes to his vision on the road to Damascus;[*] and in the Second, when he speaks of "having known Christ after the flesh" (v. 16), he refers to his pre-conversion ideas respecting the Messiah.[†] This Pharisaical young Hebrew student, with his deep attachment to tradition, and his pride of birth and race, would assuredly hold himself aloof from the vulgar crowd of Samaritans, "publicans, and sinners" that followed the footsteps of our Lord; and if any rumours reached him of the miracles He was said to be working, would shrug his shoulders in serene contempt of the credulity and ignorance of the multitude.

On his return to the flowery banks of the Cydnus, he must have found that during the years of his studentship many changes had been wrought among his friends; but the only change that had taken place in himself was

---

[*] And to those "visions" and "appearances" of which he speaks in Acts xxii. 18, and possibly on other occasions (*see* 2 Cor. xii.), οὐ μικρὸν δὲ καὶ τοῦτο ἀξίωνα ἦν.—St. Chrysostom, *Homilies*, xxi.

[†] When he supposed him to be simply Jesus of Nazareth. In the original, the words used are κατὰ σάρκα Χριστόν,—not τὸν Χριστόν, *the* Christ. *See* Stanley, "Commentary on the Galatians," *in loco*.

that he had acquired a fuller knowledge of the law, a more burning zeal, a greater strictness of life. And these things marked him out for distinction above his fellows.

Soon after the death of Christ, we meet, pre-eminent in the ministry of the Church, a certain Hellenistic Jew, named Stephen,—who has justly been called, in many respects, the forerunner of St. Paul, and was one of the leading teachers and upholders of the new faith. He especially directed his arguments against the Pharisees, and Libertines, or enfranchised Jews;* urging them with extraordinary eloquence and success. The learned members of the foreign synagogues, and especially of the Cilician, endeavoured to outreason and silence him; but, we are told, were unable "to resist the wisdom and the spirit by which he spake" (Acts vi. 9, 10). We can hardly doubt that in those discussions Saul of Tarsus, who had again returned to Jerusalem, bore a foremost part; and it may be surmised that he shortly afterwards received, as a reward of his zeal, an important appointment from the Sanhedrim.

The Jewish authorities, unable to silence Stephen by argument, resolved upon crushing him by force,—the usual resource of power when unable to refute reason. The great Council was assembled to try him as a blasphemer; and a general excitement prevailed in Jerusalem, where the people, the scribes, and the elders had been stirred up by the artifices of the priests (Acts

* That is, the Western Jews, who generally spoke Greek. They had been expelled from Italy by a decree of the Senate (Tacitus, *Annales*, ii. 85), in A.D. 19. The natives of Palestine, or Aramaic Jews, spoke the Syrian dialect, as well as Greek. *See* Dr. Roberts' "Discussions on the Gospels."

vi. 12). The Council met in the hall *Gazith*, or the "Stone Chamber," which was situated partly within the Temple court and partly without it, to the east of the Most Holy Place. There sat the high-priest, and around him, in a semicircle, the seventy judges; at the gate were placed the armed guards; and in front of the tribunal, Stephen, with a glory upon his face like that of an angel,* stood before his accusers. After these had been heard, the judicial question, to which he was bound to plead, was put by the president: "Are these things so?" Then, with a wonderful eloquence, he began his defence, recapitulating in animated language the principal points of the national history, enlarging upon the privileges, and setting forth the crimes of the race of Israel, and their persecution of the prophets; and especially commenting upon their greatest crime, the consummation of their iniquity, in the rejection of the Messiah, and the murder of the Son of God.†

Filled with a divine anger as he recalled this last terrible manifestation of impenitence, ‡ he suddenly turned from the course of his narrative to inveigh against

* Some commentators think the text (Acts vi. 15) refers only to Stephen's Christian calmness and composure, but it is more reasonable to suppose that the martyr's countenance was kindled with a supernatural radiance.

† It has been remarked that Stephen, in his defence, curiously anticipated, both in form and substance, that of St. Paul. 1st, He engaged the attention of the Jews by adopting the historical method, as St. Paul did in the synagogue at Antioch (Acts xiii. 16-22). 2nd, Compare Stephen's assertion of the true doctrines of the Hebrew faith with that of the Apostle, when addressing Agrippa (Acts xxvi. 22). 3rd, Compare Stephen's language with that used by St. Paul at Athens (Acts xvii. 24). 4th, Compare Stephen's declaration, that the Jews had received but not fulfilled the law, with Paul's, in Romans xi. 17-29. 5th, Compare Acts vii. 44 with Hebrews viii. 5; Acts vii. 5-8 with Romans iv. 10-29; Acts vii. 60 with 2 Tim. iv. 16.

‡ This is the view taken by Neander (p. 92).

his judges as the real and only violators of the law. At this audacious charge they broke forth into a tempest of rage: they "were sawn asunder in their hearts;" they "gnashed on him with their teeth;" they loaded him with threats and curses. But of the tumult which swelled around him Stephen took no heed; he was upheld by a prophetical ecstasy: and looking steadfastly up into heaven, he "saw the glory of God revealed, and Jesus *standing** on the right hand of God,"—as if, says Chrysostom, the Saviour had risen from his throne to welcome and receive his faithful servant.† And as the vision, in all its unutterable splendour, broke upon the martyr's inner sight, he exclaimed aloud, "Behold! I see the heavens opened, and the Son of man standing on the right hand of God!" ‡

This to the Jews was unutterable blasphemy, and their passions could no longer be controlled. "They cried out with a loud voice, and stopped their ears, and ran upon him with one accord." No formal judgment seems to have been pronounced; but the crowd, with the approval of the Sanhedrim, seized upon their victim, dragged him from the council-hall, hurried him through

* In all other places the Saviour is represented as *sitting*; unless, indeed, we interpret Romans viii. 34, and 1 Peter iii. 22, as referring to a standing posture. *See* Pearson, "On the Creeds," art. vi., *Notes.*

† The same explanation of our Lord's unusual attitude is given by Gregory the Great,—"Stephanus stantem vidit, quem adjutorem habuit." So in the Collect for St. Stephen's Day:—"To thee, O blessed Jesus, who standest at the right hand of God to succour all those that suffer for thee."

‡ This is the only time that our Lord is called "the Son of man" by human lips after his ascension. Dean Alford thinks the reason is, that Stephen, full of the Holy Ghost, speaking *now* not of himself at all, but entirely by the utterance of the Spirit, uses the words in which Jesus himself, before this Council, had foretold his glorification (Matt. xxvi. 64).

the streets to one of the gates of the city, and on the rocky brink of the valley of Jehoshaphat—perhaps near the brook Kidron; the exact spot is uncertain—with stones which they gathered from the ground, they stoned to death the first Christian martyr.* His end was worthy of his life, was worthy of a disciple of his Lord; for while the cruel stones rained pitilessly upon him, he turned a loving gaze on the wolfish faces of his murderers, and kneeling down, cried with a loud voice, "Lord, lay not this sin to their charge." Then he fell asleep. †

> "Who best can drink Christ's cup of woe,
>   Triumphant over pain?
>
> "The martyr first, whose eagle eye
>   Could pierce beyond the grave;
> Who saw his Master in the sky,
>   And called on Him to save.
>
> "Like Him, with pardon on his tongue,
>   In midst of mortal pain,
> He prayed for them that did the wrong!" ‡

In this sanguinary and illegal act § Paul was not a whit behind the most violent. He "was consenting unto his death" (Acts viii. 1). Some writers are of opinion that he held a place among the Sanhedrim, and gave his vote

---

* Dean Milman observes:—"Whether legal or tumultuary, the execution of Stephen was conducted with so much attention to form, that he was first carried beyond the walls of the city; the witnesses, whose office it was to cast the first stone, put off their clothes, and, perhaps, observed the other forms peculiar to this mode of execution."—" History of Christianity," i. 365, 366.

† This is the first occurrence of the phrase, "he fell asleep," since applied to the departure of all Christians, but here the more remarkable from the bloody scenes in the midst of which the death took place.—Dr. Smith, "Bible Dictionary," art. *Stephen*.

‡ Bishop Heber, "Hymns and Poems," p. 17 (edit. 1827).

§ Illegal, because the Sanhedrim do not seem to have possessed the power of inflicting capital punishment.

against the martyr; if so, he must have been married, as none but married men could sit in this high council. We take it, however, that at the age of thirty or thirty-one (A.D. 33) Paul would scarcely have been promoted to a post of so much importance. But in some prominent capacity he was undoubtedly present, and "consenting unto Stephen's death." That the event made a deep impression upon him, we know from his pathetic allusion to it in his subsequent vision within the precincts of the Temple:—" And it came to pass...I was in a trance... And I said, Lord, they know that I imprisoned and beat in every synagogue them that believed on thee: and when the blood of thy martyr Stephen was shed, I also was standing by, and consenting unto his death, and kept the raiment of them that slew him." The impression was burned in upon his soul, yet at the time it did not influence his conduct. It in no wise mitigated his fanatic zeal against the Christians. He arrested all he could lay his hands upon; he imprisoned them, and scourged them; when they were condemned to death he voted against them* (Acts xxii. 4; xxvi. 10). And, bitterest of all, he endeavoured to make them blaspheme that Holy Name whereby they were called.

His fame as a persecutor spread far and wide. Even at Damascus, Ananias had heard "how much evil he had done to the saints at Jerusalem" (Acts ix. 13); how he had destroyed those who confessed Christ. Who can wonder that, in after-years, he remembered with keen repentance the immeasurable ferocity with which he had

---

* He was elected a member of the Sanhedrim immediately *after*, if not before, St. Stephen's martyrdom.

persecuted the Church, and laid it waste (Gal. i. 13). Who can wonder that, oppressed with such memories, he declared himself not meet to be called an Apostle, because he had wrought so much woe upon the servants of God (1 Cor. xv. 9)?

Despite of wrong, and torture, and bloodshed, the followers of Christ rapidly increased in number. Like a wave of light, the gospel spread over the land of Judea. Its confessors and witnesses travelled even as far as Phœnicia and Syria. Then Paul addressed himself to his colleagues in the Sanhedrim, and, "breathing out threatenings and slaughter against the disciples of the Lord," of his own accord solicited letters of authorization to the presidents of synagogues at Damascus, that he might be permitted, if he discovered there any Christians, to bring them bound unto Jerusalem (Acts ix. 2; xxii. 5; xxvi. 12). The letters were willingly granted, and the persecutor set forth on his mission of evil; his mind inflamed with the bitterest animosity against every apostate from the faith of their ancestors (A.D. 36).*

But this great enemy of the new faith was suddenly to be converted into its most eloquent and earnest Defender, its greatest and most successful Apostle.

Let us follow him on his road to the Syrian capital. His journey must have brought him, as Conybeare remarks, into the vicinity of the beautiful Lake of Gennesaret, whose smiling shores had been so frequently visited by Christ. We do not know whether he crossed the Jordan where it flows through the deep ravine of the

* The date of Paul's conversion is fixed as the year 36 A.D., by Neander; Archbishop Usher places it in 35; the German, Michaelis, in 37.

Ghor, or where its mazy course brightens the wooded country at the base of snow-crowned Hermon. It is most probable, however, that he went by the usual route, crossing the river by Jacob's Bridge—*Jisr el Yakoob*—and traversing the undulating plain which stretches to the very spurs of Anti-Libanus. It was a six days' journey of 136 miles; and after the Jordan was passed, the principal stations would be at Gadara—where Christ healed the demoniac—at Neve, and at Acre. The country all around is barren and desolate; a region of stony hills and thirsty plains, through which the withered stems of the scanty vegetation hardly penetrate. "Over this desert," says our authority,* "under the burning sky, the impetuous Paul holds his course, full of the fiery zeal with which Elijah travelled of yore on his mysterious errand through the same 'wilderness of Damascus.' 'The earth in its length and its breadth, and all the deep universe of sky, is steeped in light and heat!' When some eminence is gained, the vast horizon is seen stretching on all sides, like the ocean, without a boundary; except where the steep sides of Lebanon interrupt it, as the promontories of a mountainous coast extend into a motionless sea. The fiery sun burns overhead; and that refreshing spectacle is anxiously looked for,—Damascus, seen from afar, within the wild circumference, resting, like an island of paradise, in the green embrace of its radiant gardens."

And here, with Damascus glittering before our eyes, let us pause to think of its history, and survey its streets and gardens. It is the oldest city in the world; older than Abraham, in whose time it

* Conybeare and Howson, "Life and Epistles of St. Paul," i. 94.

would seem to have been already a place of some importance. Its annals began long before the Hellenes had colonized Greece;* nay, it may be, long before the Egyptian monarchs had reared their huge sepulchres on the bank of the Nile. During the period of the Hebrew monarchy it was the head or capital of Syria (Isa. vii. 8); and the ruler of Syria is called the "king of Damascus" (2 Chron. xxiv. 23). But we find that it was sometimes captured by the Israelites; and, during the reigns of David and his successors, was frequently attached to the Jewish territory. About B.C. 740, it was taken by Tiglath-pileser, king of Assyria, and thenceforward it shared the fortunes of the Assyrian monarchy.

Happily for Damascus, it did not occupy a position of any military value, and the storms of war accordingly passed it by, leaving its inhabitants to the peaceful enjoyment of their sunny skies and genial atmosphere, their groves, and gardens, and translucent rivers. Few references to it occur in the classical writers; Pliny mentions it as one of the cities of the Decapolis, and as celebrated for its alabaster. In the days of Paul it was governed by an ethnarch under Aretas, the king apparently of Arabia Nabatæa; but how it had come into the possession of this petty sovereign, history has omitted to record.† It is certain, however, that it was subject to the Roman rule until the reign of Heraclius, A.D. 634, when it was taken by the Saracens; from which time—it has been remarked—as if to compensate for the neglect or indifference of the Romans, it has become "the delight and glory of the East," and Arabian poets have loved to celebrate it as "the terrestrial paradise." A favourite legend relates that Mahomet, while yet a camel-driver from Mecca, was so struck with its beauty, as he looked down upon it from the mountain range, that he turned away without entering the city. "Man can have but one paradise," he said, "and *my* paradise is fixed above." And a modern writer—Mr. Buckle—enraptured with the beautiful prospect, exclaims: "This is indeed worth all the toil and danger it has cost me to come here!"‡

* Gen. xiv. 15; xv. 2.
† It may have been bestowed on Aretas by his patron, the Emperor Caligula, as Wieseler suggests.
‡ Dean Stanley, "Syria and Palestine," 414.

A GENERAL VIEW. 25

From the brink of the last ridge of Anti-Libanus we do indeed survey a scene which the world can scarcely equal.

Graceful minarets and shapely domes, surmounted by gilded crescents, start up in every direction from a labyrinth of terraced roofs, or, like silver shafts and curved diamonds, glitter in the midst of embowering foliage. In the centre of all, says Dr. Porter,[*] stands the noble structure of the Great Mosque, contrasting vividly with the massive towers and heavy battlements of the old castle. Away in the south the eye traces the long narrow suburb of the *Medân*, at whose extremity rises the "Gate of God," where the great pilgrim-caravan, on each returning year, takes leave of the city. Nearly all the buildings of Damascus are snowy white, which furnishes a bold relief against the background of perennial verdure. The fragrant gardens and prodigal orchards, which have been famous from all antiquity, extend on both sides of the Barada[†] for some miles eastward, and cover an area of nearly twenty-five miles in circuit.

Damascus internally is a congeries of narrow and winding streets. It is celebrated, says Colonel Chesney,[‡] for its numerous coffee-houses and shops of confectioners and bakers, besides its profuse supplies of rice, meat, fruits, and vegetables. There are nearly 400 cook-shops, in which ready-made dishes are prepared for sale. Of juster repute are its manufactories of silk, and the skill and artistic elegance of its jewellers and silversmiths: it can also boast of its white and copper smiths, its carpenters, and trunk and tent makers; but especially of its extensive leather manufactures. The Damascene artists are great in leather. They make boots and shoes, and richly embroidered slippers, fit for the feet of Circassian beauties; they make bridles ornamented with cowry shells, and all the trappings of camels, and equipments for a caravan,—tents, net-bags, water-skins, and the like.

Eight synagogues exist in modern Damascus, one Latin and three

---

[*] Dr. Porter, "Five Years in Damascus" (ed. 1855).
[†] The *Abana* of Scripture, and the *Chrysorrhoas* of the classic writers.
[‡] Chesney, "Expedition up the Euphrates."

Franciscan convents, besides four Greek churches, and some others now converted into mosques. Of the latter nearly two hundred may be counted; the finest, to which we have already alluded, was once a cathedral, dedicated to St. John of Damascus; it has a noble dome and two handsome courts. The houses are mostly built of sun-dried bricks, and those of the richer inhabitants are luxuriously fitted up and embellished.

Mr. Eliot Warburton* pronounces Damascus to be even more thoroughly Oriental in character than Cairo itself. It is like a page from "The Arabian Nights," set in motion, and filled with sunny life.

As Paul, breathing threatenings and slaughter, was approaching this beautiful city,—the pearl of the East,—behold, at mid-day, he was suddenly startled by a great light, a glory, which shone from heaven (Acts xxii. 6; xxvi. 13). Wonderful, indeed, must have been that light which could outshine the brightness of an Eastern sun, could out-dazzle the glare of an Eastern noon! So terrible, so awful was it, that Paul's companions fell to the ground in a panic, or stood dumb with amazement (Acts xxvi. 14; ix. 7). "They were afraid;" they instinctively recognized it as a manifestation of supernatural power. Then out of the ineffable radiance came a voice which spoke to Paul, and Paul alone; or which, if heard by his companions, was not understood by them (Acts xxii. 9; ix. 7); probably they were too confused and stunned to heed its utterances.† But clear and distinct

---

* Eliot Warburton, "The Crescent and the Cross."

† The Greek phrase used in the New Testament account implies the *hearing of sound*, but not the *apprehension of its meaning*. When St. Paul says his companions "heard not the voice of Him that spake to me," he means that they heard an inarticulate utterance, but knew not its signification. So a person in a large hall may hear a speaker at the other end without understanding a word he says.

enough were its accents to the arch-persecutor as he lay prostrate on the earth (Acts ix. 6, 8 ; xxvi. 16); and in the light which blinded others, his purged eyes saw plainly the Redeemer whom he had blasphemed. Then he knew that what he had so long derided was very truth ; that Christ had lived, and suffered on the cross, and died, and had risen from the grave to sit at the right hand of the Father.

"Saul, Saul, why persecutest thou me ? it is hard for thee to kick against the goad" (Acts xxvi. 14).

Thus spake the Saviour, making use of the Hebrew tongue, the language he had been accustomed to use to Peter and John ; the language in which, perhaps, he had addressed the blind man by the walls of Jericho, and the woman who washed his feet with her tears.

And Paul, trembling and astonished, said, "Lord, what wilt thou have me to do ?"

"Arise, and go into the city, and it shall be told thee what thou must do" (Acts ix. 6).

Then Saul, suddenly changed in spirit, arose from the earth. He opened his eyes, which had been unable to bear the full splendour of the revelation vouchsafed to him ; but, like one who has gazed on the sun at noon, he could see nothing; all around him was void and darkness ; and his companions were forced to take him by the hand and lead him into Damascus.

And it was thus he entered the city which he had designed to visit with full authority; no longer burning with a bigot's hate, no longer proud of his mission and his power ; but helpless and trembling, like a child guided by the hands of others, he passed under the gateway, and through the street called "Straight," to the house of Judas (Acts ix. 11).

> Here we pause to observe that the street called Straight may still be discovered by the visitor to Damascus. From the Eastern to the Western Gate, a long thoroughfare, called the "Street of Bazaars," strikes through the heart of the city. Both of its gates exhibit evidences of Roman workmanship. That on the west, we are told, is now so blocked up with buildings as to be almost undistinguishable.* That on the east, however, shows distinctly the triple archway: the large central arch opening on the broad central thoroughfare; the lesser arches on each side leading to the side thoroughfares, divided from the central one by colonnades. This, says Porter,† is the *Via Recta*—deriving its name from the directness of its course; and in this street a house is still shown as the house of Judas, which contains a square room with a stone floor, partly walled off as the "Tomb of the Apostle," to receive the offerings of the faithful.

Referring to this extraordinary event, Dean Milman well observes that no other in Christian history, from the apparent improbability of the conversion of so bitter a persecutor, would so demand, if the expression may be used, the Divine intervention, as the conversion of St. Paul.‡ Humanly speaking, a man such as Paul was essentially necessary to the development of the Christian scheme. Neither the self-suggested workings of the imagination, even if coincident with some extraordinary but fortuitous atmospheric phenomena; nor any worldly notion of future aggrandisement at the head of a new and powerful sect; nor that more noble ambition, which might anticipate the moral and social blessings of Christianity, and,

---

* Dean Stanley, "Syria and Palestine," p. 414.
† Porter, "Five Years in Damascus," i. 48.
‡ Dean Milman, "History of Christianity," i. 370, 371.

once conceived, would strike resolutely into the scheme for their advancement,—furnish even a plausible theory for the total change of such a man, at such a time, and under such circumstances. To deny the divine mission of Paul, in whatever manner it occurred, would be, as Dean Milman says, to discard all providential interposition in the design and propagation of Christianity.

And it is to be observed that the revelation to St. Paul was not the effect of any mere trance or ecstasy. The future Apostle was admitted, as it were, into the *visible presence* of the Saviour. He says in his First Epistle to the Corinthians (ix. 1), "Am I not an apostle? have I not seen Jesus Christ the Lord?" And in his famous argument for the truth of the resurrection, he exclaims: "He [the Lord] was seen by Cephas, by James, by all the apostles; and last of all by me, as of one born out of due time" (1 Cor. xv. 5, 7, 8). When the reality of his conversion was doubted by James and Cephas, "Barnabas brought him to the apostles, and related to them that he had *seen* the Lord in the way, and that he had spoken to him" (Acts ix. 27). Ananias recognizes the fact as one confirmed by the divine authority: "The Lord hath sent me [to thee], even Jesus, who *appeared to thee* in the way as thou camest" (Acts ix. 17). And again: "The God of our fathers hath chosen thee, that thou shouldest *see* that Just One, and shouldest hear the voice of his mouth" (xxii. 14). Thus, specially and pre-eminently favoured, chosen by the Lord Himself, Paul went forth on his mission, to plant the gospel of Christ among the nations of the Gentile world.

The signal importance of Paul's conversion, which marks, indeed, an epoch in the history of Christianity, has been clearly demonstrated by an eminent theological writer.* He points out that it is memorable, in the first place, as "a triumph over the enemy." "When God would convert the world, opening the door of faith to the Gentiles, who was the chosen preacher of His mercy? Not one of Christ's first followers. To show His power, He put forth His hand in the very midst of the persecutors of His Son, and seized upon the most strenuous among them." In the second place, Paul's conversion must be regarded as a fitting introduction to the work he was called upon to do. "Who could so appropriately fulfil the purpose of Him who came to call sinners to repentance, as one who esteemed himself the least of the apostles, that was not meet to be called an apostle, because he had persecuted the Church of God? When Almighty God, in His infinite mercy, purposed to form a people to Himself out of the heathen, as vessels for glory, first He chose the instrument of this His purpose as a brand from the burning, to be a type of the rest." And lastly, Paul was rendered, by his previous course of life, a more fitting instrument, after his conversion, of God's purpose towards the Gentiles, as well as a more striking example of it. "His awful rashness and blindness, his self-confident, headstrong, cruel rage against the worshippers of the true Messiah, then his strange conversion, the length of time that elapsed before his solemn ordination,—all this constituted a peculiar preparation for the office of preaching to a lost world, dead in sin.

* Newman, "Parochial Sermons," ii. 97, *et seq*.

It gave him an extended insight, on the one hand, into the ways and designs of Providence; and, on the other hand, into the workings of sin in the human heart, and the various modes of thinking in which the mind is actually trained."

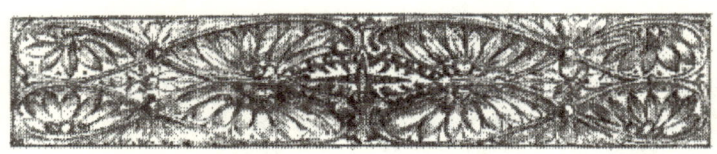

CHAPTER II.

OPENING YEARS OF THE APOSTLE'S MINISTRY.

In Damascus—Retirement into Arabia—At Antioch.

FOR three days Paul remained stricken with blindness. We may well imagine that this interval was allowed him for thought and meditation, and for the full completion of the change which had been wrought in his soul by the wondrous Vision. It is not difficult to conjecture that he must have been torn by overwhelming emotions, when he saw, as in a glass, the whole history of the life of God made man; when he reflected on the stubbornness of his disbelief in that Saviour who had now manifested Himself to his bodily eyes with so awful a revelation; when he remembered the cruelty with which he had persecuted that Saviour's followers, and the manner in which he had consented unto the death of Stephen. So violent were these emotions, that they deadened the natural promptings of the flesh, and for three days Paul neither ate nor drank. He sat in silence and in solitude; he fasted and he prayed. He sought no communion with his fellows; he knew that none could understand or sympathize with the strange phases of his present mental condition. And so the three days passed by, and Paul was alone.

At this time there lived in Damascus a Jew named Ananias, who had become a "disciple" of Christ (Acts ix. 10), and who, by all the Jewish inhabitants of the city, was held in high repute as "devout according unto the law" (Acts xxii. 12). Tradition, which has been so busy with the early Christians, affirms that he afterwards became Bishop of Damascus, and suffered martyrdom—being first tortured and then stoned—during the governorship of Licinius (or Lucianus). But the only authentic record of him which we possess is in connection with Paul's reception into the Christian Church. The Lord, we are told, appeared to this devout Jew in a vision, and bade him seek in the house of Judas for one Saul of Tarsus, for, "behold, he was praying," and had "seen in a vision a man named Ananias coming in, and putting his hand on him, that he might receive his sight." Fully aware of Saul's character as a bitter persecutor, Ananias would fain have declined the mission; but the Lord announced that the former enemy of Christ was thenceforth a changed man, and a man specially chosen to proclaim the truths of God before the Gentiles, and kings, and the children of Israel (Acts ix. 11–16). Therefore Ananias, though, doubtless, with some misgivings, repaired to the house of Judas, and finding the exhausted persecutor, worn with fasting and spent with emotion, he laid his hands upon him, and said: "Brother Saul, the Lord hath sent me, even Jesus, who appeared to thee in the way as thou camest, that thou mayest receive thy sight, and be filled with the Holy

Ghost" (Acts ix. 17). Immediately the scales fell from the eyes of the new disciple, and new hopes entered into his heart. He awoke, as it were, to a new life; and going forth, he was formally received into the Church by baptism;* and having eaten meat, was strengthened for the work he had to do (Acts ix. 18, 19).

How long Paul remained at Damascus after this event, we are unable to determine. It is certain that he began his apostolic mission without delay, bringing to bear in the service of Christ that fiery zeal and unresting energy which he had previously devoted to a very different purpose. At first he was received by the Christians of Damascus with coldness and suspicion, with doubt and amazement; but as he entered the synagogues, day after day, and boldly declared that Jesus, whose servants he had formerly persecuted, was in truth the Son of God, their fears were banished; they owned that the change he had undergone was not the result of a transient impulse, but of deep and earnest conviction; they gladly welcomed this new and important recruit to the thin ranks of the Christian army (Acts ix. 21, 22).

Very different was the effect produced by his conduct upon the unconverted Jews. They were filled with a bitter hatred against this renegade from the old faith, and resolved on his assassination. Happily, he obtained intelligence of their designs, and, " without conferring with flesh and blood," without visiting Jerusalem to con-

---

* Here we may see a significant testimony to the importance of baptism; not even St. Paul, though specially called by our Lord Himself, being allowed to dispense with this " appointed way of admission" into the Church.

sult with those who had been apostles before him, he went into Arabia (Gal. i. 16, 17).

Over this visit to Arabia, as Professor Lightfoot remarks,* a veil of thick darkness hangs. Of the scenes among which he moved, of the thoughts and occupations which engaged him while there, of all the circumstances of a crisis which must have shaped the whole tenor of his after-life, absolutely nothing is known. "Immediately," says St. Paul, "I went away into Arabia." The historian Luke passes over the event without a word of notice. "It is a mysterious pause, a moment of suspense in the Apostle's history; a breathless calm which ushers in the tumultuous storm of his active missionary life."

With what object did he go to Arabia; and what part of Arabia did he visit?

He may either have gone, as St. Chrysostom supposes, to proclaim the gospel in Petra, the city among the rocks, whence "Arabians" sometimes came to the festivals at Jerusalem; or, as seems to us more probable, feeling the need of further solitary communion with God, of further examination of his own heart and conscience, he may have retired to the mountain solitudes of the Sinaitic peninsula. There, in the shadow of Sinai and Horeb, where Moses had received the tables of the Law amid fire, and tempest, and thick darkness,—where Elijah, the "typical prophet," listened to the Divine voice, and then went forth refreshed on his mission of righteousness,—St. Paul, the greatest preacher of Him whom both the Law and the

---

* Lightfoot, "On Galatians," *in loc.* (c. i., verses 17, 18); Rev. J. Ll. Davies, in Smith's "Bible Dictionary."

Prophets foretold, was strengthened and sanctified for his mighty work, was taught the breadth and depth of the riches of God's wisdom, was transformed from the champion of a bigoted and narrow tradition into the Apostle of the universal Gospel.

After his sojourn in Arabia, Paul returned to Damascus, and probably a second time preached in the synagogues of that city, increasing in strength, and confounding the Jewish zealots who sought to oppose him in argument. The old hostility against him soon revived, and again they laid snares for the Apostle's life. To prevent his escape, they kept watch at the gates; and he only eluded their murderous fury through the assistance of his fellow-Christians, who, under the cover of night, let him down in a basket from the wall—that is, from the window of a house overhanging the wall. In their designs against him the Jews had secured the co-operation of the ethnarch who governed Damascus for Aretas the king (2 Cor. xi. 32); but Paul escaped both the Jewish spies and the Arabian soldiers, and went on his way to Jerusalem in safety. Between his conversion and his escape from Damascus a period of nearly three years seems to have intervened (Gal. i. 17, 18).

Paul's motive for visiting Jerusalem was to become acquainted with the great Jewish Apostle, St. Peter, who at this time seems to have been regarded as the principal adviser of the Christian Churches. But when he essayed to join the Apostolic fellowship, he met with cold looks and colder words. He was remembered as a leading spirit of the Sanhedrim, as one of the persecutors of

Stephen, and his profession of faith in Christ was openly discredited. Then Barnabas—destined afterwards to be his fellow-worker and lieutenant, and who appears to have known him at Damascus, and to have become acquainted with his conversion and its results—stood forward as his sponsor. He declared unto the Apostles how Paul had seen the Lord in the way, how he had been privileged to hear the Divine voice, and how at Damascus he had preached boldly in the name of Jesus (Acts ix. 27). Then, indeed, he was gladly welcomed as a fellow-soldier in the great battle, and was constantly in the society of the Apostles,* sharing with them their prayers, their ministrations, their daily labours; and expounding, with fervour and heroic courage, the gospel to all unbelievers.

It is impossible to think, without emotion, of the intercourse which must have taken place between Paul and Peter, between the new convert and the old disciple, between the past persecutor of the Galileans and the saint who had zealously followed the steps of Jesus upon earth. Who but must wish that some faint record of their conversation had descended to our times? What Peter must have had to tell! With what earnest eagerness must Paul have listened! We know something of the impulsive energy and fiery zeal of Peter's character, and can understand with what moving eloquence he would narrate the events of the Saviour's earthly career— His miracles, His teachings, His sufferings, His crucifixion, His ascension. Had Paul wavered or hesitated

---

* Namely, Peter, and James the Lord's brother (Gal. i. 18, 19). No other Apostles seem to have been then at Jerusalem; if so, Paul would have named them.

before, such a narrative—so full, so glowing, so pathetic—would have amply sufficed to confirm his faith.

We may also imagine the deep and tender interest with which the Apostle of the Gentiles visited the places hallowed by their associations with his Lord and Master. The Mount of Olives, the Garden of Gethsemane, Calvary, the new tomb of Joseph of Arimathea—with what new and profound interest must he have gazed upon them! Formerly he had trodden the streets of the Holy City with a bitter scorn and hatred for the unlettered disciples of the Nazarene, with a vehement disbelief in the Divine claims urged by their great Master: now he knew in his heart of hearts that those claims were true; now he was proud to call himself one of the least of these disciples! What thoughts must have risen in his mind as he compared the present with the past! From how intolerable a burden must he have felt relieved! How enthusiastically he must have devoted himself, under the rush of such thoughts and such emotions, to the service of Christ the Lord!

The appearance of Saul the persecutor in the strange character of Paul the preacher aroused the relentless animosity of his former coadjutors, and a plot was formed for his assassination. The brethren urged him to flee, but at first he was reluctant to quit his work in the Holy City. Oppressed and anxious, he sought relief in prayer, and retired into the holy calm of the Temple to commune with his God. And while he prayed, he fell into a trance or ecstasy; and the Lord appeared unto him, saying, "Make haste, and get thee quickly out of Jerusalem: for they will not receive thy testimony concerning me." He hesitated to obey the command, "his desire to do God's will leading him to struggle against the hindrances of God's providence;"* and the memory of Stephen, which still was fresh in his mind, furnishing him with an argument. The reply was a second and more peremptory injunction: "Depart: for I will send thee far hence unto the Gentiles." This was the second intimation which the Apostle received of the peculiar nature of the work to which he was appointed (Acts xxii. 17–21; xxvi. 17).

He now complied with the earnest solicitations of the disciples, and suffered them to convey him to Cæsareia-on-the-sea, or Cæsareia-Stratonis, where he took ship and sailed to Tarsus.

CÆSAREIA-ON-THE-SEA must not be confounded with the smaller and less important city of Cæsarea Philippi, the modern *Banias*. It received its name of Cæsareia from its founder, Herod the Great, in honour of Cæsar Augustus. Its site, we are told,† was formerly occupied by a town named Turris Stratonis, which Herod greatly enlarged, and embellished with palaces of white marble, and other magnificent structures. Its harbour was, in those days, a miracle of engineering science. It was defended from the prevalent south-west winds by a massive breakwater, two hundred feet long, and formed of blocks of stone more than fifty feet in length, by eighteen in width, and nine in thickness, sunk in water twenty fathoms deep. One half of this mole or breakwater was exposed to the billows; the other half was adorned with towers at certain intervals, with a terrace walk commanding a view of the whole harbour, and of the blue sea beyond.

The city, built all of polished stone, encircled the harbour, and was furnished with an agora, or market-place, a prætorium, and other public buildings. Conspicuous on a central mound rose a

---

* Conybeare and Howson, i. 114.
† Dr. Smith, "Dictionary of Greek and Roman Geography," i. 470.

temple of Cæsar, with statues of Rome and the Emperor. A rock-hewn theatre, and a spacious circus to the south of the harbour, completed the adornment of Cæsareia, on the improvement of which Herod spent twelve years of zealous labour, and vast sums of money.[*]

It became, through the agency of Paul, the place where "the door of faith was first opened to the Gentiles;" and remained, for generations, illustrious from the devotion and constancy of its martyrs and confessors.

Its ruins are still of great extent, and more than ordinary interest, and the substructions of the breakwater may readily be traced.

At Tarsus, Paul was once more among the scenes of his childhood. As Conybeare and Howson remind us, it is the last time we are distinctly told he was there. Now, at least, if not before, he would come into direct contact with its philosophers and men of letters, who, according to Strabo, were so zealous in the study of philosophy and the whole circle of education, that they surpassed both those of Athens and Alexandria. Himself of cultivated intellect, and no ordinary acquirements, we may be sure that he met the wise men of Tarsus on their own ground, and demonstrated the vast superiority of the Christian morality to the system of the Stoics and the Epicureans.[†] Nor can we suppose that he neglected to visit the Jewish synagogues, or preach the new faith among his own kinsmen and friends. At this time it may have been that he gathered into the fold of Christ the members of his family whose names have been handed down to us— his sister, and his sister's son. Probably he also travelled about Cilicia and Syria on the same holy and blessed

---

[*] Josephus, "Antiquities," xv. 10; "Wars of the Jews," book i., c. 21, §§ 5, 6, 7.
[†] For proofs of this superiority, see Prebendary Gregory Smith's "Characteristics of Christian Morality" (Bampton Lectures for 1872. London: Parker and Co., 1873).

mission. The fame of his labours, at all events, spread far and wide among the scattered communities of Christians, and though he was personally unknown to them, they felt how precious a reinforcement their cause had gained, and "glorified God in him" (Gal. i. 22–24).

But we must now take leave of Tarsus, and carry the reader with us to the great Pisidian capital, Antioch, or Antiocheia.

> This beautiful city was founded by Seleucus Nicator, who called it after his father Antiochus. It belonged to the Seleucid kings of Syria, until captured by the Romans, who made it a *colonia*, with the title of Cæsarea. It was a place of considerable commerce, and of much luxury. Its public buildings were spacious and handsome; vast and massive walls surrounded it; the country in its neighbourhood was not only fertile but picturesque. The situation of the city was peculiar. It lay in a broad valley, with the Orontes washing its walls on one side, and on the other a rugged barrier of hills, belonging to the Casian range, crowned by towers and ramparts, and adorned with gardens and orchards. On the north, the valley, which opened seaward, was closed in by the bold heights of Amanus.
>
> The remains of Antioch (now Antakia) are numerous, and include a large building, supposed to have been a church, two or three temples, a small theatre, and twenty arches of an aqueduct.*

When Christianity first travelled beyond the borders of Palestine, Antioch was one of the places where it planted itself most firmly. Gentiles as well as Jews became hearers of the Word; and such was the increase in their numbers, that the Apostles at Jerusalem considered it advisable to despatch one of their number on a special mission.

---

* Arundell, "Discoveries in Asia Minor," i. 280, *et sqq.*; Lewin, "Life and Epistles of St. Paul," i. 108, *et sqq.*

For this purpose Barnabas, "the Son of Consolation," —"a good man, and full of the Holy Ghost and of faith," —was selected (A.D. 44). He repaired to Antioch—was much amazed and delighted at the work which had been wrought by the grace of God—and he exhorted the new converts that "with purpose of heart they would cleave unto the Lord" (Acts xi. 23). But soon becoming aware that for the work to be done a stronger than he was needed,—one better fitted to cope with the subtlety and reasoning of the Greeks,—he went away to Tarsus for his friend and fellow-labourer Paul. The two returned together to the Syrian metropolis, where they laboured unremittingly for a whole year (Acts xi. 26), mixing with the constant assemblies of the believers, and teaching "much people." So successful were their joint exertions, that the numbers of the faithful were daily augmented, until they could no longer be confounded with the Jews, but were recognized by the Romans as a sect apart. To distinguish them, a new and ever-famous appellation was invented— a name first given in scorn and derision, but now regarded as honourable above all other names—that of *Christiani*, or *Christians* (Acts xi. 26)*—*i.e.*, the followers, or partisans, of Christ.

The form of the word, we are told,† implies that it came from the Romans, not from the Greeks. "The word 'Christ' was often in the conversation of the believers, as we know it to have been constantly in their letters. 'Christ' was the title of Him whom they avowed as their leader and their chief. They confessed that this

---

* *See* Tacitus, "Annales," xv. 44.—" Quos vulgus Christianos appellabat."
† Conybeare and Howson, i. 130.

Christ had been crucified, but they asserted that He was risen from the dead, and that He guided them by His invisible power. Thus 'Christian' was the name which naturally found its place in the reproachful language of their enemies. It is remarkable that the people of Antioch were notorious for inventing names of derision, and for turning their wit into the channels of ridicule. And in every way there is something very significant in the place where we first received the name we bear. Not in Jerusalem, the city of the Old Covenant, the city of the people who were chosen to the exclusion of all others, but in a heathen city, the Eastern centre of Greek fashion and Roman luxury; and not till it was shown that the New Covenant was inclusive of all others: then and there we were first called Christians, and the Church received from the World its true and honourable name."*

We have now arrived at the age of Claudius, whose reign was marked, either from bad harvests or other causes, by a great number of local famines. In the fourth year of his reign (A.D. 44), the distress, according to Josephus, was so severe, that great numbers perished of hunger. It was at this time that certain " prophets," or expounders of the Word, came down from Jerusalem to Antioch; and one of them, named Agabus, foretold that a season of want and suffering was close at hand (Acts xi. 28). The Gentile Christians of Antioch, inspired by that feeling of charity which the gospel of Christ so warmly inculcates, resolved to minister out of their abundance to the wants of their Jewish brethren at Jerusalem; and their contri-

* The Christians always designated themselves as οἱ μαθηταί, οἱ πιστοί, οἱ ἀδελφοί, and the like. They, however, soon adopted the honourable appellation.

butions were accordingly conveyed to the elders of that Church by the hands of Paul and Barnabas. This was the first practical recognition of the unity which ought to exist between all the members of Christ's Church.* Having discharged their errand,† the two missionaries returned to Antioch, taking with them, as a fellow-worker, John, surnamed Mark, the nephew of Barnabas. Then they resumed their labours, prophesying and teaching, expounding the way of God, and organizing the rapidly augmenting Church.

* Baumgarten comments upon this incident as the first stretching forth of the hand by the Gentile world across the deep gulf which separated it from Israel.

† While they were at Jerusalem, Herod Agrippa (the 'Ηρώδης of the Acts, and 'Αγριππας of Josephus) died (Acts xii. 23), A.D. 44. While sitting in state, in the theatre of Cæsarea, clothed in a robe of silver stuff, he was seized with sudden pains, and died five days afterwards, in exceeding agony (Josephus, *Antiq.*, xix. 8).

CHAPTER III.

PAUL'S FIRST MISSIONARY JOURNEY.

Salamis—Paphos—Perga—Antioch—Iconium—Derbe—Lystra—Jerusalem.

WE now enter upon a fresh development, a new stage, in the career of the Apostle. Hitherto his labours have been confined to a limited sphere; we are now to follow up the extending circle of his operations, as it gradually embraced a considerable portion of the Roman Empire. He is to be recognized henceforth as, emphatically, the Apostle of the *Gentiles*. Events, under the providence of God, had been slowly converging towards one great end,—the revelation of Christ to the outer world. To accomplish this mighty work, St. Paul had been called and chosen, had been instructed and trained, until, with a steadfast faith, and a burning enthusiasm, and a matured intellect, he was fit to gather in the harvest.

It has been well remarked [*] that something of direct expectation—both of the work to be done, and of the workers to do it—seems to have animated the leaders of

---
[*] Rev. J. Ll. Davies, art. *Paul*, in Smith's "Bible Dictionary."

the Church at Antioch while they were "ministering to the Lord, and fasting" (Acts xiii. 2); so that, when the Holy Ghost bade them "separate Barnabas and Saul," it was with instant alacrity, and, seemingly, without surprise, that, after fasting and prayer, they laid their hands upon them, and sent them away. Away,—into unknown lands and unknown cities, to preach the gospel to the heathen,—ignorant of all the trials that were in store for them, though not unconscious, we may be sure, of the danger and difficulty of their enterprise, but relying in the protection of Him whom they so faithfully served! One thing, at all events, was clear to them,—whatever else might be clouded and obscure,—that "they were sent forth to speak the word of God." This was Paul's profound conviction, and in this conviction he lived and taught.

Either by land, along the base of the Pierian hills, or by water, following the sinuous course of the river Orontes, in the shadow of lofty cliffs clothed with the vine, the myrtle, the ilex, and the arbutus, Paul and his companion proceeded to Seleucia, the port of Antioch, from which it was fifteen miles distant.

SELEUCIA was both a fortress and a sea-port; it stood on a rocky eminence, which on the north-east rose into high and craggy summits, and the only easy approach to it was by the level ground on the west, where it was protected by strong artificial defences. Seleucus, its founder, gave his own name to this maritime fortress, this Syrian Gibraltar, which grew in importance under the Seleucidæ and the Ptolemies, and by the Romans was made a free city (*urbs libera*). It retains many interesting memorials of its ancient greatness.

Here they embarked for Cyprus, the native island

of Barnabas, and the scene where they designed to commence their apostolic labours. A few hours' easy sailing brought them to Salamis, the eastern port and ancient capital of the island, which, according to Horace,* was founded by the Greek chieftain Teucer. It occupied the inner sweep of a fine bay, with a background of dark blue mountains sloping downward into a pleasant breadth of orchards and corn-fields. In the days of Paul it was a prosperous town, with a numerous and opulent population, who traded in fruit, flax, wine, and honey; but in the reign of Trajan it was partially destroyed during an insurrection of the Jews,† and an earthquake shortly afterwards completed its ruin. In the Middle Ages it was rebuilt by a Christian emperor, who named it Constantia.

In the synagogues of Salamis the Apostles preached the Word of God, assisted by John who was surnamed Mark; and thence they travelled to Paphos, situated at the south-western extremity of the island, the seat of the Roman government, and the residence of the proconsul,‡ Sergius Paulus. At his court they met with a Jewish sorcerer or astrologer, named Bar-jesus ($\beta\alpha\rho\iota\eta\sigma o\hat{\upsilon}s$), or, in Arabic, Elymas,—that is, "the wise,"—who, when he found the proconsul desirous of hearing the Word of God (Acts xiii. 7, 8), endeavoured to dissuade him. Then Paul, looking intently upon him, from under his overhanging eyebrows, and impelled by the Holy Ghost, exclaimed,—" O thou child of the devil, thou enemy

---

* Horace, "Odes," i. 7, 29.

† The revolt was suppressed by Hadrian, who expelled every Jew from the island.

‡ The proconsul was a civil governor; the propraetor, a military commander.

of all righteousness, full of subtilty and mischief, wilt thou not cease [even in the presence of His servants] to pervert the right ways of the Lord? Behold, the hand of the Lord is upon thee, and thou shalt be blind, not seeing the sun for a season" (Acts xiii. 10, 11). And as the Apostle spake, the judgment came to pass: there fell upon Elymas a mist, and then a total darkness; and he went about seeking some one to lead him by the hand.

The proconsul, already inclined to listen to the teaching of the Apostles,—he seems to have been a man of acute and inquiring intellect,—was convinced by this miracle, and embraced the faith of Christ. It can hardly be doubted that many of his servants and subjects followed his example; and we may well believe that the foundations of Christianity were effectually and boldly laid in Cyprus.

The scholar will always regard with peculiar interest the establishment of the religion of Jesus in a town which had formerly been the seat of the most degrading superstition. Paphos was the principal home of the worship of Aphrodite, or the Paphian Venus, who here, according to the poets, rose from the sea,—

> "To the soft Cyprian shores the goddess moves,
> To visit Paphos and her blooming groves;
> Where to her power an hundred altars rise,
> And breathing odours scent the balmy skies."[*]

The town was accordingly the favourite residence of the lewd and profligate, who resorted to it from all parts of the civilized world. The temple of the goddess was at Old Paphos, now called *Kuklia*, some little distance from the harbour and chief town, New Paphos, now called *Baffa*.

The conversion of Sergius Paulus, it must be noted, is

---

[*] Homer, "Odyssey," viii. 362.

made, by the writer of the Acts, to mark a special crisis in the history of the Apostle. Henceforth the name of Saul occurs no more; henceforth, in the record, Paul takes precedence of Barnabas. "Nothing is said," remarks Llewellyn Davies,* "to explain the change of name. No reader could resist the temptation of supposing that there must be some connection between Saul's new name and that of his distinguished Roman convert. But on reflection, it does not seem probable that St. Paul would either have wished, or have consented, to change his own name for that of a distinguished convert.† If we put Sergius Paulus aside, we know that it was exceedingly common for Jews to bear, besides their own Jewish name, another from the country with which they had become connected. Thus we have Simeon also named Niger, Barsabas also named Justus, John also named Marcus. There is no reason, therefore, why Saul should not have borne from infancy the other name of Paul. In that case he would be Saul among his own countrymen, Paulus amongst the Gentiles. And we must understand St. Luke as wishing to mark strongly the transition point between Saul's activity amongst his own countrymen, and his new labours as the Apostle of the Gentiles, by calling him Saul only during the first, and Paul only afterwards."

Their work in Cyprus done, Paul "and his company" sailed in a north-westerly direction to the harbour of Attaleia, on the coast of Pamphylia,—founded by Attalus Philadelphus, and now named Satalia,—and thence

* Smith's "Bible Dictionary," art. *Paul*.
† Though, as we have already stated, both St. Jerome and St. Chrysostom adopt this explanation.

ascended the river Cestrus some six or seven miles, to the town of Perga.

As Paphos was celebrated for the worship of Venus, so was Perga for that of Artemis or Diana, in whose honour was held a yearly festival, and whose magnificent temple was situated on an eminence at a short distance from the town. The position of Perga was one to charm an artist's eye: it occupied both declivities of a narrow valley, with the Cestrus flowing between, and the snow-capped mountains of the Taurus resting like huge clouds upon the horizon. Its site is now known as *Eski-Kalesi*, where considerable ruins of walls and towers, theatre, stadium, and aqueduct, are still extant.*

Here Mark abandoned the Apostles, and returned to Jerusalem; either because afraid to persevere "in journeyings often, in perils of rivers, and in perils of robbers;" or because drawn back to Jerusalem by the claims of domestic affection. We shall see, hereafter, that his defection deeply wounded the earnest and steadfast spirit of Paul, and led to a temporary estrangement between that Apostle and Barnabas.

The two Apostles, continuing their adventurous journey, arrived at Antioch in Pisidia; a town of some importance, erected by the founder of the Syrian Antioch, and possessing a large population of Greeks, Romans, Jews, and Pisidians. It is represented by the modern *Valobutch*, about six hours distant from Ak-Shero, and easily identified by the ruins of its aqueduct, discovered by Mr. Arundell in 1833.

On the Sabbath following their arrival in this town, Paul and Barnabas repaired to the Jewish synagogue.

The synagogue worship, we may here explain, was

* Sir Charles Fellows, "Asia Minor," pp. 190, 191.

conducted in the following manner:—On entering, the people bowed towards the veil which screened the ark containing the Book of the Law, and took their places in the body of the building. The elders then ranged themselves on a raised platform in the centre; the Pharisees and the wealthy going up to the chief seats immediately in front of the veil. A prayer was said, a psalm sung. Then the *chazzan*, or deacon, drew aside the veil with reverence, and removed from the ark the Book of the Law; which, as he carried it to the platform, where stood the *sheliach*, or officiating minister, every one pressed forward to kiss or touch with his hand.

The sheliach then opened the roll in the sight of all the people, and read the Law of God distinctly, and gave the sense, and caused them to understand the reading (Neh. viii. 4–8); addressing them first in Hebrew, and afterwards in the vulgar tongue. The writings of the prophets formed what may be called a second lesson. Then came an exhortation, or exposition, from one of the elders (Luke iv.); after which the roll of the Law was replaced in the ark, and the service concluded with the reading of prayer.

In the synagogue of Antioch, after the reading of the Law and the Prophets, the elders or rulers of the synagogue sent to Paul and Barnabas,—to whom, as strangers, many eyes had already been directed,—and invited them, if they had "any word of exhortation" or encouragement, to address the people (Acts xiii. 15). Paul immediately stood up, and, with an emphatic gesture of his hand to arouse attention, he delivered a striking discourse, the substance of which has, fortunately, been preserved for us by St. Luke (Acts xiii. 16–41).

Like the discourse which Stephen addressed to the Sanhedrim at Jerusalem, it was founded on the history of the Jewish nation. He referred, in succession, to the exodus from Egypt, to the forty years of toil and wandering in the wilderness, to the conquest of the land of Canaan and its division by lot, to the period of the Judges, the election of the first Jewish king, the accession of David, and the promise of God to raise up a Saviour from the seed of David. Then he spoke of the appearance of John, and the coming of the Saviour; whom they "that dwelt at Jerusalem, and their rulers," had, in ignorance of the voices of the prophets, condemned and crucified. But, though dead, this Saviour had risen from the tomb, and had been seen by many witnesses. Thus were accomplished, he continued, the ancient prophecies. Be it known, then, that through this risen Saviour was henceforth to be preached the forgiveness of sins; and that all who believed in Him should be justified from all transgressions, from which by the law of Moses they could not be justified. Woe unto them who should *not* believe!

This fervid and eloquent address deeply moved the congregation, and many besought Paul to preach again on the following Sabbath; while others, following him into the street, questioned him respecting the solemn truths he had preached, and received an earnest exhortation to continue in the grace of God (Acts xiii. 43).

With what pleasure, as Dr. Arnold remarks,* the

---
* Dr. Arnold, "Sermons," No. xxiv.

Apostles must have observed these hearers of the Word, who seemed to have listened to it with so much earnestness! How gladly must they have talked with them,—entering into various points more fully than was possible in a public address,—appealing to them in various ways which no one can touch upon who is speaking to a mixed multitude! Yet with all their hopefulness and all their pleasure, their knowledge of the heart of man must have preserved them from over-confidence. Therefore, they would implore them to abide in the grace of God; to keep up the impression which had already outlasted their stay within the synagogue; to feed it, and keep it alive, and make it deeper and deeper, that it should remain with them for ever. What the issue was, we know not, nor does that concern us; only we may be sure that here, as in other instances, there were some in whom their hopes and endeavours were disappointed; there were some in whom they were to their fullest extent realized."

So great and so general was the interest excited by this new teaching, that on the following Sabbath the synagogue was crowded, and almost the whole city came together to hear the Word of God (Acts xiii. 44). Not only proselytes were present, but Gentiles; at whose appearance the more bigoted Jews could no longer restrain their fury, but broke out into torrents of invective and blasphemy. Paul was neither cowed nor silenced; but recognizing once for all that his work could not lie among his own countrymen, who had openly rejected him, he exclaimed: "It was necessary that the Word of God should *first* have been spoken to you; but seeing ye put it from you, and judge yourselves unworthy of eternal life, lo, we turn to the Gentiles. For so hath the Lord commanded us, saying,* I have set thee to be a light of the Gentiles, that thou shouldest be for salvation unto the ends of the earth."

We can imagine with what enthusiasm this announcement was received by the Gentiles; how they rejoiced at the brightness of the new day which was dawning on their world. Many became believers; and from one to another the glad tidings spread, like the electric spark from wire to wire, until they were published abroad throughout the entire region.

The Jews had expelled Paul and Barnabas from the synagogue, but with this act of hostility they were not content. Availing themselves of the influence which the female sex enjoyed in the cities of Western Asia, through some "devout and honourable women"—Jewish proselytes—they carried their complaints to the chief men of the city, and raised against the Apostles a storm of persecution which forced them to retire beyond the borders of the colony.

In taking their farewell of Pisidian Antioch, the Apostles, in obedience to their Master's injunction,† lifted up their testimony against its impiety: they shook off the dust of their feet against it. Leaving the infant Church which they had founded filled with joy and the Holy Ghost, and exulting in their new and purer life, Paul and Barnabas once more resumed their pilgrim-staves, and bent their steps eastwards towards Lycaonia. After a brief journey, they arrived at Iconium.

---

* Compare Isa. xlii. 6, and xlix. 6; and Luke ii. 32.
† *See* Matthew x. 14.

VISIT TO ICONIUM.

ICONIUM, the modern *Konía*, in the Pauline era was a commercial centre of very great activity. It was situated on the great line of communication between Ephesus and the western coast of the peninsula on the one side, and Tarsus, Antioch, and the river Euphrates on the other. It continued to preserve its importance for centuries, and, under the Seljukian sultans, played an important part in the foundation of the Ottoman Empire. It is still a large and populous town; the residence of a pasha; contains some Byzantine memorials and inscriptions; and is surrounded by cultivated fields and pleasant gardens.[*]

At Iconium the order of events seems to have closely resembled what occurred at Antioch. The Apostles taught in the Jewish synagogues with characteristic eloquence and characteristic success; great numbers both of Jews and Greeks took up the yoke of Christ, and found it easy to be borne. Encouraged by these evidences of Divine support, they remained in the city for a considerable period, speaking boldly in the name of the Lord, who attested His approval of their mission by the signs and wonders which He allowed their hands to work. Meantime, the unbelieving Jews were busy with their machinations, and contrived to enlist the support of many of the Greeks, so that the town was divided into two factions; and, eventually, the anti-Christian, which was led by the magistrates, proceeded from verbal insults to personal injuries, and Paul and Barnabas only escaped Stephen's fate by a sudden withdrawal from the town.

In connection with Paul's residence at Iconium, a curious legend is recorded by some of the Roman Catholic historians.

When the Apostle arrived at Iconium, a virgin named

[*] Leake, "Asia Minor," p. 48.

Thekla was betrothed to a Greek youth, named Thamyris. Spell-bound by the eloquent appeals of the Christian missionary, whom she heard in a neighbouring house, she remained at her window day and night, forgetful of her earthly passion. By the contrivance of two false disciples, St. Paul was summoned before the Roman proconsul, and, by his orders, cast into prison. Bribing the jailer with her golden ear-rings, she obtained admission to the Apostle, and was instructed by him in the truths of Christianity. St. Paul was next condemned to be scourged and banished, Thekla to be burned; but a terrible earthquake and storm of rain occurring at the intended time of her martyrdom, she escaped, hastened after Paul, and overtook him on the road to Daphne. Thence they travelled together to Antioch, where a certain citizen called Alexander fell in love with Thekla; and, because she resolutely spurned him, exerted his influence to procure her death. She was thrown to the wild beasts; but the lions, refusing to touch her, crouched at her feet; and the monsters in the water died when she entered it, and floated to the surface.

Thekla being thus preserved, was received by a lady, called Tryphœna, into her house,* and in return Thekla instructed her in the truths of the gospel. After this, she repaired to Myra, in Lycia, where she rejoined Paul. Eventually she returned to Iconium, to find Thamyris dead, and to fail in an attempt to convert his mother. Thence she journeyed to Seleucia, and in its neighbourhood lived an anchorite's life, working many miracles,

---

* *See* Jones, "On the Canon," ii. 371. The "Actio Pauli et Theklæ" is given at full length by Jones, who shows that it is not authentic.

and gaining many disciples, until her death at the age of ninety.

From Iconium, Paul and Barnabas travelled into the land of the uncivilized heathen, to Lystra and Derbe, "cities of Lycaonia,"—a cold, cheerless, barren plain among the mountains of Taurus,—where, amongst a rude population, they preached with undaunted faith the truths of Christ.

<small>The exact situation of LYSTRA is unknown; but most writers identify it with the ruins called *Bin-bir-Kilisseh*, near the volcanic mountain of the *Kara-dagh*. The remains of numerous churches have been discovered here. DERBE lay further to the south-west, at *Divlé*, near the lower spurs and buttresses of the great Taurus range.*</small>

A remarkable incident inaugurated the apostolic work at Lystra. A certain man, who had been a cripple from his birth, and had never walked, hearing Paul speak, and looking steadfastly upon the inspired countenance, was so moved and stirred by the words which fell upon his eager ear, that Paul perceived he had faith enough to be healed. Therefore, with a loud voice, he exclaimed: "In the name of the Lord Jesus Christ, Stand upright on thy feet" (Acts xiv. 10). And immediately, with a loud shout of exultant belief, the cripple leaped to his feet, and walked.

Now, of old, it was a tradition that Jupiter and Mercury had descended from Olympus to wander among the hills and plains of Lycaonia;† and the people,

---

* Hamilton, "Researches in Asia Minor," ii. 313.

† "Jupiter huc, specie mortali, cumque parente
   Venit Atlantiades positis caducifer alis."
                              Ovid, *Metam.*, viii. 626, 627.

when they saw this wonder wrought, lifted up their voices, and exclaimed: "The gods have again come down to us in human form." And Barnabas, probably on account of his reverend aspect, they called Jupiter, the Father and Ruler of the Gods; to Paul, on account of his persuasive speech, they gave the name of Mercurius,* the God of Eloquence. In front of the city gates stood a Temple of Jupiter, and its chief priest, hearing of what had taken place, hastened, with bulls and garlands, with musicians and incense-bearers, to do sacrifice in honour of the divine strangers before their residence. As soon as Paul and Barnabas understood the object of the tumult, they hastened forth; they met the singing and dancing procession as it approached the gate or vestibule, which opened from the street into their house, and with garments torn, they rushed in among the people, and cried:—

"Ye men of Lystra, why do ye these things? We also are men of like passions with you; and we are come to preach to you the glad tidings, that you may turn from these vain idols to the living God, who made the heavens, and the earth, and the sea, and all things that are therein. For in the generations that are past, he suffered all the nations of the Gentiles to walk in their own ways. Nevertheless, he left not himself without witness, in that he blessed you, and gave you rain from heaven, and fruitful seasons, filling your hearts with food and gladness."

To this eloquent appeal the people listened, but they listened reluctantly; and though they led away the sac-

---

* "Mercuri facunde nepos Atlantis."—Horace.

rificial victims, it was still with a feeling that they ought to have been offered up to these disguised divinities. Such a feeling, however, like all sudden popular impulses, did not endure. Jewish emissaries came from Antioch and Iconium, and easily excited the minds of the Lystrans against the Apostles; representing, probably, that they accomplished their wonderful works by magical arts, and were the servants and ministers of evil. With the hasty violence of a half-savage race, the Lystrans rise against the men whom they had just been ready to worship, and stoned St. Paul until they thought him dead, when they dragged the insensible body through the city gates, and cast it outside the walls.* There the faithful gathered round him, the men and women whom he had baptized to Christ, and there they sheltered and tended him until he suddenly recovered from his swoon.† By this time the crowd of persecutors had departed, and Paul was able to return into the city. Though persecuted, he was not forsaken; though cast down, he was not destroyed. But it was evident he could no longer remain securely at Lystra.‡ The next day, therefore, he and Barnabas departed for Derbe.

Whether their stay at Derbe were long or brief, the historian does not tell us; but long or brief, the Apostles lost not a moment in fulfilling the great object of their mission. They taught the gospel; they instructed many.

---

* This is the occasion to which Paul alludes in 2 Cor. xi. 25: "Once I was stoned."

† The words of Acts xiv. 20 (ἀναστὰς εἰσῆλθεν εἰς τὴν πόλιν) seem to imply that his recovery was miraculous.

‡ It is supposed that during this first visit to Lystra, Timothy was converted. (Acts xvi. 1.)

Recruits to fight under the new banner of love and mercy they enlisted here as elsewhere; and then, to complete the organization of the Christian communities they had founded, they returned to Iconium—where we may suppose the temporary excitement to have subsided—and Antioch, exhorting the disciples to continue earnest in the faith they had embraced, and reminding them that through much tribulation they must enter into the kingdom of God. The crown was to be worn only by those who did not refuse to bear the cross. In each Church they appointed grave and reverend men to act as overseers (ἐπίσκοποι, Acts xx. 28), ordaining them to their office* with the solemn rites of prayer and fasting, and commending them heartily to the Lord in whom they believed.

Having discharged these important apostolic duties, Paul and Barnabas descended through the Pisidian mountains to the plain of Pamphylia, just as the deeper hues of autumn were beginning to empurple the fruit and embrown the leaves.† It was in this lovely time of the year, while the littoral plain was still blest with the warm breezes of the sea, that they arrived at Perga. Here they preached the Word as usual, but apparently, from Luke's silence, with little success.

From Perga they proceeded to the sea-port of Attaleia.

ATTALEIA, now *Satalia*, is the largest maritime town on the south coast of Asia Minor. It was founded by Attalus Philadelphus,

* They had been previously chosen by show of hands (χειροτονήσαντες).—Acts xiv. 23. At least, such is the interpretation which some authorities put on this passage.
† Conybeare and Howson, i. 213.

king of Pergamus, and perpetuates his name. The coast scenery here is very romantic; long lines of bold and broken cliffs extending on either hand, with numerous calcareous streams falling over them in sparkling and resounding cascades. In the rear is a wide plain, through which the Catarrhactes flows in constantly-shifting channels.

The Apostles took ship at Attaleia, and across the Pamphylian Gulf, and along the picturesque coast of Pamphylia and Cilicia, they sailed to Seleucia, whence they repaired to Antioch.

Immediately on their arrival they gathered together the brethren, and poured into their eager ears the stirring story of all they had done and suffered; of all their trials and successes; of the dangers they had escaped, and the new Churches they had founded; of how the great work of Christianity had been begun among the Gentiles (Acts xiv. 27): and we can well believe that every Christian as he listened felt his faith strengthened, and his hope confirmed.

At Antioch, SS. Paul and Barnabas remained for three years (A.D. 47-50), extending and organizing the Christian community in that wealthy and populous city, and engaged in a religious struggle on the result of which much of the future happiness and prosperity of the Church undoubtedly depended.

The historian of the Acts of the Apostles opens his account of the great contest thus :—

"And certain men* which came down from Judea taught the brethren, and said, Except ye be circumcised after the manner of Moses, ye cannot be saved. When

---

* The "false brethren" (ψευδάδελφοι) of Galatians ii. 4.

therefore Paul and Barnabas had no small discussion and disputation with them, they determined that Paul and Barnabas, and certain other of them, should go up to Jerusalem unto the apostles and elders about this question" (Acts xv. 1, 2).

It is probable that the "certain men" above referred to were converted Pharisees, who had carried into their new religion all the narrowness and intolerance of the old. The Jewish proselytes at Jerusalem had sought from the first to infuse the spirit of Judaism into Christianity; to choke out its free and vigorous life with ceremony and ritual. Before they would admit the Gentiles to be on an equality with themselves, these Judaizing Christians insisted that they should be circumcised; and not content with this, they presumed to assert that circumcision was necessary to salvation,—thus making the blood of Christ of no account. The imposition of such a burden, in direct violation of the spirit of all Paul's teaching, necessarily provoked the Apostle to resistance.

Arriving at Jerusalem, in company with Barnabas, Paul held conferences with the leading members of the Christian community, and to them he expounded the principles of the gospel, as he had preached it—as he was still preaching it—to the Gentiles; these great principles being, the doctrine of grace, and the freedom from the ceremonial law. In this course of conduct he had but one object in view: that the gospel might have free course among the Gentiles; that his past and present labours might not be thwarted by any opposition or misunderstanding.* (Gal. ii. 1-10.)

* Professor Lightfoot, "On Galations," p. 102.

A solemn meeting, or synod, was afterwards held (A.D. 50), at which the apostles and elders (and, most probably, the whole Church) were assembled. The principal speakers were Paul and Barnabas, who again set forth in public the arguments they had previously enunciated in private, and who impressively confirmed their arguments by references to the good work they had done in Christ's name at Paphos, at Iconium, and at Lystra; St. Peter, who gave his decision in favour of Paul and Barnabas;* and James the Just, who, though emphatically, like St, Peter, an Apostle of the Circumcision,† nevertheless protested against the views of the Judaizing Christians.

The result, after much discussion, was an Apostolic decree which relieved the Gentile Christians from the burden of Jewish observances.

And then, says Paul, when James, Cephas, and John, who seemed to be pillars of the new Temple of Christ, perceived the grace that was given unto me, they gave pledges to me and Barnabas that henceforth we should confine ourselves to separate spheres of labour; that they would restrict their mission to the Jews, while we went forth on the more glorious enterprise of converting the Gentile world. (See Gal. ii. 9, 10.)

Accompanied by certain chief men among the brethren, —Judas surnamed Barsabas, and Silas or Silvanus ‡,— and bearing with them the Apostolic letter, Paul and Barnabas returned to Antioch, where they were received

---

* See Acts xv. 11.

† "The representative of the strictest adherence to, and loftiest appreciation of, the pure standard of legal morality."—Dean Alford, "Greek Testament," ii. 165.

‡ A Roman citizen (Acts xvi. 37), supposed to be mentioned again in 1 Peter v. 12.

with the greatest enthusiasm. Judas and Silas encouraged the brethren in the enjoyment of the freedom they had earned by Paul's exertions, and after a few days' sojourn, returned to Jerusalem; leaving the apostles of the Gentiles to continue their missionary labours, and to add daily new members to the Church of Christ (Acts xv. 22–35).

During their further residence, Peter, for some unexplained reason, paid a visit to Antioch (Gal. ii. 11). Here, at first, he lived on terms of cordial fellowship with the Gentile converts: he ate with them and drank with them; he visited them at their houses, and joined with them in their public worship. But certain intriguers came down from Jerusalem,*—men to whom the Law was still more than the Gospel,—and bringing their influence to bear on the impulsive nature of the Apostle of the Circumcision, Peter gradually withdrew himself from the familiar intercourse he had held with the Gentile community.

Such conduct—conduct so timid and vacillating—deeply provoked the earnest, steadfast soul of Paul. And his indignation grew still more intense when he saw that Peter's example was affecting, not only the Jewish converts at Antioch who had hitherto mixed freely with their Gentile brethren, but even Barnabas, his own friend and colleague,—he who had shared with him so many perils and persecutions, and who had so recently gone up to Jerusalem, protesting against this very Judaizing spirit.

* It is not improbable that they came invested with some power from James, which they abused.—Lightfoot, p. 111.

It is not impossible, as Lightfoot remarks,* that this incident, by producing a temporary feeling of distrust, may have prepared the way for the dissension between Paul and Barnabas which shortly afterwards led to their separation.

But neither the powerful influence and many claims of Peter, nor the defection of his fellow-labourer, could shake the manly, steadfast, vigorous mind of Paul. He stood up in defence of the freedom of the gospel, and withstood Peter to his face, because he was in the wrong.

"But when I saw that they walked not uprightly according to the truth of the gospel,"—that they diverged from the straight path of the gospel truth,—"I said unto Peter, before them all, If thou, being a Jew, livest after the manner of the Gentiles, and not as a Jew, why art thou compelling the Gentiles" to adopt Jewish customs? For, take our own case. We were born to all the privileges of the Hebrew race; *we* were not "sinners," as, in our pride and haughtiness, we call the Gentiles. What then? We clearly saw that by the mere observance of the law no man could be justified—that *faith* was the sole means of justification. Therefore, we turned to a belief in Christ the Lord. And thus our Christian profession is in itself an open acknowledgment that such ceremonial observances are empty and profitless. (Gal. ii. 14–16.)

The conduct of St. Peter at Antioch, remarks Professor Lightfoot,† has been a great stumbling-block both

---

* Professor Lightfoot, "On Galatians," p. 112.
† Professor Lightfoot, "On Galatians," pp. 127, 128.

in ancient and modern times. And, certainly, at first sight it seems strange that the very Apostle to whom God had specially granted the revelation that He looks upon nothing He has made as common or unclean, and who, only a short time before this meeting at Antioch, had openly declared himself in favour of Gentile liberty, should have acted in so vacillating and inconsistent a manner. But, in fact, St. Peter's character, as we trace it in the Gospel narrative, explains the apparent difficulty. "It is at least no surprise, that he who at one moment declared himself ready to lay down his life for his Lord's sake, and even drew his sword in defence of his Master, and the next betrayed Him with a thrice-repeated denial, should have acted in this case, as we infer he acted from the combined accounts of St. Luke and St. Paul. There is the same impulsive courage, followed by the same shrinking timidity. And though St. Paul's narrative (in the Epistle to the Galatians) stops short of the last scene in this drama, it would not be rash to conclude that it ended, as the other had ended,—that the revulsion of feeling was as sudden and complete, and that again he went out and wept bitterly, having denied his Lord in the presence of these Gentile converts." *

Thenceforth the two Apostles, who played so great a part in the building up of the Christian Church—though so widely separated in character, and so unequally endowed with intellectual gifts—were divided in their lives as in their work; nor did they meet again until they were called upon, at Rome, to seal with their blood the

* Professor Lightfoot, "On Galatians," p. 129.

testimony they had so heroically borne to the truth of the Gospel of Christ.*

Soon after this memorable event,—when Peter, in all probability, had returned to Jerusalem,—Paul resolved on undertaking another missionary journey. "Let us go again," he said to Barnabas, "and visit our brethren in every city where we have preached the Word of the Lord, and see that they remain constant in the faith" (Acts xv. 36). Barnabas assented, but was fain to take with them his relative John Mark (Acts xv. 37), who, as we have seen, had shrunk from their labours in Pamphylia. An earnest man like Paul could work only with earnest men. He had no sympathy with lukewarm natures like John's. He felt that they are an incumbrance and a hindrance when a great enterprise has to be carried out. It is with the lever of enthusiasm that genius moves the world, and in this timid kinsman of Barnabas enthusiasm was wanting. Paul, therefore, refused his companionship; and the consequence was a "sharp contention," ending in a temporary separation. Accompanied by John Mark, Barnabas set sail for Cyprus; while the great Apostle of the Gentiles, choosing Silas as his colleague, departed through Syria and Cilicia, confirming the Churches (Acts xv. 39–41).

* It is well we should here call the reader's attention to the circumstance pointed out by Conybeare and Howson (i. 242), that Peter, afterwards, was not ashamed to refer the Church to the epistles of his "beloved brother Paul," though in those epistles a censure of himself was recorded. Rightly may this be designated "an eminent triumph of Christian humility and love."

CHAPTER IV.

THE APOSTLE'S SECOND MISSIONARY JOURNEY.

A.D. 50.

Lystra—Troas—Samothrace—Nicopolis—Philippi—Thessalonica—Berea—Athens—Corinth—Cenchrea—Antioch.

> "This is His will: He takes and He refuses,
> Finds Him ambassadors whom men deny;
> Wise ones nor mighty for his saints He chooses,
> No, such as John, or Gideon, or I."
>
> F. W. MYERS, *St. Paul.*

OF the Churches which St. Paul visited, as he traversed the mountain-passes and deep romantic valleys of Cilicia, the historian has preserved no record, but we may well believe that he availed himself of the opportunity of visiting Tarsus, his native city, where many families had already cast aside their idols to worship the only true and living God.

Through that famous gap or portal in the grand mountain-barrier of the Taurus, known to the ancients as the "Cilician Gates,"—a rent or fissure, extending due north and south for some eighty miles,—the wayfarers descended into Lycaonia, and Paul began to approach the well-remembered scenes of his former labours. Near the rocky base of the Kara-dagh, or the "Black Mountain," they came to Derbe, and from thence they repaired to Lystra, where Paul and Barnabas had formerly been welcomed as the deities Mercurius and Jupiter. In this town a prosperous Christian community was established; the seed sown on a previous occasion had taken root and ripened under the Divine blessing. A prominent agent in the work was one Timotheus, the son of a Greek father and a Jewish mother.* He had become a convert on Paul's former visit, and had since laboured so earnestly in the diffusion of the faith of Christ, that his good repute had spread to Iconium. Paul, like all great men, had a quick eye for instruments suitable to the work he wanted done. He approved of the earnestness, sobriety, and regulated enthusiasm of Timotheus, and perceived that he would be a valuable assistant in his missionary labours. Therefore, because of the Jews,—that is, the Jewish Christians,—who were numerous in these parts, and whose scruples Paul did not hesitate to satisfy, he took Timotheus and circumcised him (Acts xvi. 3).†

If this fact, says Llewellyn Davies,‡ had been omitted in the sacred narrative, but stated in some other record, how utterly irreconcilable it would have been considered by censorious critics with the history in the Acts! Paul and Silas were actually delivering the Apostolic decree of

---

* Named Eunice,—who, it is probable, had carefully instructed him in the Old Testament Scriptures (2 Tim. i. 5).

† He was afterwards solemnly ordained by the laying on of hands of the whole assembly of elders, and of the Apostle himself.(1 Tim. iv. 14; 2 Tim. i. 6).

‡ Llewellyn Davies, in Smith's "Bible Dictionary," ii. 740, 741.

freedom of conscience to all the Churches they visited. They were no doubt rejoicing in the liberty which St. Paul's firmness had secured to the Gentiles. Yet at this very time the Apostle had the wisdom of mind and the largeness of heart to conciliate the sympathies of the Jewish converts by circumcising Timothy. Many Jews in Lycaonia were well aware that Timothy's father was a Greek, his mother a Jewess. That St. Paul's principal companion should be one who was uncircumcised, would of itself have been an obstacle to him in preaching to Jews; but it would have been a still greater stumbling-block if that companion were half a Jew by birth, and had professed the Christian faith. Therefore, in this case, St. Paul "became unto the Jews as a Jew, that he might gain the Jews."

Accompanied by Silas and his new colleague, the Apostle traversed Phrygia and the region of Galatia, in each city delivering to the Christian Churches—which "increased in number daily"—the decrees that had been ordained by the apostles and elders at Jerusalem.

Galatia, or Eastern Gaul, is a wide expression, and susceptible of a double interpretation. It may mean either the Roman province, so called, or Galatia proper. The former was of very great extent, including the central regions of Asia Minor; the latter, which is probably the Galatia visited by the Apostles, measured about two hundred miles in length, from north-east to south-west, and had for its three chief towns,—Ancyra, Pessinus, and Tavium. It was occupied by the Gauls in the third century before Christ.

It does not seem that St. Paul had had any intention

of preaching the gospel to the wild Celtic inhabitants of this comparatively unknown region. But he was detained among them by a return of his old malady—" the thorn in the flesh, the messenger of Satan sent to buffet him" (2 Cor. xii. 7),—which may very probably have been some acute epileptic seizure, that at once and completely prostrated his physical strength. Professor Jowett has pointed out that the description of its effects, given in various passages of the Pauline Epistles (Gal. iv. 13, 14; 1 Cor. ii. 3; 2 Cor. i. 8, 9; 2 Cor. x. 10; 2 Cor. xii. 7; and 1 Thess. ii. 18), bears a striking resemblance to Asser's account of the mysterious illness which afflicted Alfred the Great.

In spite of this infirmity, however, he was eagerly welcomed by the Galatians. "They did not despise nor loathe the temptation in his flesh. They received him as an angel of God, even Christ Jesus. They would have plucked out their very eyes, if they could, and have given them to him" (Gal. iv. 14, 15). With all that impetuous eagerness which we commonly attribute to the Celtic character, they embraced the new religion preached to them by the afflicted servant of Christ.

This, Paul's first visit to Galatia, was, in all probability, a very brief one. Having been detained by illness, he would be desirous of resuming his journey as soon as his restored strength permitted; and, all unknown to himself, under Divine guidance, he was pressing towards a broader and more important field of missionary labour in the hitherto unexplored continent of Europe.

At first, indeed, Paul intended to visit the rich and

populous cities which studded the western coast of Asia; but this was not the work reserved for him. He received a special intimation (Acts xvi. 6), which induced him to bend his steps in a different direction. Being on the borders of Mysia, he thought of returning by the north-east into Bithynia, but again was prevented by the "Spirit of Jesus." So passing by Mysia, without attempting to evangelize it, he came down to Troas (Acts xvi. 8).

The full name of the city was ALEXANDRIA TROAS, but sometimes it was called simply Alexandria, and sometimes, as in the New Testament, simply Troas. It was founded by Antigonus, one of the generals of Alexander—who inherited a portion of the great conqueror's empire—and was peopled with inhabitants from the neighbouring cities. Lysimachus altered its name to Alexandria Troas, and embellished it with those public buildings in which the Greeks so greatly delighted. Situated on the Mysian coast, opposite the south-eastern extremity of the island of Tenedos, it became, under the Romans, a very wealthy and important town; it was connected by good roads with many places in the interior, and it was the principal port of communication between Western Asia and Macedonia. For these reasons, Constantine the Great at one time conceived the idea of erecting here the "seat of Empire;" an idea which seems also to have occurred to Julius Cæsar and Augustus, probably influenced by its proximity to the supposed site of ancient Troy.

It is now called *Eski-Stamboul*. Its walls enclose a rectangular area, about a mile from east to west, and nearly a mile from north to south. Its ruins are numerous and considerable; and its harbour may still be traced in a basin about 400 feet long by 200 feet broad. *

While at Troas, all uncertainty as to his future desti-

---

* Lewin, "Life and Epistles of St. Paul," 192, *et sqq.*

nation was dispelled from the mind of Paul by a vision which appeared to him at night; a vision, or unreal apparition, of "a man of Macedonia," who besought him, saying, "Come over into Macedonia and help us."

Paul lost no time in obeying the mysterious summons. With St. Luke * added to his little band, he immediately took ship at Troas, and touching at Samothrace and Neapolis, sailed for Philippi, an important city of Macedonia, and a Roman colony.

SAMOTHRACE is one of the beautiful islands which stud the waters of the blue Ægean; situated to the north-east of Lemnos, and about thirty miles from the coast of Thrace. Its outline is oval, and it measures some eight miles in length by six in breadth.† It is remarkable for its lofty elevation, which renders it a conspicuous landmark to the seamen of the Archipelago; so that Paul must have had it in full view during his voyage from Troas to Neapolis. Homer refers to the prospect which its picturesque summits commanded:—

> "Wondering, he viewed the battle, where he sat
> Aloft on wooded Samos' topmost peak,
> Samos of Thrace; whence Ida's heights he saw,
> And Priam's city, and the ships of Greece."‡

NEAPOLIS, in northern Greece, is the first place in Europe where Paul and his companions landed; a circumstance which ought to render its name familiar to every Christian. It was the port of Philippi, and is now represented, according to the best topographical authorities, by the modern town of Cavallo. Among the principal antiquities are the ruins of an aqueduct, eighty feet in height. The harbour, a mile and a half wide at the entrance, lies on the west

---

* So we may conjecture from the adoption, in Acts xvi. 10, of the first personal pronoun, "We."
† Admiral Smyth, "The Mediterranean," p. 74.
‡ Homer, "Iliad," Book xiii., 12-15 (Earl of Derby's translation).

side of a rocky promontory, whose base is washed by the waters of the Ægean.

Through a defile in the hills passes the tree-shadowed road from Neapolis to PHILIPPI.

As the scene of the great battle between Cassius and Brutus on the one side, and Antony and Octavius on the other,—the great battle which crushed the hopes of the aristocracy of Rome (B.C. 42), —Philippi has always attracted the attention of travellers. Its Turkish name is *Felibidjik*.* It was founded by Philip, the father of Alexander the Great. It lies on a steep hill, which was at one time bordered northward by dense forests, and looks across an undulating and well-watered surface, to the Ægean Sea.

Its site is thickly covered with ruins, and the walls may still be traced through the gates of which Paul and his companion passed to the "prayer-meeting" on the river-side, where they made the acquaintance of Lydia, the Thyatiran vendor of purple. These walls were built by Augustus, who refounded the city soon after his power was firmly established, and, in memory of his great victory over Brutus, endowed it with the privileges of a Roman *colonia*. Traces of a theatre and amphitheatre, erected about the same time, are visible on the north-east side, and the ground is strewed with fragments of columns and slabs of marble.

At the time of Paul's visit to Philippi, the Jewish inhabitants, who were few in number, had no synagogue in the city; but met in a *Proseuchē*, or "Place of Prayer," outside the gate, on the bank of the river Gangites.†
The worshippers were chiefly women; and among them was a Jewish proselytess of Thyatira, who conducted an establishment at Philippi for the sale of the celebrated dyed stuffs of her native city. These, on the Sabbath, were joined by the Apostle, who sat down among them, and poured into their ears the wondrous tale of the life

---

* Leake, "Northern Greece," iii. 215, *et sqq.*
† Conybeare and Howson, i. 315.

and death and resurrection of Christ. And the heart of Lydia was opened, so that she listened willingly to Paul's pathetic eloquence, and finally expressed her anxiety to become a Christian. And straightway, along with her household, she was received into the Church by baptism; and, in proof of her sincerity, she then besought the Apostle to take up his abode in her house so long as he remained in Philippi (Acts xvi. 15, 40).

A few miles from Philippi, among the spurs of the Hæmus range, dwelt a tribe, called the Satræ, who were worshippers of the heathen god Dionysus,* and had among them an oracle of great repute. One of the *hierodules*, or attendants, of this establishment, who was skilled in the art of divination, chanced to come across the path of Paul and his companions as they went to prayer, and felt herself constrained, by an inner power, to acknowledge them as "the servants of the most high God, showing unto men the way of salvation" (Acts xvi. 16, 17). And for several days she followed them to and fro, bearing this testimony involuntarily, or, perhaps, in scorn and derision, until Paul, grieved in spirit, turned round upon her, and exclaimed to the evil demon that possessed her, "I command thee in the name of Jesus Christ to come out of her."

Then, indeed, it was seen that the witness she had borne was literally true; for the evil demon, recognizing the Name of Power, immediately came out of her.

But the masters who owned her—for she was a Thracian slave, hired by some citizens of Philippi to impose on the peasants attending the country market—

* Not the Greek Bacchus, but the prophet-god of the Thracians.

perceiving that all hope of future gain was gone, fell in their rage upon Paul and Silas, dragged them into the Forum, and laid their complaint before the *decemviri*, or magistrates.

"These men," they said, "being Jews, do exceedingly trouble our city, and teach customs which are not lawful for us as Romans to receive or observe."

Such a charge was sufficient to stir up the worst passions of the multitude; and the uproar became so great that the magistrates shrank from doing justice. The Apostles had in no wise disturbed the public peace; yet their clothes were torn off them, they were scourged with many stripes,* and finally they were thrust into prison; where, for their safe custody, the jailer flung them into an inner cell, and made their feet fast in the stocks.

Though thus "shamefully entreated," though spent with ill usage, and bleeding from the scourge, neither Paul nor Silas bated one jot of heart or courage, but strengthened themselves with prayer — raising their voices in praise of God, and filling the vaults of the prison with the echoes of the sacred melody.†

And all the prisoners heard them (Acts xvi. 25).

And suddenly God manifested himself on behalf of His suffering servants. A great earthquake shook the foundations of the prison; and all the doors sprang open; and the fetters were miraculously loosened from the limbs of the captives. Aroused from his sleep, the first thought of the jailer on finding the doors open was, that his prisoners had escaped; and knowing the conse-

---
* Compare Acts xvi. 23, and 1 Thess. ii. 2.
† "In their prayers were singing praises" (προσευχόμενοι ὕμνουν τὸν θεόν).

quences to himself, he drew his sword with the intention of ending his life, when Paul's voice was heard, "Do thyself no harm: for we are all here" (Acts xvi. 28).

The jailer had already felt that the new-come prisoners were no ordinary men. He now called for lights; leaped into the inner prison; and, falling at the feet of Paul and Silas—whom he recognized as, indeed, the messengers of God—he exclaimed, "Sirs, what must I do to be saved?" How simply eloquent, how full of meaning, how all-important in itself, and in its illustration of Paul's cardinal teaching, was the reply: "Believe in the Lord Jesus, and thou shalt be saved." And Paul proceeded to explain what this salvation meant, and what this faith (Acts xvi. 32), until the heart of the rude Roman soldier was touched to the quick. He led them into the outer prison,* and washed the blood from their scourged backs. He and his whole family were next baptized; and afterwards they all retired into his private house, where he set meat before the Apostles, and rejoiced in the knowledge he and his family had received of the way of eternal life.

The next morning, as soon as it was day, the magistrates sent their lictors to the prison with an order for the release of Paul and Barnabas. Perhaps they had gathered a more accurate idea of the true character of the complaint against the Apostles; perhaps they connected their unjust decision with the sudden earthquake, and trembled with superstitious fear lest fresh calamities should occur. Gladly did the jailer convey the intimation of their freedom to the Apostles; but, to his sur-

---

* Dean Alford, "Greek Testament," ii. 183.

prise, he found Paul in no haste to take advantage of it. "They have scourged us uncondemned," he said; "they have scourged *us*, who are Roman citizens,* and have cast us into prison. Now, indeed, conscious of their wrong-doing, they would privily get rid of us; but we were punished openly, and our innocence shall be openly proclaimed: let them come in person, and formally release us."

Great was the alarm of the magistrates when they found that, in their precipitation, they had condemned unheard, and unjustly punished, two Roman citizens. They knew how jealous was the imperial power of the rights and immunities of the *cives Romani;* they knew how far the arm of Rome could reach, and how heavily it could strike. In all haste they repaired to the prison, and petitioned the Apostles to accept of their release. They brought them at once out of the dungeon, and implored them to quit the city.

Before Paul complied with their abject request, he and his companion retired to the house of Lydia, where they addressed the Christian brethren in some farewell words of exhortation (Acts xvi. 40).

In this manner, and under these striking circumstances, was founded the Philippian Church (A.D. 52).

Leaving Philippi, the Apostles † proceeded along the

---

* By the *Lex Valeria*, passed A.U.C. 254, and *Lex Porcia*, passed A.U.C. 506, Roman citizens were exempted from the scourge until the result was known of an appeal to the people.—See Cicero, *Pro Rabirio*, c. 3; *In Verrem*, v. 62, 63.

† Paul and Silas seem to have left Luke behind them at Philippi to make short missionary excursions along the coast. We think Timotheus accompanied them, though some writers represent him as staying awhile with Luke, and afterwards rejoining Paul and Barnabas at Berea.

great Roman road—the *Via Egnatia*, which skirted the sea-coast—and avoided as much as possible the rugged mountain-spurs, to Amphipolis and Apollonia, and thence to Thessalonica.

AMPHIPOLIS was situated on a considerable ascent, which rose from the left bank of the Strymon, some three miles inland from its mouth, and about thirty-three miles from Philippi. Leake describes its position as one of the most important in Greece; for it stood in a pass which traverses the mountains bordering the Strymonic Gulf, and commanded the only easy communication from the coast of that gulf into the great Macedonian plains, which extend, for sixty miles, from beyond Meleinko to Philippi. It was anciently called, from the number of roads converging to it, the "Nine Ways."

"Some of the deepest interest in the history of Thucydides, not only as regards military and political movements, but in reference to the personal experience of the historian himself, is concentrated on this spot. And again, Amphipolis appears in the speeches of Demosthenes as a great stake in the later struggle between Philip of Macedon and the citizens of Athens. It was also the scene of one striking passage in the history of Roman conquest: here Paulus Emilius, after the victory of Pydna, publicly proclaimed that the Macedonians should be *free*. And now another *Paulus* was here, whose message to the Macedonians was an honest proclamation of a better liberty, without conditions and without reserve." *

The exact position of APOLLONIA is not known. It stood somewhere on the Via Egnatia, between Amphipolis and Thessalonica, thirty miles from the former, and thirty-seven miles from the latter. The surrounding scenery is rich in those features which inspire the poet's strain and adorn the painter's canvas: in shining river-waters, foaming through a rocky valley, under the shadow of oaks and plane trees; in lofty mountains, of bold, romantic aspect; in level spaces, smiling with rich verdure; and gently rising hills, clothed with the dark-green olive.

* Conybeare and Howson, i. 341, 342.

AT THESSALONICA.

Thessalonica is the modern *Saloniki* (population, 70,000). It is still the most important town of European Turkey—next to Constantinople—and commands an extensive trade both by land and sea.

Its original name was Therma. Its later appellation it derived from Thessalonica, the sister of Alexander the Great, and the wife of its second founder, Cassander, king of Macedonia. Under the Romans it became the capital of the Macedonian province. It was the scene of the exile of Cicero; and after the battle of Philippi, was visited both by Antony and Octavius. From its position, it was destined to be a great commercial emporium. Half-way between the Adriatic and the Hellespont, it held the keys of the trade of Asia and Europe. A more appropriate starting-point for the apostles of Christianity in Europe could hardly be selected; and hence we may appreciate the full force of Paul's language in his First Epistle to the Thessalonians, that "from them the word of the Lord had sounded like a trumpet, not only in Macedonia and Achaia, but in every place."

Our limits do not permit us to dwell at any length on the history of the various places visited by Paul in the course of his apostolic labours, or that of Thessalonica, from its absorbing interest, would supply us with a sufficient theme for several pages. We cannot deny ourselves, however, a brief reference to the terrible massacre of its inhabitants, executed by order of the Emperor Theodosius, in A.D. 390.

Their great city, the metropolis of all the Illyrian provinces, was at this time protected by strong fortifications and a numerous garrison. In a popular revolt, the Roman general and some of his principal officers were slain. As the authors of the crime could easily have been discovered, an impartial judge would have ordered their arrest, trial, and execution; but the choleric and fiery Theodosius resolved that the blood of his lieutenant should be immediately expiated by the blood of the guilty Thessalonians. In the name of their sovereign, they were treacherously invited to witness the games of the circus; and such was their insatiate avidity for these amusements, that every consideration of fear or suspicion was disregarded by the numerous spectators. As soon as the assembly was complete, says Gibbon, the soldiers, who had been secretly posted round the circus, received the signal of a general massacre.

For three hours the slaughter continued, without discrimination of strangers or natives, age or sex, innocence or guilt: the lowest accounts estimate the number of the slain at seven thousand, while some authorities bring it up to fifteen thousand.

"A foreign merchant, who had probably no concern in the murder of the imperial lieutenant, offered his own life and all his wealth to supply the place of *one* of his two sons. But while the father hesitated with equal tenderness, while he was doubtful to choose, and unwilling to condemn, the soldiers determined his suspense by plunging their daggers at the same moment into the breasts of the defenceless youths." *

When the news of the massacre reached Milan, Ambrose, its illustrious archbishop, with a courage worthy of a Christian prelate, insisted that the emperor should perform a public act of penitence. Stripped of his royal insignia, Theodosius appeared in the midst of the church, and, with sighs and tears, acknowledged the greatness of his sin. Nor was he restored to the Christian communion until he had meditated over the terrible consequences of his unrestrained fury for a period of eight months.

At Thessalonica the Jews had a synagogue, and thither Paul repaired for three successive Sabbaths, reasoning with them out of their own Scriptures, and showing how the prophecies of the Old Testament had been fulfilled in Jesus Christ (Acts xvii. 1–3). He pointed out to them that, according to these very prophecies, it was necessary that Christ should be no triumphant "King of the Jews," leading a warrior host to universal victory, but a Saviour who must needs suffer for the sins of man, and rise again from the dead to comfort man with the certain hope of a resurrection.

As at Antioch, his eloquent teaching—and it was elo-

* Gibbon, "Decline and Fall of the Roman Empire," c. 27.

quent, because he threw into it all the force of his fiery soul and passionate genius—produced a very different effect upon different classes of hearers. All were moved and excited by it, and a large number of Greek proselytes and many devout and influential women accepted it with ardour. On the other hand, the Jews waxed indignant at his declaration against a temporal Messiah and an earthly "kingdom of God." They felt that Judaism was being slowly but surely undermined; and gathering a crowd of idlers and loiterers from the markets and landing-places, they assaulted the house of Jason,* where the Apostle and Silas were lodging, with the view of bringing them before the *demus*, or assembly of the people.

Paul and Silas were absent. But the fury of the mob was not to be denied; and, seizing upon Jason and certain of his brethren, they dragged them before the magistrates on the charge, false but plausible, of having been guilty of treason by asserting that there was another king than Cæsar—namely, Jesus (Acts xvii. 7). As Thessalonica was a "free city," its "politarchs" had the power of life and death; but an erroneous decision in the case of a dispute between two religious sects might, nevertheless, have provoked the anger of the Roman government. They did not, therefore, venture to inflict any punishment on Jason, but contented themselves with "taking security"—in the form, probably, of a deposit of money—from him and his companions, that they would attempt nothing against the supremacy of Rome, nor compromise the peace of the city.

---

* Jason was probably a Hellenist Jew, and his name seems to be the Grecianised form of Joshua. He is supposed to be the Jason of Romans xvi. 21.

But though the danger had temporarily passed over, the position of Paul and Silas was still precarious. They might at any time fall victims to the secret knife, while their longer stay in the city could not advance the good cause, inasmuch as they were bound by the agreement of Jason and his friends to make no further appearances in public. Under cover of night, therefore, they departed in a south-westerly direction to the city of Berœa.

We may remark, however, that Paul was not dissatisfied with the work he had accomplished in Thessalonica. Afterwards, when writing to the Church of the Thessalonians, he referred to it in warm and glowing terms:— "Remembering without ceasing," he writes, "your work of faith, and labour of love, and patience of hope* in our Lord Jesus Christ, in the sight of God and our Father; knowing, brethren beloved, your election of God. For our gospel came not unto you in word only, but also in power, and in the Holy Ghost, and in much assurance; as ye know what manner of men we were among you for your sake. And ye became followers of us, and of the Lord, having received the word in much affliction, with joy of the Holy Ghost: so that ye were ensamples to all that believe in Macedonia and Achaia" (1 Thess. i. 3–7).

BERŒA, now called *Verria* or *Kara-Verria*, is a city of some 20,000 inhabitants, situated on the eastern slope of the mountain range of Olympus, whence it commands a view of an extensive and fertile plain, rich in groves and gardens, and shining with many streams.†

---

* "Your faith, hope, and love: a faith that had its outward effect on your lives; a love that spent itself in the service of others; a hope that was no mere transient feeling, but was content to wait for the things unseen, when Christ should be revealed."—Professor Jowett, *in loco*.

† Leake, "Northern Greece," iii. pp. 290, *et sqq*.

It is one of the most prosperous towns in European Turkey, and surrounded by scenery of a very varied and agreeable character.

At Berœa, as at Thessalonica, there was a synagogue; but its Jewish worshippers were of a nobler character, more desirous of learning the truth, and better acquainted with the Scriptures, which they "searched daily." Paul's preaching attracted numerous listeners, and many of these listeners became believers. And not only did he make converts among the Jews, but also among the Greeks, both male and female. The Thessalonians, however, no sooner heard of his success than they resorted to Berœa, and began to plot and intrigue against him among the ignorant multitude. "The Jews came like hunters upon their prey, as they had done before from Iconium to Lystra." Once more the great Apostle—for, observe, it was against Paul individually that the wrath of the Jews was stirred up—in danger of his life, was hurried away to the sea-shore; leaving Silas and Timotheus behind him for awhile to complete the organization of the Church his labours had founded. Once at the sea-coast, St. Paul's attention was naturally directed to Athens, the great central seat of intellectual culture, and taking ship at Dium, or some neighbouring port, he sailed along the beautiful Grecian coast, and past the rock-bound island of Eubœa, until he reached the famous harbour of the Piræus.

ATHENS, the capital of Attica, the most famous city of ancient Greece, and the fountain of our modern civilization, would supply us with an abundance of subjects for reflection and illustration, if our space permitted us to take them up. Easily might we devote page upon page, and volume upon volume, to its stirring history, to its glorious literature, to the aspirations of its philosophy, to the biographies of its worthies, to the description of its numerous masterpieces of art. And easily, too, might we point the moral and adorn the tale by an examination into the causes which led to its fall from the high place it enjoyed in the world of the past. For it was fallen when visited by the great Apostle; its power and its independence were like vanished dreams; and only its statues, its temples, and its beautiful edifices remained to attest its ancient splendour. To some of these, which Paul must have examined with all the interest and delight of a cultivated mind,—of a mind familiar, moreover, with Greek literature,—we shall briefly direct the reader's attention, prefacing our remarks with that admirable passage in which the glorious city has been so fitly celebrated by the poet of *Paradise Regained*:—

SITUATION OF ATHENS.

" Behold !
Where on the Ægean shore a city stands,
Built nobly: pure the air, and light the soil:
ATHENS, the eye of Greece, mother of arts
And eloquence, native to famous wits,
Or hospitable, in her sweet recess,
City or suburban, studious walks and shades."

ITS MEMORABLE PLACES.

" See there the olive grove of *Academe*,
Plato's* retirement, where the Attic bird †
Trills her thick-warbled notes the summer long;
There flowery hill *Hymettus*, ‡ with the sound
Of bees' industrious murmur, oft invites
To studious musing; there *Ilissus* rolls
His whispering stream:"

THE SCHOOLS OF ITS SAGES.

"Within the walls then view
The schools of ancient sages;—his,§ who bred

---

* Plato, the greatest of the Greek philosophers, flourished about B.C. 427-347.
† The nightingale,—still very frequently found in Attica.
‡ Hymettus was famous for its exquisite honey.
§ Aristotle, the founder of a famous school of logic and criticism, was the tutor of Alexander. He lived B.C. 384-322.

Great Alexander to subdue the world,—
Lyceum there,*—and painted *Stoa*† next:—
There shalt thou hear and learn the secret power
Of harmony, in tones and numbers hit
By voice or hand; and various measured verse,
Æolian charms, and Dorian lyric odes,
And his who gave them breath, but higher sung,
Blind Melesigenes, thence *Homer* called,‡
Whose poem Phœbus challenged for his own:"

ITS TRAGIC DRAMATISTS.

"Thence what the lofty grave tragedians taught §
In Chorus or Iambic, teachers best
Of moral prudence,—with delight received
In brief sententious precepts,—while they treat
Of fate, and chance, and change in human life;
High actions and high passions best describing:

ITS ORATORS.

Thence to the famous orators repair,— ‖
Those ancient,—whose resistless eloquence
Wielded at will that fierce democracy,
Shook the arsenal, and fulmined over Greece,
To Macedon and Artaxerxes' throne:"

ITS PHILOSOPHERS.

"To sage Philosophy next lend thine ear,
From heaven descended to the low-roofed house

---

* The *Lyceum* was a celebrated school, dedicated to Apollo Lyceius. Here Aristotle taught his disciples while walking about,—whence they were named *Peripatetics*.

† The *Stoa Pœcile*, or painted porch. The disciples of Zeno were called Stoics, because he taught them in the Στοα; but the real founders of the sect were his predecessors Cleanthes and Chrysippus.

‡ Homer was born near Smyrna, on the banks of the Meles, and thence called "Melesigenes." The name "Homeros" means, it is said, the "blind man."

§ The three great tragic dramatists were Æschylus (B.C. 525-456), Sophocles (B.C. 495-405), and Euripides (B.C. 480-406).

‖ The most famous orators were Pericles, Demosthenes, Æschines, Themistocles, and Alcibiades. It was Demosthenes who "fulmined over Greece to Macedon."

> Of *Socrates*;* see there his tenement,
> Whom well inspired the oracle pronounced
> Wisest of men ; from whose mouth issued forth
> Mellifluous streams, that watered all the schools
> Of Academics old and new, with those
> Surnamed Peripatetics, and the sect
> Epicurean, and the Stoic severe."†

The ruins of the wall with which Themistocles united the city of Athens to the harbour of the Piræus were, in Paul's time, far more extensive than they now are. Passing these, the Apostle entered the city by the Peiræic gate, and emerging from under the shadow of the black rocks which served as a foundation for the Parthenon, he saw before him the "heaven-kist" Acropolis : its *Propylæa*, or vestibules, enriched with white marble ; every compartment adorned with the finest sculpture; the stately columns, as smooth and polished as when they left the hands of the sculptors in B.C. 457.

The grand staircase in the Propylæa led, on the right, to an elevated wall, on which was erected the small but graceful temple of the Wingless Victory (Νίκη 'Απτερος). Originally it was dedicated to Pallas Athene, the tutelary divinity of Athens, but in course of time the dedication was forgotten, and a new deity was invented. It is supposed to have been erected about the time of Timon, whose period of rule was antecedent to that of Pericles, and whose genius gave the impulse to that long and glorious era now unjustly connected with the latter's name alone. Small in dimensions, this temple is one of the most ancient Greek examples of that beautiful Ionic order which has left too few memorials of its perfection.

The whole area of the Acropolis was covered, in Paul's time, as in our own, with monuments of ancient art ; but in Paul's time they had not suffered from the ignorant fury of barbarian conquerors.

The hill, thus adorned with the finest works of the artistic genius of the Greek, rises high above the city, like the Castle-rock above Edinburgh, and is equally conspicuous from every point. It forms a square and craggy mass, of remarkably bold outline, one hundred and

---

* Socrates flourished about B.C. 468-399. All we know of him is from the writings of his pupils, Xenophon and Plato.

† Milton, " Paradise Regained," Book iv.

fifty feet in height, with a tolerably level summit, one thousand feet in length, and five hundred feet in breadth. Here might the Athenian plant himself, proudly conscious of the glory of his native city, the heir of a thousand memories of pride and power, and survey, as in a panorama, the scene around and beneath,—a scene so full of life, vigour, and motion. Here we may well believe that St. Paul not unfrequently stood, and gazed upon the glowing landscape with mingled emotions and thick-coming thoughts. Yonder, to the south-west, he would see the harbours of Athens, still crowded with the ships of Europe and Western Asia; and beyond, the bright and gleaming deep, to which the city had formerly owed so much of its prosperity and influence. These harbours were three in number: the Phaleros, nearest the city; the Piræus; and the strong defensive port of Munychia. To the east the Apostle's eye would track the wanderings of the sacred Ilissus; to the west, the more direct course of the river Cephissus. Southward his glances rested on the green slopes of Hymettus, whose flowers nourished a winged population, and whose undulating ridge stood out in sharp clear outline against the sapphire sky. To the north-east extended the historic plain of Marathon,—

> "The mountains look on Marathon,
> And Marathon looks on the sea,"—

where Miltiades and his heroes overthrew the Persian hosts. To the west towered the "rocky brow" which commanded the bay of Salamis; the rocky brow where Xerxes sat and counted his thousand ships on the morning of that eventful day which saw them irretrievably shattered and dispersed by the Greek fleet. To St. Paul, as he gazed, may have recurred the lines of the dramatist Æschylus, commemorating the great event:—

> "Deep were the groans of Xerxes, when he saw
> This havoc; for his seat, a lofty mound
> Commanding the wide sea, o'erlooked the hosts.
> With rueful cries he rent his royal robes,
> And through his troops embattled on the shore
> Gave signal of retreat; then started wild,
> And fled disordered."

The most conspicuous object on the Acropolis was the *Parthenon*, or "House of the Virgin," built by the architects Callicrates and

Ictinus, under the superintendence of the great sculptor Phidias. It was the most perfect expression of Greek art, the truest realization of its highest ideal. Nowhere else, we are told, has architecture assumed a greater harmony, been inspired with a nobler serenity, or more successfully combined nobility and grace with truth. Nowhere else has stone so eloquently embodied poetry.

It is built entirely of white marble. The *metopes*, or interspaces of its pediment, are enriched with raised sculptures representing divers religious and historical subjects; and, among others, the combats of the Centaurs and the Lapithæ. At another part was depicted the struggle between Athene and Poseidon for the supremacy of Athens; at another, the birth of Athene, or the presentation of that goddess to the assembled divinities of Olympus.

Within the Parthenon stood the colossal statue of Athene, of ivory and gold, the work of Phidias, unrivalled for its beauty of conception and perfection of execution.

Of two other statues of the goddess the Acropolis boasted. The oldest was preserved in the temple of the *Erechtheium*, which contained, moreover, Athene's mystic olive-tree; it was believed to have fallen from heaven. The third, fashioned from the "brazen spoils" of Marathon, rose conspicuous above all the buildings of the Acropolis, and with spear and shield—the tutelary divinity of Athens—caught the seaman's eye, as his vessel doubled the headland of Sunium, and sailed toward the harbour of the Piræus.

But how shall we enumerate all the wonders of Athens, which must, undoubtedly, have arrested the attention of St. Paul?

We conjecture that he must have seen,—

The grove of Academe, the favourite retirement of Plato, beautifully rich in the dark-green foliage of the olive;

The Lyceum, where Aristotle loved to walk, and where a famous statue of Apollo Lyceius was erected;

The venerable Areopagus, the seat of the Greek court of judicature;

The Pandroseion, dedicated to the nymph Pandrosa;

The Horologium, or octagonal Temple of the Winds, built by Andronicus Kyrrhestes;

The magnificent Temple of Zeus, three hundred and fifty-four feet long, by one hundred and seventy-one feet broad, in whose sanctuary was preserved another of the masterpieces of Phidias, a colossal statue of the god in ivory and gold;

The Temple of Theseus, immediately outside the walls of Athens, —at once a tomb and a temple, a tomb for the hero and a temple to the demi-god, erected a few years after the battle of Marathon; and,

The Choragic Monument of Lysicrates, a circular building of great beauty, exhibiting the best characteristics of the rich Corinthian order.*

But, assuredly, the feature which specially aroused the astonishment of the Christian philosopher and apostle was, the extraordinary number of statues dedicated to gods, and demi-gods, and deified heroes. For the Athenians were *over*-religious. As Paul himself told them, they carried their religious veneration to an excess ($\delta\epsilon\iota\sigma\iota\delta\alpha\iota\mu\omicron\nu\epsilon\sigma\tau\acute{\epsilon}\rho\omicron\upsilon\varsigma$).† In the *Agora*, or market-place, where they met for the purposes of philosophical teaching, idleness, conversation, or business, memorials abounded to Heracles, and Theseus, and others of their reputed worthies; besides statues of Hermes, statues dedicated to Apollo, and the celebrated altar of the Twelve Gods.‡ On the Areopagus, moreover, rose the temple of the great deity, Ares, from whom that eminence had received the name of "Mars' Hill" (Acts xvii. 22). Every public place and building was likewise a shrine or a sanctuary. We are reminded by an eminent authority§ that the Record House was a temple of the Mother of the Gods. The Council House contained an altar of Vesta, and statues of Jupiter and Apollo. The Theatre at the base of the Acropolis was dedicated to Bacchus; and the Pnyx, on whose Bema, or platform, the Athenian orators "fulmined," to Jupiter the Lofty. Even abstractions were deified, and held in religious honour. Altars were erected to Fame, Modesty, Energy, Persuasion, and Pity. Everywhere the Athenian

---

* Compare Leake, "Topography of Athens;" Stuart and Revell, "Antiquities of Athens;" Ferguson, "History of Architecture;" Dr. Dyer, "Ancient Athens;" and art. *Athens* in Smith's "Dictionary of Geography."

† Acts xvii. 22.—*See* Alford, *in loc.*

‡ Wordsworth, "Athens and Attica," p. 129.

§ Conybeare and Howson, L 381, 382.

found some sacred place—some shrine or statue—to remind him of the "immortal gods."

Replete as the whole of Greece was, says Bishop Christopher Wordsworth, with objects of devotion, there were more gods in Athens than in all the rest of the country, and the Roman satirist hardly exaggerated when he declared it was easier to find a god there than a man. This misdirected religious feeling was very grievous to the Apostle, who longed to turn it towards the worship of the only true God; and to this end he began to labour—while waiting for Silas and Timotheus to join him—both in the Jewish synagogues, and among the crowds assembled in the Agora (Acts xvii. 17). In some respects he found a fitting audience, for the Athenians were eager to learn whatever was new in religion or philosophy, though, perhaps, from no better motive than that of curiosity (Acts xvii. 21). And the doctrine which Paul enunciated was, in truth, novel: he spoke of God made Man, of Christ suffering for the sins of His creatures, of His Resurrection from the dead, and the brotherhood of the human race. It has been well said that the philosophers encountered him with contempt, perhaps, but also with curious interest. "The Epicurean, teaching himself to seek for tranquil enjoyment as the chief object of life, heard of One claiming to be the Lord of men, who had shown them the glory of dying to self, and had promised to those who fought the good fight bravely a nobler bliss than the comforts of life could yield. The Stoic, cultivating a stern and isolated moral independence, heard of One whose own righteousness was proved by submission to the Father in heaven, and who had promised to give His righteousness to those who trusted not in themselves, but in Him. To all, the announcement of a Person was much stranger than the publishing of any theories would have been."*

All this was new and striking, and it awakened the curiosity of the speculative Athenians. Here was "a setter forth of strange gods" (ξένων δαιμονίων καταγγελεὺς); might it not be worth while to listen to his babbling? Not, indeed, to profit by it, but to gain some fresh theme for argument or ridicule. They took him, therefore, to the Areopagus, as to a place where a large assembly could conveniently be seated, and requested him to expound at length the strange doctrine of which he had been speaking.

And there, alone among thousands of subtle and critical Athenians, alone among the altars and statues of the deities which for centuries had been connected with all the traditions of Athenian life and history, the Apostle began that celebrated discourse which even the sceptic is forced to praise for its lucidity and power, and which the Christian feels to be a masterly exposition of some of the great truths of his religion.

"The oration of Paul before this assembly," says Neander, "is a living proof of his apostolic wisdom and eloquence: we see here how he, according to his own words, could become a Gentile to the Gentiles, to win the Gentiles to the gospel."

Stier remarks: "It was given to the Apostle in this hour what he should speak; this is plainly to be seen in

* Llewellyn Davies, "Dictionary of the Bible," ii. 743.

the following discourse, which we might weary ourselves with praising and admiring in various ways; but far better than all so-called praise from our poor tongues is the humble recognition that the Holy Ghost, the Spirit of Jesus, has here spoken by the Apostle, and therefore it is that we have in his discourse a masterpiece of apostolic wisdom."

"It was in the midst," says Milman,[*] "of elevating associations—to which the student of Grecian literature in Tarsus, the reader of Menander and of the Greek philosophical poets, could scarcely be entirely dead or ignorant—that Paul stood forth to proclaim the lowly yet authoritative religion of Jesus of Nazareth. His audience was chiefly formed from the two prevailing sects,—the Stoics and the Epicureans,—with the populace, the worshippers of the established religion. In his discourse, the heads of which are related by St. Luke,[†] Paul, with singular felicity, touched on the peculiar opinions of each class among his hearers; he expanded the popular religion into a higher philosophy; he imbued philosophy with a profound sentiment of religion."[‡]

This famous speech ran as follows:—[§]

"Ye men of Athens, I perceive that in every point of view ye carry your religious veneration to an extreme. For as I passed by I beheld your objects of religious worship: I observed, in addition to the numerous altars to your own and foreign deities, one to 'an unknown

---

[*] Dean Milman, "History of Christianity," i. 437, 438.
[†] St. Luke was probably at this time a companion of St. Paul.
[‡] Even Renan, the French sceptic, is constrained to do justice to this grand oration.
[§] Our paraphrase is partly founded on Dean Alford, *in loc.*

God.'* This unknown God, whom ye ignorantly worship, I am now manifesting to you.

"The God that made the world and all things therein, inasmuch as He is Lord of heaven and earth, dwelleth not in temples made with hands; neither is He really and truly served with men's hands, as though He needed anything, seeing He is the Preserver as well as the Creator of all; and hath caused every nation of men [sprung] of one blood to dwell on all the face of the earth, prescribing to each its period of endurance and its limits of territory, in order that they should feel after Him, if haply they might find Him:

"Though, in truth, He is not far from any one of us; in Him we live, and move, and have our being, as certain of your own poets have said,—†

'For we are also His offspring.'

"As the offspring of God, then, we ought not to suppose that the Godhead is like unto gold, or silver, or stone, fashioned by human art and workmanship.

"This ignorance hitherto God hath overlooked (ὑπεριδὼν ὁ Θεὸς), but *now* He commandeth all men everywhere to repent, seeing that He hath appointed a day wherein He will judge the world in righteousness by the Man whom He hath ordained, and of this hath given a certain pledge and assurance in that He hath raised Him from the dead." (Acts xvii. 22–31.)

Here the orator was suddenly interrupted. When

---

* On the occurrence of any plague, calamity, or even deliverance, if not easily explicable, the Athenians would erect an altar to its supposed author as to "an unknown God."

† The phrase occurs both in the "Phænomena" of Aratus and in the "Hymn to Jupiter" of Kleanthes.

Stoics and Epicureans heard him speak of the "resurrection of the dead" as of a thing feasible, probable, and which, indeed, had taken place, they broke out into loud laughter, and openly jested at him. Some there were, however, whose reason was struck by the cogency of the Apostle's argument, and it produced, at all events, so much impression upon them that they expressed a desire to hear him again upon the matter. And a few there were—the nucleus of the future Church—who *clave* unto him (to use the strong expression of the historian), and believed; and among them Dionysius the Areopagite, and a woman named Damaris.*

His work in Athens completed, and the good seed sown, Paul repaired to Corinth, another of the great centres of Grecian civilization, situated on the narrow isthmus which connects the Morea with the Peloponnesus —northern with southern Greece.

CORINTH, in the days of Paul, was "the Venice of the Ancient World," in whose streets continuous streams of commerce, either flowing from or to Imperial Rome out of all the eastern territories, met and crossed one another.

It was originally a Phœnician settlement; was afterwards occupied by an Ionian tribe; and finally, under Sisyphus, by the Æolians. It grew rapidly in wealth and power, nor was its prosperity checked by the Dorian conquest. The Dorians ruled from B.C. 1074 to B.C. 747; and were followed by the Bacchiadæ (747–657), who fostered a spirit of commercial enterprise, and founded the important colonies of Corcyra and Syracuse. Then came the reigns of Cypselus (657–627) and Periander (627–583), who still further developed the re-

---

* Of Damaris nothing is known. Dionysius, according to Eusebius, was the first Bishop of Athens. It is said he suffered martyrdom.

sources of Corinth, so that it was recognized as one of the leading states in Greece. During the wars between Athens and Sparta it favoured the latter. As Macedonia rose into importance, Corinth declined, and eventually it became a Macedonian city. At a later period it stood forward as the head of the Achæan League, and rashly entering upon hostilities against Rome, was entered by Lucius Mummius (B.C. 146), and completely destroyed. All the male inhabitants were put to the sword, and the women and children sold as slaves. Its statues, and paintings, and other works of art were carried to Rome; its public and private buildings set on fire. Thus was extinguished the *lumen totius Græciæ* — the "light of all Greece."

In B.C. 46, Julius Cæsar, recognizing the value of its position, determined on rebuilding Corinth, and despatched thither a "colony" of veterans and freedmen. Henceforth it was called *Colonia Ivlia Corinthvs*, and it quickly regained much of its former importance. When Paul visited it, the prosperous and populous city was the residence of Junius Gallio, the proconsul of Achaia. It lay then, as now, in the shadow of a steep and picturesque mountain,—the Acrocorinthus,*—whose summit was crowned with a temple to Aphrodite, and whose elevation above the sea-level is computed at 1886 feet. It was adorned with temples, and theatres, and amphitheatres; was defended by massive fortifications; and contained a population of about 100,000. An aqueduct, 20 miles in length, supplied its baths and fountains with pure and abundant water. Its bazaars were crowded with the costliest wares of the

* Thus described by Colonel Mure:—" Neither the Acropolis of Athens, nor the Larissa of Argos, nor any of the more celebrated mountain-fortresses of western Europe, not even Gibraltar, can enter into the remotest competition with this gigantic citadel. It is one of those objects more frequently, perhaps, to be met with in Greece than in any other country of Europe, of which no drawing can convey other than a very faint notion. The outline, indeed, of this colossal mass of rugged rock and green-sward, interspersed here and there, but scantily, with the customary fringe of shrubs, although from a distance it enters into fine composition with the surrounding landscape, can hardly be called picturesque. Its vast size and height produce the greatest effect, as viewed from the seven Doric columns, standing nearly in the centre of the wilderness of rubbish and hovels that now mark the site of the city which it formerly protected."

East; its inhabitants were wealthy, and spent their wealth in the most luxurious enjoyments.

The social and moral condition of this remarkable city in the Pauline era has been admirably depicted by Robertson. In the following sketch we shall attempt to indicate the various points which he brings out more fully in his elaborate picture.*

Owing to the importation of veterans and freedmen from Rome, the population of the new city was Roman, not Greek; democratic, not aristocratic; and held within it all the vices as well as the advantages of a democracy. It was only in such a city, therefore, that these public meetings could have taken place, in which each one exercised his gifts without order; it was in such a city only that the turbulence, and the interruptions, and the brawls which we read of, and which were so eminently characteristic of a democratic society, could have existed.

Again: the population was not only democratic, but, as the site of Corinth necessitated, commercial. The isthmus connecting northern and southern Greece had two ports—Cenchreæ on the east, and Lechæum on the west. Corinth lay between them, and all the commerce from north to south, and east to west, was compelled to pass through it. From this circumstance arose another feature of its society: its aristocracy was one of wealth, not of birth; were merchants, not manufacturers; and worshipped Mammon with an absolute and all-absorbing devotion.

In addition to this lust of gold, there were all the demoralizing influences of a sea-port. The city was "the hot-bed of the world's evil, in which every noxious plant, indigenous or transplanted, rapidly grew and flourished; where luxury and sensuality throve rankly, stimulated by the gambling spirit of commercial life, till Corinth now, in the Apostle's time, as in previous centuries, became a proverbial name for moral corruption."

Another element to be considered is the Greek population, who were divided into two widely separated parties: the uncultivated and poor, still clinging to their old pagan creed of gods and goddesses, nymphs, fauns, and satyrs, omens and prodigies; and the

---

* F. W. Robertson, "Lectures on the Epistles to the Corinthians," Introd.

cultivated and wealthy, looking upon the whole with scornful contempt or sceptical indifference. "The energy," says Robertson, "which had found a safe outlet in war now wasted itself in the amphitheatre. The enthusiasm which had been stimulated by the noble eloquence of patriotism now preyed on glittering rhetoric. Men spent their days in tournaments of speeches, and exulted in gladiatorial oratory. They would not even listen to a sermon from St. Paul unless it were clothed in dazzling words and full of brilliant thought. They were in a state not uncommon now with fine intellects whose action is cramped. Religion, instead of being solid food for the soul, had become an intellectual banquet. That was another difficulty with which Christianity had to deal."

An element not to be overlooked in this complex community was the Jews, of whom a numerous body seem to have been settled at Corinth. *Their* religion had become a thing of forms and ceremonies: had lost all energy, and force, and heart. So far as it was vital at all, its vitality consisted in the passionate longing for a world-prince, a temporal Messiah, who should restore the lost glories of the Jewish kingdom, and reign in visible pomp over all the lands. As St. Paul says, the Jews required a sign.

At Corinth, however, *one* influence existed which worked in favour of Christianity: that of the Roman Government. Nothing is more remarkable in the polity of Rome than the tolerance, almost contemptuous, with which it treated the various creeds of its subject nations, so long as they did not affect the public order or threaten the supremacy of the state. And, as yet, the doctrine of Christ had not come into collision with Roman paganism. Its teachers and followers were obscure men and women, of simple habits and peaceful lives, who paid apparently the greatest reverence to the "powers that be." When we read in St. Luke's history of persecution coming from the Greeks, we invariably find that the Greeks had first been stirred up and excited by the Jews. And until it became evident that in Christianity there was a Power before which all the "principalities of evil"—all wrong and oppression and injustice—must vanish, the Roman magistrates generally defended the Christians, and interposed their authority between them and their enemies.

Into this complex community, then—a community made up of such widely different elements, and swayed by such widely different influences—came Paul the Apostle as the preacher of a new religion. For a task of so much difficulty a man like Paul was eminently needed: a man of fiery heart and brain, of iron will and unquailing energy, with an intellectual force that could break down the barriers erected by Jewish selfishness and Greek subtlety. John, the apostle of love and mercy; Peter, the apostle of the Circumcision; James, the austere prophet of justice and the law,—would assuredly have failed (humanly speaking) on a stage so wide and so crowded as Corinth. But Paul, strong in Jesus Christ, and gifted with mental powers which both the Jew and the Greek could respect and understand, had here the work to do for which he was eminently fitted—a work which he wrought "in all patience, in signs, and wonders, and mighty deeds," and which resulted in the foundation of one of the largest and most prosperous of the early Christian Churches.

The number of Jews at Corinth, at this time, was very large, owing to the decree of the Emperor Claudius, issued in A.D. 52, which had ordered their expulsion from Rome, "because they were constantly raising tumults under the leadership of one Christus."* Among those who had taken refuge in Corinth were two natives of Pontus, in Asia Minor, named Aquila and Priscilla. They were engaged in the manufacture of tents—probably of the *Cilicium,* or hair-cloth, which we have already described as woven from the wool of the Cilician goats. It does not appear that they were Christians when Paul entered the city, and, attracted by the similarity of occupation, went to reside at their house. But his preaching and example soon converted them to

---

* Suetonius, "Claudius," c. xxv.:—"Judæos Chresto duce, assidue tumultuantes, Româ expulit." The *Chresto* is, almost unquestionably, a mistake for *Christo.*—See Milman, "History of Christianity," i. 296.

the new faith.; and they remained devoted to *it* and to *him* during the whole of Paul's life.

While thus occupying himself with manual labour (1 Cor. iv. 12), Paul did not forget the great mission which had been specially intrusted to him. Every Sabbath-day he discoursed in the synagogue (Acts xviii. 4); not, as he himself tells us, "with enticing words of man's wisdom, but in demonstration of the Spirit and of power," knowing nothing, preaching nothing, but "Jesus Christ, and him crucified" (1 Cor. ii. 2–4). His labours were crowned with success. The simple beauty of Christ's life and doctrine was felt both by Jew and Gentile. Many sheep were gathered into the fold; and among the "first fruits" of his apostolic zeal were "the house of Stephanas" (1 Cor. xvi. 15), all of whose family were baptized by his own hand (1 Cor. i. 16); Crispus, a ruler of the synagogue (Acts xviii. 8); and Gaius, or Caius, with whom he afterwards lodged (1 Cor. i. 14).

Let not the reader think these gains were small. Has he ever considered the enormous difficulties of the enterprise undertaken by the pioneers of Christianity? Unless their faith had been fed by Divine inspiration, assuredly they must have looked upon their work as hopeless.

This has been finely put by Milman in one of his earlier works.* "Conceive," he says, "the Apostles of Jesus Christ—Paul the tentmaker, or Peter the fisherman—entering as strangers into one of the splendid cities of Syria, Asia Minor, or Greece; into Athens,

---

* Milman, "Bampton Lectures," pp. 269, 273.

Ephesus, or Corinth. Conceive them, I mean, as unendowed with miraculous powers, having adopted their itinerant system of teaching from human motives, and for human purposes alone. As they pass along to the remote and obscure quarter, where they expect to meet with precarious hospitality among their countrymen, they survey the strength of the established religion, which it is their avowed purpose to overthrow. Everywhere they behold temples, on which the utmost extravagance of expenditure has been lavished by succeeding generations; idols of the most exquisite workmanship, to which, even if the religious feeling of adoration is enfeebled, the people are strongly attached by national or local vanity. They meet processions, in which the idle find perpetual occupation; the young, excitement; the voluptuous, a continual stimulant to their passions. They behold a priesthood numerous, sometimes wealthy. Nor are these alone wedded by interest to the established faith; many of the trades, like those of the makers of silver shrines at Ephesus, are pledged to the support of that to which they owe their maintenance. They pass a magnificent theatre, on the splendour and success of which the popularity of the existing authorities mainly depends; and in which the serious exhibitions are essentially religious, the lighter as intimately connected with the indulgence of the baser passions. They behold another public building, where even worse feelings—the cruel and the sanguinary—are pampered by the animating contests of wild beasts and of gladiators, in which they themselves may shortly play a dreadful part,—

'Butchered to make a Roman holiday!'

"They encounter, likewise, itinerant jugglers, diviners, magicians, who impose upon the credulous to excite the contempt of the enlightened;—in the first case, dangerous rivals to those who should attempt to propagate a new faith by imposture and deception; in the latter, naturally tending to prejudice the mind against all miraculous pretensions whatever: here, like Elymas, endeavouring to outdo the signs and wonders of the Apostles, thereby throwing suspicion on all asserted supernatural agency by the frequency and clumsiness of their delusions.

"They meet philosophers, frequently itinerant like themselves; or teachers of new religions, priests of Isis and Serapis, who have brought into equal discredit what might otherwise have appeared a proof of philanthropy —the performing laborious journeys, at the sacrifice of personal ease and comfort, for the moral and religious improvement of mankind—or, at least, have so accustomed the public mind to similar pretensions as to take away every attraction from their boldness or novelty. There are also the teachers of the different mysteries, which would engross all the anxiety of the inquisitive; perhaps excite, even if they did not satisfy, the hopes of the more pure and lofty minded.

"Such must have been among the obstacles which must have forced themselves on the calmer moments of the most ardent; such the overpowering difficulties of which it would be impossible to overlook the importance or elude the force; which required no sober calculation to estimate, no laborious inquiry to discover; which met and confronted them wherever they went, and which, either in desperate presumption or deliberate reliance on their own preternatural powers, they must have condemned and defied."

In the growth of Christianity under circumstances such as these, we see a striking proof of its Divine origin. In the perseverance of the Apostles in the face of such tremendous obstacles, we see a no less striking proof of their Divine calling.

For the Apostles could not know, what *we* now know, as we look back to the epoch at which they lived, how wonderfully God had made all things converge to the accomplishment of His purpose in the incarnation of the Saviour. They could not see, what *we* now see, that the old order was rapidly breaking up, and preparing the way for the new; that Paganism was losing its grasp upon the people; that behind its apparent prosperity and pomp it was rapidly sinking from its own inherent corruption; that, in like manner, Judaism was growing soulless and effete; and that men's minds were everywhere restless and disturbed—men's souls aching with a desire for some purer faith to satisfy their purer aspirations. Nor could they see, what *we* now see, that in the extension of the Roman supremacy over all the known world, and the consequent cohesion of nations under the pressure of a common law and order, God had made a direct provision for the safer and surer diffusion of Christianity.* Before them were shadows and a thick

---

* See these points most admirably brought out and illustrated in the Very Rev. Dean Merivale's Hulsean Lecture, "On the Conversion of the Empire." See also Neander, "Church History," ii. 275 (ed. Clark). In further study of the same subject, the reader should consult Mackay's "Rise and Progress of Christianity," and Farrar's "Witness of History to Christ."

darkness, illuminated only by their faith in their Divine mission, and their consciousness of Divine support.

After Paul had toiled in his Master's service for two or three months, Silas and Timotheus returned from Macedonia (Acts xviii. 5), bringing tidings of the Churches founded there by Paul, which greatly revived his spirit. They informed him that these Churches were zealous in the truth, that their faith and love had undergone no diminution, and that they anxiously desired to see him (1 Thess. iii. 6). He had begun his work at Corinth in weakness, and in fear, and in much trembling (1 Cor. ii. 3); but now he was comforted by his knowledge of their faith. Relieved, too, by their liberal contributions, from the pressure of manual labour, he was able to devote his whole time to the preaching of the word.*

But the intelligence brought by Silas and Timotheus from Thessalonica was not wholly satisfactory. Into the newly-founded Church some errors had obtruded, and certain irregularities were allowed to prevail. Some of the converts had lost their friends and relations, and conceived that their departed spirits would lose the felicity of witnessing the Saviour's Second Advent, which they, like so many of the early Christians, supposed to be close at hand (1 Thess. iv. 13-18). Many there were who, under the stimulus of this belief, had abandoned their daily occupations, and looked for support to the charity of their wealthier brethren (1 Thess. iv. 11, 12).

* Such seems to be the exact meaning of the words συνείχετο τῷ λόγῳ (Acts xviii. 5), rendered in our English version, "Paul was pressed in the spirit."

Others attempted, with a profession of Christianity, to combine the indulgence of their passions and desires (1 Thess. iv. 1-8); others showed an inclination to underrate the "gift of prophesying," and exalt less useful but more showy gifts (1 Thess. v. 19, 20); and others, again, seem to have been tempted to listen too readily to every fluent speaker (1 Thess. v. 21).

In these circumstances Paul sat down, in the midst of all his pressing labours, to write his first apostolic letter—the First Epistle to the Thessalonians (A.D. 52, 53)*—which is remarkable for its practical and earnest character, and its simple, direct, and emphatic style. Its contents may be thus indicated:—

PART I.—Narrative (1st, 2nd, and 3rd chapters, to verse 13).

1. The Apostle gratefully records the conversion of the Thessalonians to the gospel, and their progress in the faith (i. 2-10).

2. He reminds them of the purity and blamelessness of his ministry among them (ii. 1-12).

3. He repeats his gratitude for their conversion, and rejoices in the faith with which they had endured their numerous persecutions (ii. 13-16).

4. He describes, as a sequence to this, his own exceeding anxiety, the mission of Timotheus to Thessalonica, and the good tidings with which he had returned (ii. 17-iii. 10).

5. He prays that they may be made to increase and abound in love toward one another, and toward all men; and that their hearts may be established in holiness unblameable before God (iii. 11-13).

PART II.—Hortatory (4th and 5th chapters to end).

1. He warns them against impurity of conduct (iv. 1-8).

2. He exhorts them to righteous living and brotherly love (iv. 9-12).

* See the Introductions of Jowett and Alford.

3. He sets forth the true Christian doctrine of the second coming of our Lord (iv. 13-v. 11).

4. He repeats his counsel as to the proper performance of their duties as citizens and Christians (v. 12–15).

5. He enlarges on their spiritual obligations (v. 16-22); and,

6. Concludes with a general prayer on behalf of the Thessalonian Church.*

The Apostle continued his exertions among the Jews, and openly testified to them that the Jesus they had crucified was indeed the Christ. He was met with a storm of obloquy and blasphemy, against which he found it useless to persevere. Turning round upon them, as with the awful indignation of one of the old Hebrew prophets, he "shook his raiment"—to show that he abandoned them altogether—and declaring that their blood must be upon their own heads, announced his intention of devoting himself to the Gentiles. For this purpose he took up his residence with a Christian convert, named *Justus*, whose house stood near the synagogue, the place of his public teaching (Acts xviii. 6, 7). The chief ruler of the synagogue—Crispus—had already renounced Judaism, and among the Corinthians the little body of Christian warriors enlisted numerous recruits; but still the difficulties of the Apostle's position were so many and so formidable, and his spirit—perhaps from physical infirmity—was so depressed, that he seems to have thought of quitting Corinth. But in such moments of despondency on the part of His servants, God ever comes to their help and renewal; and He now appeared to Paul in a vision of the night, breathing into his soul

* See Smith's "Dictionary of the Bible," 3rd vol., *in loc.*

words of inspiration and comfort. "Be not afraid," He said, "but speak, and hold not thy peace. I am with thee, and no man shall do thee harm; for I have many in this city who believe in me" (Acts xviii. 9, 10). Refreshed and reinvigorated by this intercourse with Him whom he served, Paul continued at Corinth, abiding there in all a year and six months (Acts xviii. 11).

At this time the proconsul at Corinth was Annæus Novata—a brother of the philosopher Seneca—who, having been adopted into the family of Junius Gallio, was known by the name of his patron. Gallio was probably a man of culture and refinement, as, according to the testimony of his brother, he was certainly a man of gentle and amiable disposition, whom "every one loved too little, even he who loved him most."* Before this humane and upright magistrate—presuming, perhaps, upon his easy disposition—the Jews, with one accord, dragged the Apostle, accusing him of "persuading men to worship contrary to the law" (Acts xviii. 13). But, without requiring Paul to enter upon his defence, the proconsul recognized the folly and injustice of the charge, and proceeded to dismiss it as the offspring of sectarian prejudice. "Ye have charged this man," we may imagine him to have said, "with violating your law. Now, had ye accused him of immoral or dishonest conduct, I would have patiently heard you—it would have been my duty; but for this trivial matter of words and names,† and supposed breach of your law, why, look ye to it. I will in no wise meddle with the matter"

---

* Seneca, "Naturales Quæstiones," iv. præf.
† That is, whether Jesus was or was not the Christ.

(Acts xviii. 14, 15). And he dismissed them contemptuously from before the judgment-seat.

When the Gentile population, who at all times hated the Jews, found them so indifferently treated by the Roman proconsul, they immediately attacked them, and beat their leader, Sosthenes, even in Gallio's presence, without let or hindrance (Acts xviii. 17). After this unexpected termination to their artful movement, the Jews thought it advisable not again to interfere with the Christians or their Apostle, and Paul remained peacefully in Corinth, building up his rapidly-increasing Church.

At this time, too, he indited his Second Epistle to the Thessalonians, with the view of removing some difficulties which the former had left untouched, and of enlarging on some points of the greatest practical importance. In this epistle, as in the former, it may perhaps be said that we see more of Paul the Administrator than of Paul the Teacher. And it is noticeable that in his fulfilment of his apostolic duties, he strictly enjoins, "in the name of the Lord," that his epistle shall be read "to all the brethren," so that none may plead ignorance of his views or injunctions.

Like the first, it is divided into two distinct parts :—

PART I.—Explanatory (chapters i. and ii.).

1. After thanking God for their progress in the faith, he encourages them to remain patient under persecution, and prays they may prepare themselves to meet the judgment to come (i. 3-12).

2. Of this judgment, however, erroneous notions prevail,—such as, that it is close at hand,—which Paul proceeds to correct (ii. 1-13).*

---

* Here occurs the celebrated "Apocalyptic passage." The "Man of Sin," or Antichrist, may probably be understood as referring to Judaism.—Professor Lightfoot.

3. He repeats his thanksgiving, and concludes with a prayer (ii. 13-17).

PART II.—Hortatory (chapter iii.).

1. He calls upon his brethren to pray for him; and confidently anticipates their continued advancement in a knowledge and love of the truth (iii. 1-5).

2. He reproves the idle, disobedient, and disorderly, and charges the faithful to eschew their companionship (iii. 6-15).

3. He closes with a prayer and benediction.

His work at Corinth finished, Paul prepared to resume his missionary enterprise. He therefore took an affectionate leave of the brethren whom he had gathered into Christ's Church, and accompanied by Aquila, and Aquila's wife Priscilla, by Silas and Timotheus, he took his departure for Jerusalem, to keep there the great national feast of the Pentecost (Acts xviii. 20, 21). Before leaving Greece, he stopped at Cenchreæ (now *Kichnis*)—a small town about nine miles from Corinth—and fulfilled a religious vow, whose purport is not known, by shaving off his hair.*

Thence, a voyage of thirteen or fourteen days brought him and his companions to Ephesus, where Aquila and Priscilla remained; while Paul—after one visit to the Jewish synagogue, and promising the Jews that he would return to them again—sailed, with Silas and Timotheus,

---

* This vow *may* refer to Aquila, and is so understood by some of the commentators. "A passage in Josephus, however, if rightly understood, mentions a vow which included, besides a sacrifice, the cutting of the hair, and the beginning of an abstinence from wine thirty days before the sacrifice. If St. Paul's were such a vow, he was going to offer up a sacrifice in the Temple at Jerusalem, and the 'shaving of his head' was a preliminary to the sacrifice" (Smith's "Bible Dictionary," ii. 745. See also Alford, ii. 188; and Neander, p. 348). Yet it seems improbable that the eloquent and steadfast opponent of Jewish formalism would have complied with any such ceremonial rite.

to Cæsarea. From Cæsarea he journeyed by land to Jerusalem, in time to assist at the Pentecostal celebrations. After examining into the condition of the Christian Church, he again quitted the Holy City, and went down to Antioch, the starting-point of his third missionary journey, from which he had been so long absent (Acts xviii. 21, 22).

CHAPTER V.

PAUL'S THIRD MISSIONARY JOURNEY.

A.D. 54-57.

Galatia — Ephesus — Troas — Illyricum — Corinth — Troas — Mitylene — Chios — Samos — Miletus — Cos — Rhodes — Tyre — Ptolemais — Cæsarea — Jerusalem.

"To St. Paul was committed the task of explanation, defence, and assertion of all the doctrines of the Christian religion, and especially of those metaphysical ones touching the will and grace; for which purpose his active mind, his learned education, and his Greek logic, made him pre-eminently fit."—S. T. COLERIDGE, *Table Talk.*

AFTER a residence at Antioch of, I suppose, a few weeks, Paul again resumed his missionary labours. That brain of fire — that earnest, tender heart — could not be at rest. He counted every moment lost which was not spent in proclaiming abroad the ineffable love of Christ. Accompanied by Timotheus, and, probably, by Titus,* he visited the Churches which he had founded in Galatia and Phrygia, "strengthening all the disciples" (Acts xviii. 23), and ordaining a weekly collection from every

---

* Also, perhaps, by Erastus, Gaius, and Aristarchus.

Church in behalf of their poorer brethren in Judea (1 Cor. xvi. 1, 2).

Meanwhile, at Ephesus, a certain Jew had made his appearance, named APOLLOS :* a native of Alexandria—that great Oriental seat of the Hellenistic language, literature, and philosophy ; a Jew, and thoroughly versed in the law and the prophets; eloquent and learned; and a disciple of John the Baptist. Of Christianity he knew no more than John the Baptist had known,—that is, he had received the Hebrew doctrine of the Messiahship; but of the Cross, and the Resurrection, and the descent of the Holy Spirit, he had learned nothing. What he knew, however, he expounded earnestly and faithfully in the synagogue ; where Aquila and Priscilla heard him, and feeling how much he had yet to learn of the truths of Christian doctrine, they took him home with them, and explained to him more perfectly the way of God (Acts xviii. 26). Filled with gladness and sympathy, he longed to teach to others the gospel which had done so much for himself, and he chose for the theatre of his labours the historical region of Achaia ; probably having heard much from Aquila and Priscilla of the wide field for exertion which lay at Corinth. Thither, then, he repaired, furnished with commendatory letters from the brethren of Ephesus ; and by his success fully demonstrated his fitness for the work he had undertaken. He watered those whom Paul had planted (1 Cor. iii. 6). He greatly helped those who had believed through grace ; and more, with the assistance of his extensive

---

* Abbreviated from Apollonius, or Apollodorus.

Biblical erudition, he convinced many of the Jews, and that publicly, proving, from the evidence of the Scriptures themselves, that Jesus was indeed the Christ (Acts xviii. 27, 28).

In the course of his travels, Paul now came to Ephesus —thus fulfilling a promise which he had made on a former visit (Acts xviii. 21)—and met with his indefatigable assistants, Aquila and Priscilla. Here he found twelve Jewish proselytes, who had received only John's baptism, like Apollos, and had had no proof of the descent of the Holy Spirit, nor knowledge of His gifts.* To Paul's question, "Did ye receive the Holy Ghost when ye became believers?" they replied, "On the contrary, we did not so much as hear Him mentioned." "To what, then," continued the Apostle, "were ye baptized?" They said, "Unto John's baptism,"—that is, unto repentance for sins, and a belief in Jesus as still to come. The Apostle then proceeded to speak of that loftier baptism, of which John's was only the type and foreshadowing; of the baptism in Christ Jesus, Who died that He might make satisfaction for the sins of men. And when they heard of the Saviour, they were much moved, and desired to be baptized in His name. Whereupon the Apostle solemnly laid his hands upon them; and in proof of the efficacy of this new baptism, they received the gifts of the Holy Spirit, and spake with tongues, and prophesied (Acts xix. 2–7).

In reference to this striking incident, Mr. Llewellyn

---

* His miraculous gifts,—that is, such as were bestowed on Cornelius and his household after their baptism.

Davies remarks that it may obviously be compared with the apostolic act of Peter and John in Samaria, and regarded as, on St. Paul's part, a full assertion of the apostolic dignity. But, he adds,* besides this bearing of it, we see in it indications which suggest more than they distinctly express as to the spiritual movements of that age. Mention is made of these twelve disciples immediately after Apollos, who, as we have seen, was an Alexandrian, learned in the Hebrew Scriptures, and fostered by the Greek culture of that capital. Hence we may well suppose that a knowledge of John's baptism and of the ministry of Christ had spread far and wide, and been favourably received by some of those who knew the Scriptures most thoroughly, before any information had reached them of Christ's resurrection and ascension, and of the outpouring of the Holy Ghost. We cannot, indeed, determine what was the exact belief of Apollos and the "twelve" concerning our Saviour's work and character, but it seems certain that it was wanting in a recognition of the power of the Spirit and the supreme lordship of Jesus.

As EPHESUS was the goal of the Apostle's travels in Asia Minor, and afterwards the seat of what may be called the mother Church of the Asiatic cities, the reader will wish to gain some information respecting it.

"What would have been the astonishment and grief," says a modern writer,† "of the 'beloved Apostle' and Timothy if they could have foreseen that a time would come when there would be

* Rev. J. Ll. Davies, in Smith's "Dictionary of the Bible," ii. 746, 747.
† Rev. F. V. J. Arundell, "A Visit to the Seven Churches in Asia" (ed. 1828).

in Ephesus neither 'angel,' nor Church, nor city,—when that great city would become 'heaps, a desolation, a dry land, and a wilderness; a land wherein no man dwelleth, neither doth any son of man pass thereby.' Once it had Christian temples, almost rivalling the pagan in splendour, wherein the image that fell from Jupiter lay prostrate before the cross; and as many tongues, moved by the Holy Ghost, made public avowal that 'great is the Lord Jesus!' Once it had a bishop, the 'angel of the Church,' Timothy, the disciple of St. John; and tradition reports that it was honoured with the last days of both these great men, and of the mother of our Lord......

"Some centuries passed on, and the altars of Jesus were thrown down to make way for the delusions of Mahomet; the Cross is removed from the dome of the church, and the Crescent glitters in its stead......

"A few years more, and all may be silence in the mosque and the church. A few unintelligible heaps of stones, with some mud cottages, untenanted, are all the remains of the great city of the Ephesians. The busy hum of a mighty population is silent in death. 'Thy riches, and thy fairs, thy merchandise, thy mariners, and thy pilots, thy calkers, and the occupiers of thy merchandise, and all thy men of war, are fallen.' Even the sea has retired from the scene of desolation, and a pestilential morass, covered with mud and rushes, has succeeded to the water which brought up the ships laden with merchandise from every country."

Such is the Ephesus of to-day,—"fallen from her high estate."

Ancient Ephesus excelled even luxurious Smyrna in wealth and magnificence. Seated near the mouth of the river Cayster,—looking forth upon the isle-studded waters of the Mediterranean,—embosomed in leafy groves and fragrant gardens, sheltered inland by the green flanks of an undulating range of mountains,—its position was rich in every charm that could gratify the cultivated taste. We can fancy that it was the amenity of the spot which led an Ionian tribe to settle there—some ten centuries before the birth of Christ—and to found a city, which grew with a truly marvellous growth. Its fame spread throughout Western Asia for the splendour of its palaces, the treasures of its marts, and especially for its magnificent Temple of Diana or Artemis, the tutelary divinity of the city. The history of this temple is singular; for no less than seven times was it destroyed, and seven times rebuilt with augmented grandeur. The edifice, which must often have attracted Paul's sorrowful gaze, was restored in the third century before Christ. It was built on immense foundations, and measured 425 feet in length, by 220 feet in breadth. One hundred and twenty-seven marble columns adorned it, each 60 feet in height. Thirty-six were cunningly carved by the most skilful artists. The folding-doors were of cypress wood, which had been treasured up for four generations, and highly polished. The ceiling was of fragrant cedar, considered indestructible. The steps which led up to the roof were wrought from the giant stem of a single vine. The masterly sculptures of Praxiteles enriched the altar, which blazed, moreover, with ornaments in gold and silver. Among the offerings was a picture by the famous painter Apelles, representing Alexander the Great as armed with Jove's thunderbolt.* So rich, so glorious was this temple within and without, that Philo of Byzantium pronounced it "the only Home of the Gods" (μόνος θεῶν οἶκος); and the city, in acknowledgment of its pious zeal, was called the νεώκορος, or Custodian of Diana.

Not less famous was the statue of the goddess which it enshrined, like a gem in a superb casket. Its sanctity was great, for the priests asserted that it had fallen from heaven. It now lies in the British Museum, and may be described as bearing a general resemblance to an Egyptian mummy. A circle round its head denotes the *nimbus* or halo of Diana's glory; the griffins inside express its brilliancy. On its breast are depicted the twelve signs of the Zodiac, of which those visible in front are Aries, Taurus, Gemini, Cancer, Leo; they are separated by personifications of the Hours. A chaplet drooping from the neck is composed of acorns, the primeval food of man. Lions on the arms typify the goddess's power; and the outstretched hands, that she is ready to receive all who come to her. The body is covered with various beasts and monsters—as sirens,

---

* For these details, consult Vitruvius, bk. iv., sect. 1.

sphinxes, and griffins—to prove that she is the source of all things, and the generative power of nature. The head, hands, and feet are of bronze, and the rest of the statue of alabaster—emblematic of the ever-varying light and shade of the lunar disc. It is crowned with a turret, to denote the supremacy of Artemis over terrestrial objects.[*]

In the eleventh century Ephesus was captured and razed to the ground by the Turks, and its present desolation is in strange and impressive contrast with its ancient pride of place. The sea has retired from its former shore; the harbour, once thronged with masts, is now a dreary marsh; and the original extent of the once busy city can only be traced by a solitary watch-tower, and some fragments of masonry on the grassy hill. Part of its site is a ploughed field; part a wilderness, where, when the shades of night steal over the scene, the mournful cry of the jackal resounds, and the night-hawk and the owl flit among the shattered columns. Of the Temple of Artemis, with its marble pillars and cedar roof, some interesting and valuable remains have lately been discovered. There are extant, moreover, considerable ruins of the theatre, which, as we shall see, was connected with a memorable event in St. Paul's history. A wretched Turkish village, called *Aisaluk*, is situated at a short distance inland; and these are all the signs the stranger can discover of the once luxurious centre of heathen worship.

The Ephesians themselves are now represented by a few Greek peasants, living in extreme wretchedness, despondence, and insensibility. Some dwell in huts which rest on the foundations of once glorious edifices; others lurk in the vaults of the huge *stadium*, or amphitheatre;[†] and others conceal their poverty in the tombs of their wealthy ancestors. "We employed a couple of them," says Dr. Chandler,[‡] "to pile stones, to serve instead of a ladder, at the arch of the stadium, and to clear the pedestal of a portico near the theatre from rubbish. We had occasion for another to dig at the Corinthian Temple, and sending to the stadium, the whole tribe, ten or twelve in number, followed, one playing all the way before them on a rude lyre, and at times striking the sounding-board with

---

[*] Falkner.   [†] It measured 687 feet in length.
[‡] Dr. Chandler, "Travels in Asia Minor."

the fingers of his left hand, in concert with the strings. One of them had on a pair of sandals of goat-skin, laced with thongs, and not uncommon. After gratifying their curiosity, they returned as they came, with their musician in front.

"Such," says Dr. Chandler, "are the present citizens of Ephesus, and such is the condition to which that renowned city has been gradually reduced. Its streets are obscured and overgrown. A herd of goats was driven to it for shelter from the sun at noon, and a noisy flight of crows from the quarries seemed to insult its silence." *

At the epoch of St. Paul's visit Ephesus was still renowned for the worship of Artemis, but it was scarcely less famous for its numerous professors of magic. On the crown, the girdle, and the feet of the goddess's statue, certain mysterious symbols, called "Ephesian letters," † were engraved; which, like the runes of the Norsemen, were regarded, when pronounced, as a powerful charm, and as an exorcism against evil spirits. When written, they were carried about as amulets. Curious stories of their supposed influence are told by Suidas and Eustathius. It is said that Crœsus repeated them on his funeral pile; and that an Ephesian wrestler was always successful against an antagonist from Miletus, until he lost the scroll which had acted as a talisman of victory.

In connection with the worship of Artemis a profitable trade was carried on by certain workers in silver and copper, who manufactured portable shrines, in imitation of the goddess's, for strangers to carry back to their

* See also Tristram's "Seven Churches of Asia," and Von Lennep's "Travels of a Missionary in Asia Minor."
† 'Εφέσια γράμματα.

native countries, or devotees to set up in their houses. Public games, moreover, were celebrated in her honour; probably in the month of May, which was sacred to her. At these were present the Asiarchs (Acts xix. 31), or "chiefs of Asia," who presided over the games held in different parts of Asia, just as the ædiles did at the Roman shows. The office was annual, and subject to the approval of the Roman proconsul. It was always conferred upon some wealthy citizen able to defray the expenses connected with the festivities.

It was in this luxurious, superstitious, and motley-peopled city that Paul took up his residence in 56 A.D., and resumed his apostolic work. He began, according to his custom, by preaching in the synagogue, where, Sabbath after Sabbath, for three whole months, he argued with the Jews from their own Scriptures, in demonstration of the important facts that the "kingdom of God" had actually commenced, and that the long-promised Messiah was no other than Jesus Christ. Some believed, but others were deaf to the voice of reason and faith; and as they watched with jealous eyes the formation of a Christian Church, they sought to controvert the Apostle's teaching by openly calumniating him. To withdraw his disciples from so ill an influence, he retired to the school of one Tyrannus, who was probably a teacher of philosophy, and a convert; and here, for nearly three years, he continued to proclaim the truths of the gospel.

Meanwhile, he went from house to house in the prosecution of his divine commission, testifying to the Jews as well as to the Gentiles "repentance toward God, and faith toward Jesus Christ." A large and influential Church was founded at Ephesus, over which certain "presbyters" were appointed to preside (Acts xx. 28),* and the truths of the gospel spread from point to point, and city to city, until the whole of Asia Minor had heard them expounded (Acts xix. 10). To the labours of St. Paul in Ephesus we may probably attribute the rise of the seven great Churches of Asia. †

This extension of Christianity was greatly assisted by the miracles which God wrought through His devoted servant; miracles which were absolutely necessary in order to counterpoise the wonders wrought by the professors of magic. They were of no ordinary kind; even the garments taken from his body, such as his *sudarium*, or handkerchief, and his *semi-cinctium*, or apron, were endued with a miraculous power. That cures should be effected by such simple means is a great stumbling-block to rationalistic interpreters of Scripture; but, as Dean Alford remarks, "all miraculous working is an exertion of the direct power of the All-Powerful; a suspension *by Him* of His ordinary laws; and whether He will use *any* instrument in doing this, or *what* instrument, must depend altogether on His own purpose in the miracle— the effect to be produced on the recipients, beholders, or hearers. Without this special selection and enabling, *all instruments were vain;* with these, *all are capable.* In the present case it was His purpose to exalt His Apostle

* Subject, of course, to the authority of St. Paul, as they were, afterwards, of Timothy.—*See* Bishop Wordsworth, "Outlines of the Christian Ministry," pp. 44, 45.
† Alford, "New Testament," ii. 195.

as the herald of His gospel, and to lay in Ephesus the strong foundation of His Church."

The wonders thus effected excited the envy of the Jewish exorcists, who wandered from town to town, gaining a livelihood by their necromantic arts. Supposing the great name of Jesus to be a talisman or charm, like the Ephesian letters, they used it in their attempts to exorcise the evil spirit from demoniacs, saying, "We adjure you in the name of Jesus, whom Paul preacheth" (Acts xix. 13).

Now, there were seven sons of one Sceva, a Jewish high priest (ἀρχιερέως), who practised this deceptive trade; and on a certain occasion, when two of them (ἀμφοτερῶν, in Acts xix. 16) were endeavouring to heal a man possessed, the evil spirit cried out, "Jesus I acknowledge, and Paul I know;* but who are ye?" And immediately the demoniac flung himself upon the impostors, and with maniacal fury rent their clothes from their backs, and drove them naked, wounded, and ashamed from the house (Acts xix. 14–16).

Such an incident quickly became noised abroad throughout all Ephesus, producing a powerful impression on the minds both of Greeks and Jews, and greatly magnifying the name of the Lord Jesus. It was not only fatal to the pretensions of the Jewish exorcists, but at once put to shame all who believed and dealt in magical practices, and the manufacturers of spells and talismans. Multitudes eagerly came forward, and committed to the

---

* Such is the force of the two verbs in the Greek original, γινώσκω and ἐπίσταμαι, which in our English version are both translated by the one word "know."

flames their charms, their amulets, their images of Diana, and their magical books; in such quantities that their total value was computed at 50,000 pieces of silver* (or about £2000 of our money).

About this time (A.D. 57) Paul was much disturbed by the intelligence which reached him from Corinth. Owing to the hostility prevailing between the Jewish and Gentile converts, the Church there had split up into four parties: one of whom asserted their fidelity to, and peculiar confidence in, the Apostle himself (1 Cor. iii. 4); another claimed to be followers of Peter and the "brethren of the Lord" (1 Cor. i. 12; ix. 5); the third acknowledged as their leader the learned and eloquent Apollos (1 Cor. i. 12); while the fourth proposed to put aside all human leaders, and to own the sole authority of Christ (1 Cor. i. 12).

Nor was this all: the Gentile converts had plunged anew into the notorious profligacy of Corinth, and openly defended their conduct on the pretence of Christian freedom. They were continually at variance with one another (1 Cor. vi. 1–8), and did not hesitate to submit their differences to the jurisdiction of the Greek and Roman courts. They entertained notions subversive of all Church discipline (1 Cor. xi. 20), and even espoused erroneous doctrines (1 Cor. xv.). They displayed themselves, to the great scandal of Christianity, at the sacrificial feasts in the colonnades of the heathen temples (1 Cor. viii. 10). The women were immodest in their attire; mixed marriages were contracted with the utmost license; even the Lord's Supper was profaned by disorderly feasting;

---

* The *argurion* (ἀργύριον) was probably the silver drachma, valued at about 10d.

and those "gifts" which elevate and improve the soul were despised in favour of the more ostentatious but less profitable (1 Cor. xi. 2-16; vii. 10-17; xi. 17-34; and xii. 1; xiv. 1-4).

When this grievous intelligence was first conveyed to Paul, he despatched Timotheus and Erastus (Acts xix. 22) to Corinth, for the purpose of correcting the disorders which had arisen, and punishing the offenders.* But after their departure, some members of the "household of Chloe" arrived, with fuller particulars of the scandalous confusion prevailing in the Christian Church, and of an incestuous marriage having taken place between a man and his father's wife; an alliance which even the heathen discountenanced and condemned (1 Cor. v. 1).

Filled with a sacred indignation at these grievous sins, St. Paul sat down and addressed to the Corinthians, and the other Christian communities in Achaia, what is known as his First Epistle,†—one of the most characteristic, pregnant, and beautiful of his apostolic letters.‡

* Timotheus, however, does not seem to have reached Corinth.

† From a passage in 1 Cor. (v. 9-12), it is generally inferred that the Apostle had previously written a short letter to the Corinthian Church, which has not come down to us.

‡ This epistle has been admirably described by Conybeare and Howson (vol. ii., pp. 24, 25):—

"The letter is addressed not only to the Metropolitan Church, but also to the Christian communities established in other places in the same province, which might be regarded as dependencies of that in the capital city; hence we must infer that these Churches also had been infected by some of the errors or vices which had prevailed at Corinth. This letter is, in its contents, the most diversified of St. Paul's epistles; and in proportion to the variety of its topics, is the depth of its interest for ourselves. For by it we are introduced, as it were, behind the scenes of the Apostolic Church, and its minutest features are revealed to us under the light of daily life. We see the picture of a Christian congrega-

ANALYSIS OF THE EPISTLE.

Its contents may be briefly indicated :—

PART I.—Practical (chapters i. to xi. incl.).

1. The Apostle expresses his gratitude for the general progress made by the Corinthian Church (i. 1–9).

2. He then proceeds to notice and condemn the divisions existing among them, defending his own apostolic labours as animated by the "Spirit of God," and pointing out that the Church must not build upon Paul or Apollos, or any other "ministers," but upon the foundation of Jesus Christ (i. 10–iii. 23).

tion as it met for worship in some upper chamber, such as the house of Aquila or of Gaius could furnish. We see that these seasons of pure devotion were not unalloyed by human vanity and excitement; yet, on the other hand, we behold the heathen auditor pierced to the heart by the inspired eloquence of the Christian prophets, the secrets of his conscience laid bare to him, and himself constrained to fall down on his face and worship God; we hear the fervent thanksgiving echoed by the unanimous Amen; we see the administration of the Holy Communion terminating the feast of love. Again we become familiar with the perplexities of domestic life, the corrupting proximity of heathen immorality, the lingering superstition, the rash speculation, the lawless perversion of Christian liberty; we witness the strife of theological factions, the party names, the sectarian animosities. We perceive the difficulty of the task imposed upon the Apostle, who must guard from so many perils, and guide through so many difficulties, his children in the faith, whom else he had begotten in vain; and we learn to appreciate more fully the magnitude of that laborious responsibility under which he describes himself as almost ready to sink, 'the care of all the Churches.'

"But while we rejoice that so many details of the deepest historical interest have been preserved to us by this epistle, let us not forget to thank God who so inspired this Apostle, that in his answers to questions of transitory interest he has laid down principles of eternal obligation. Let us trace with gratitude the providence of Him who 'out of darkness calls up light;' by whose mercy it was provided that the unchastity of the Corinthians should occasion the sacred laws of moral purity to be established for ever through the Christian world;—that their denial of the resurrection should cause those words to be recorded whereon reposes, as upon a rock which cannot be shaken, our sure and certain hope of immortality."

To this we may add Dean Alford's not less impressive eulogium ("New Testament," ii., pp. 56, 57) :—

"In style this epistle ranks perhaps the foremost of all as to sublimity, and earnest and impassioned eloquence. Of the former, the description of the simplicity of the gospel in ch. ii.,—the concluding apostrophe of ch. iii. (ver. 16 to

3. He explains in what light the preachers of the gospel ought to be regarded, refers to the commission he has given Timotheus to visit them, and announces an apostolic visit of his own as in contemplation (iv.).

4. The Apostle next deals with the case of incest that had occurred among them, regretting that they had not openly condemned it, and commenting on the sin of fornication (v. 1-10).

5. He advises them that fornicators, idolaters, drunkards, and others must not be received into the Christian brotherhood (v. 11-13).

6. Their litigious habits are censured, and their evil practice of resorting to heathen tribunals (vi. 1-8).

7. Commenting on these errors, the Apostle again recurs to their prominent sin of uncleanness, and exhorts them to keep unpolluted the body as "the temple of the Holy Ghost" (vi. 9-20).

the end),—the same in ch. vi. (ver. 9 to the end),—the reminiscence of the shortness of time, ch. vii. 29-31,—the whole argument in ch. xv.,—are examples unsurpassed in Scripture itself: and of the latter, ch. iv. 8-15, and the whole of ch. ix.: while the panegyric of love in ch. xiii. stands a pure and perfect gem, perhaps the noblest assemblage of beautiful thoughts in beautiful language extant in this our world. About the whole epistle there is a character of lofty and sustained solemnity—an absence of tortuousness of construction, and an apologetic plainness, which contrast remarkably with the personal portions of the sacred epistle.

"No epistle raises in us a higher estimate of the varied and wonderful gifts with which God was pleased to endow the man whom He selected for the Apostle of the Gentile world: or shows us how large a portion of the Spirit, who worketh in each man severally as He will, was given to him for our edification. The depths of the spiritual, the moral, the intellectual, the physical world are open to him. He summons to his aid the analogies of nature. He enters minutely into the varieties of human infirmity and prejudice. He draws warning from the history of the chosen people, example from the Athenian foot-race. He refers an apparently trifling question of costume to the first great proprieties and relations of creation and redemption. He praises, reproves, exhorts, and teaches. Where he strikes, he heals. His large heart holding all, where he has grieved any, he grieves likewise ; where it is in his power to give joy, he first overflows with joy himself. We may form some idea from this epistle, better perhaps than from any other,—because this embraces the widest range of topics,—what marvellous power such a man must have had to persuade, to rebuke, to attract and fasten the affections of men."

8. Marriage he advises as a remedy against sensuality, but he nevertheless praises glowingly the comeliness of virginity, and recommends widows not to marry again (vii. 1-40).

9. Abstinence is required from the sacrificial meats of the heathen, but Christian charity is spoken of as a still higher and more important duty (viii. 1-13).

10. Out of this spirit of charity, and consideration towards weaker brethren, he has abstained from exercising many apostolic privileges (ix.).

11. Then he returns to the subject of the use of things offered to idols, showing them that they have suffered no temptation which their forefathers had not suffered, while in resisting it they might be cheered by resorting to the Lord's Table (x.).

12. Practical directions are next given respecting a decent behaviour in public worship; women are forbidden to prophesy and pray with heads uncovered; and a proper celebration of the Lord's Supper is imperatively enjoined (xi.).

13. Next follow directions, copious and minute, on the exercise of spiritual gifts, which are different in different men, but all intended for the general profit (xii. 1-27).

14. Some being apostles, some prophets, some teachers, it is obvious that this very variety of gifts should make all sympathise with one another; and especially, while seeking after the highest, should it induce them to cultivate that virtue of charity without which they are as nothing (xii. 27-31; xiii.).

15. The true use of "prophesying" and "speaking with tongues" is next expounded; and Paul concludes this part of his epistle with enunciating the general rule that "all things be done decently and in order" (xiv.).

PART II.—Doctrinal (chapter xv. to end).

1. The Apostle now proceeds to recapitulate the leading doctrines which he had formerly preached to the Christian Church (xv. 1-3);

2. And explains and defends the doctrine of the resurrection of the body in a long, eloquent, and powerful argument; pointing out that it is the keystone of Christianity: for if the dead do not rise, Christ cannot have risen; and if Christ did not rise, all faith in Christ

were vain. He concludes with a beautiful anticipation of the victory of immortality over mortality, and an exhortation to the brethren to remain steadfast and unshaken in their belief (xv. 3–58).

3. With some general instructions as to relieving the wants of the poor brethren at Jerusalem, and their due obedience to their spiritual teachers, and with the customary benediction, Paul terminates his epistle (xvi.), which seems to have been conveyed to Corinth by Stephanas, Fortunatus, and Achaicus.

In closing his Epistle to the Corinthian Church, Paul states it to be his intention to remain at Ephesus, where a "great door" had been opened, and where he had many adversaries still to contend with. But it was otherwise ordered. It was now about the month Artemisius, or of Artemis (the month of May), when votaries of Diana flocked from all quarters of the world to witness the great annual festival of the goddess. But the established religion had been rudely shaken in repute by Paul's energetic teaching and the miracles he had wrought; so that the craftsmen who manufactured the portable shrines of Diana, and depended upon their sale for subsistence, grew alarmed at the probable result to their trade. Instigated by a certain Demetrius, a silversmith, probably a leading manufacturer, who had summoned them together, and harangued them on the danger that threatened them ("lest the temple of the great goddess Diana should be despised, and her magnificence destroyed"), they rose in a frenzy of popular fury, and shouting, "Great is Diana, the goddess of the Ephesians," they seized upon Gaius and Aristarchus,* two of Paul's companions, and dragged

---

* They had probably failed in an attempt to seize Paul, who may have been received, at the risk of their own lives, by Aquila and Priscilla—as hinted at in Romans xvi. 3, 4.

them to the public theatre. The Apostle, when he heard of what had befallen them, would fain, with his usual courage, have gone to their rescue, but the disciples, assisted by the Asiarchs, prevailed upon him to remain in safe concealment.

Meanwhile the theatre was the scene of a wild, riotous tumult; some crying one thing, and some another; the whole assembly eddying to and fro in strange confusion; and the majority entirely ignorant of the cause of the disorder to which they contributed (Acts xix. 32). At length, out of the press Alexander, "the coppersmith" (2 Tim. iv. 44), was pushed forward into a conspicuous position. He seems to have had considerable influence with the Ephesians, either from his connection with Demetrius, or as being himself an "employer of labour." As he beckoned with his hand, the multitude after awhile subsided into silence. But some among the crowd knew him to be a Jew, and the Jews were even more hateful than the Christians. The uproar recommenced, and owing, it is probable, to a collision between his supporters and his adversaries, it lasted for about two hours; a single shout rising predominant above all lesser noises—just as the aggregate thunder of the sea rises above the various minor sounds of its waves beating against a rock or falling heavily on the sands,—" Great is Diana of the Ephesians!"

The recorder, or keeper of the archives of Corinth (called in our English version the "town-clerk"), now stood forward to appease the excited throng, and having to some extent succeeded, he advised them, in a well-considered speech, to resort to the proper legal courts if they had any just cause of complaint against Paul and his companions.

He reminded them that all the world knew Ephesus to be the "temple-keeper" of the great goddess Diana, and of the sacred image which had fallen from the sky. This fact could not be controverted, could not be put aside by a few aliens, possessed of neither money, rank, nor influence. Such being the case, and Paul and his companions having neither robbed the temple nor blasphemed its goddess, they should take heed that they did nothing hastily nor illegally; but if Demetrius and his craftsmen had just cause of complaint, the law was open to them; they could appeal to the magistrates or to a general assembly of the citizens. As it was, they were prejudicing their own cause, for assuredly the Roman authorities would not allow the peace of the city to be disturbed, but would probably call its local magistrates to account for that day's tumultuous proceedings.

Thus was the Apostle of the Gentiles once more saved by the all-powerful influence of the Roman name; and that the danger from which he so happily escaped was no common one, we know by his emphatic reference to it in his second letter to the Corinthian Church:— *

"For we would not, brethren, have you ignorant of the affliction which befell us in Asia, when we were oppressed out of all measure, and beyond our strength,

---

* Dr. Davidson, and most of the commentators, interpret this passage as we have interpreted it in the text—that is, as referring to the tumult at Ephesus. But though we have thus followed the generally received opinion, we venture to think the Apostle's language refers rather to some dangerous illness (*see* Dean Alford, *in loc.*). From the narrative in the Acts (xix. 35-40), it does not seem that Paul's life was really endangered.

so that we utterly despaired even of life. Moreover, we carried in our own mind the sentence of death (τὸ ἀπόκριμα τοῦ θανάτου),* in order that we might not put any trust in ourselves, but in God who raiseth the dead, who rescued us from so great a death, and will rescue us, and in whom we hope that He will also continue to rescue us."

When order once more reigned in Ephesus, Paul called together the Christian brethren, spoke his farewell words, gave them his last directions, and having embraced them tenderly, set out for Macedonia. Accompanied, probably, by Tychicus and Trophimus, he reached Alexandria Troas.

Here he appears to have remained for some time, "preaching the word." His mind, however, was not free from disturbing influences. Soon after writing his First Epistle to the Church at Corinth, he had sent thither Titus, partly for the purpose of superintending the great collection which was being made on behalf of the Christian poor at Jerusalem, and partly that he might examine into the condition of the Corinthian Church. These tasks accomplished, Titus was to return through Macedonia and join the Apostle at Troas, where he had designed to arrive shortly after Pentecost. But having left Ephesus sooner than he had expected, he was now required to wait for a lengthened period at Troas in a state of extreme suspense and anxiety respecting the difficulties and differences at Corinth. Though "a door was opened unto him of the Lord," he had no rest in his spirit through the non-arrival of Titus (2 Cor. ii. 12, 13). At

* That is, in his own mind he felt sure that death was at hand.

length he resolved to continue his journey to Macedonia; took ship at Troas, and sailed for Philippi. He stayed there "until after the days of unleavened bread" (Acts xx. 6);—an incidental statement, which shows us that Paul's sojourn in Europe on this occasion lasted about nine months; that is, from shortly after Pentecost (A.D. 59) to the Easter following (A.D. 60).

At Philippi he was received by the Christian community with filial love and reverence; but still, as the father of the prodigal son dwelt more on the sinful wanderer than on the youth who stayed in affectionate fidelity by his side, so Paul's anxiety was for the erring rather than for the prosperous Church. He could think only of Corinth. Corinth, and Corinth only, says Dean Stanley,* was the word which would then have been found written on his heart. Timotheus, it is true, was with him, but the Apostle longed for the return of Titus. Until his messenger stood before his face, he felt troubled on every side; "without were fightings, within were fears" (2 Cor. vii. 5).

But at last the Divine Father, who ever hath compassion on His depressed and despondent servants, comforted Paul with the arrival of Titus. He came, too, as the bearer of joyful intelligence, such as well might cheer Paul's loving and enthusiastic soul, and compensate him for the sorrow with which he had sorrowed. The Corinthian Church had obeyed his mandates, and deeply repented of the sins they had committed. The old spirit of love and loyalty towards their founder had revived, and poured itself forth in burning utterances of

* Stanley, "Commentary on the Corinthians" (2 Cor. ii. 13).

grief and shame. The cloud was dispelled: light had returned to Corinth, and this light broke gratefully upon St. Paul. There was only one shadow on the prospect: some Judaizing emissary had arrived from Jerusalem, and was openly impugning the Apostle's authority, accusing him of selfish and egotistical motives, of timidity, vacillation, and distrust, and ridiculing his rugged speech and the meanness of his bodily presence. For Paul was no professional orator relying on a commanding appearance, a practised delivery, and on the elocutionary arts which beguile the ignorant; he spoke direct from his soul of fire, in the full consciousness of his divine commission, and in implicit reliance upon Christ crucified and Christ risen.

It was under these conditions Paul wrote his Second Epistle to the Corinthians; and bearing these in mind, we see that the symptoms it displays, of a highly-wrought personal sensitiveness,—of a kind of ebb and flow of emotion,—are as intelligible as they are beautiful and sublime.

Nothing, says Mr. Davies,* but a temporary interruption of mutual regard could have made the joy of sympathy so deep and fresh. As the object of a personal attack, it was natural for the Apostle to write as he does in chapter ii., verses 5 to 10. In verses 11 and 12, "he that suffered wrong" is Paul himself. All his protestations relating to his apostolic work, and his solemn appeals to God and Christ, are in place; and we enter into his feelings as he asserts his own sincerity and the openness of the truth which he taught in the gospel

* Davies, art. *Paul*, in Smith's "Bible Dictionary," ii. 750.

(iii., iv.). We see what supported him in his self-vindication: he did not preach himself, but his Saviour. He adduces his very weakness as an argument of the power of God working within him; for, unless sustained by that power, how could he have accomplished so much? Knowing his brotherhood with Christ, and that the same brotherhood is the privilege of all Christians, he would be severe or persuasive, as the cause of Christ and the good of men might require (iv., v.). If he were appearing to maintain his authority against the Churches in Judea, he was more anxious that the collection he was making for the benefit of those Churches should prove his sympathy with them by its largeness. He further demonstrated that the spiritual views he enunciated, and the spiritual powers he claimed, were *real;* that if he knew no man after the flesh, and did not war after the flesh, he was not the less able for building up the Church (x.). He asked them to excuse his almost jealous anxiety, his excitement and uneasiness, while he gloried in the numerous practical proofs of his apostolic commission, and in the infirmities which made the power of God more evident; and he besought them earnestly to give him no further occasion to reprimand or correct them.

Such was the general purport of this epistle, of which Meyer says that, owing to the excitement and overflow of the affections, and probably also the haste under which Paul wrote it, the expressions are sometimes obscure and the constructions difficult; yet they serve only to raise our admiration of the great oratorical delicacy, skill, and power with which this outpouring of Paul's

ANALYSIS OF THE EPISTLE.

spirit, especially interesting as a self-defensive apology, flows and rushes onward, until, in the sequel, it completely overwhelms the opposition of his adversaries.

We subjoin an analysis of the contents:—

PART I.—Personal (chapters i. to vii.).

1. The Apostle, after the usual salutation, refers to the "trouble" he had undergone in Asia, but which is now alleviated by the intelligence he has received of their affection (i. 1–15).

2. He alludes to his proposed visit, and excuses himself for not being able to pay it (i. 15–ii. 4).

3. He alludes to certain special directions contained in his First Epistle (ii. 4–12);

4. And explains his own apostolic plans (ii. 12–17).

5. He vindicates his ministry by the success which has attended it (iii.).

6. He enlarges on the character and spirit of his own labours, on the troubles and persecutions he has endured, all tending to his "eternal glory" (iv.).

7. He explains in glowing language his hopes in Christ (v.);

8. And returning to his sufferings, claims, on their account, the affection of the Church (vi.).

9. Therefore, he exhorts them to purity of life, and shows what comfort he derived from the intelligence brought by Titus of their godly sorrow, and of the kindness they had shown to him (vii.).

PART II.—Ministerial (chapters viii. and ix.).

1. He recommends to them a liberal collection on behalf of their poorer brethren in Jerusalem, stimulating them by the example of the Macedonians (viii.).

2. He explains why he sent Titus to them beforehand, and again urges upon them to be "cheerful givers" (ix.).

PART III.—Apologetic (chapter x. to end).

1. He enters upon an elaborate defence of his ministry and himself against those who have disparaged his personal presence (x. 1–5).

2. He assures them that he is armed with authority to correct their misdoings; but if he glories, it is in the Lord, and not from any selfish motive (x. 6-18).

3. He feels himself forced into an assertion of his equality with the "chiefest Apostles;" expostulates with them for their forgetfulness of his past zeal in their behalf; and shows that to the "deceitful workers" who had been plotting against him, he is superior in the service of Christ, and in all kinds of tribulation for his ministry (xi.).

4. Though, in commending his apostleship, he might well glory in the wonderful revelations vouchsafed to him, he prefers to glory in his infirmities (xii. 1-14).

5. He promises another visit, though fearing some of them may again have relapsed (xii. 14-21), in which case he will deal with them severely (xiii. 1-10); and,

6. Concludes with the usual commendation and benediction (xiii. 10-14).

With this epistle, Titus, accompanied by Luke and Trophimus, departed for Corinth, while St. Paul resumed his apostolic labours in Northern Macedonia, or rather along the shores bordering upon the Ægean. He would seem also to have penetrated inland, and to have crossed the country to the coast of the Adriatic, "fully preaching the gospel round about unto Illyricum" (Rom. xv. 19).

It has been suggested that this portion of the Apostle's journey occupied the summer and autumn of A.D. 60. As winter approached, he returned to Achaia, and took up his abode in the house of Gaius at Corinth. Either here, or on his way from Macedonia to Achaia, he received information of the appearance of his old enemies, —the Judaizing Christians in Galatia, where they were representing a rigid observance of the ceremonial law as essential to salvation, and at the same time impugning the apostolic claims and character of St. Paul, in whom they recognized their boldest and most successful opponent. It was a bitter grief to him to learn that these false traitors had completely fascinated * the Christian brethren, and were rapidly gathering around them a large and sympathizing following. † The evil was a serious one, and required to be dealt with firmly. Paul struck at it immediately, and struck deeply, in his Epistle to the Galatians; an epistle very characteristic of his mode of thought and reasoning, of his mingled earnestness and gentleness, and full of particulars illustrative of his early career as an Apostle.

We subjoin an analysis of the contents of the epistle:—

PART I.—Narrative (chapters i. and ii.).

1. The Apostle opens with the usual salutation to the Churches (i. 1-5);

2. And plunging at once *in medias res*, he rebukes the Galatians for having listened to false teachers, and strongly affirms the truth of the gospel which he had preached (i. 6-10), and which he had received by special revelation (i. 11-12).

3. Nor, in truth, would he have otherwise received it, for he was brought up in the Jews' religion (i. 13, 14), and after his conversion

---

* St. Paul's metaphor is borrowed from the popular belief in the power of the evil eye.—Lightfoot on Galatians, iii. 1.

† "For whatever reason, the Judaism of the Galatians was much more decided than we find in any other Gentile Church. The infection was both sudden and virulent. They were checked all at once in the gallant race for the prize. It was a Judaism of the sharp Pharisaic type, unclouded or unrelieved by any haze of Essene mysticism, such as prevailed a few years later in the neighbouring Colossian Church. Great stress was laid on the observance of 'days and months and seasons and years.' In short, nothing less than submission to the whole ceremonial law seems to have been contemplated by the innovators."—Professor Lightfoot on Galatians, p. 27.

he held no intercourse with the Apostles of the Circumcision (i. 15, 16).

4. When he first visited Jerusalem, he saw only James and Peter (i. 17-20); and, afterwards, though he went into Syria and Cilicia, he was unknown even by face unto the Judean Churches (i. 21-24).

5. Afterwards, on his second visit to Jerusalem, he yielded in nothing to the Judaizers, but maintained his equality with the Apostles of the Circumcision, and extorted from James, Peter, and John the right hand of fellowship (ii. 1-10).

6. At Antioch, when Peter, under evil influence, began to give the preference to the Law, Paul openly withstood him. The mention of this incident leads him to repeat the arguments he employed, and he is thus carried into the second portion of his epistle.

PART II.—Argumentative (chapters iii. and iv.).*

1. The Galatians are stultifying themselves; are substituting the flesh for the Spirit, the works of the Law for the obedience of Faith; forgetting the experience of the past and violating the order of progress (iii. 1-5).

2. Yet as Abraham was justified by Faith, so must it be with the true children of Abraham (iii. 6-9).

3. The Law, on the contrary, did not *justify* but *condemn*, and from this condemnation we were rescued by Christ (iii. 10-14);

4. Who thus fulfilled the promise given to Abraham,—a promise given prior to the Law, and therefore incapable of being annulled by it (iii. 15-18).

5. Such being the case, what purpose was the Law intended to answer? (iii. 19).

(1.) It was an inferior dispensation, given as a witness against sin; a badge of a condition of thraldom, not as adverse to, but as preparatory for, the Gospel (iii. 19-23).

(2.) And so through the Law we are educated for the freedom of the Gospel (iii. 24-29).

(3.) Thus under the Law we were in our nonage, but now we are our own masters (iv. 1-7).

* We borrow this portion of our analysis mainly from Professor Lightfoot.

(4.) Yet to this inferior and pupil-like condition the Galatians seem bent on returning (iv. 8-11).

6. The Law, moreover, is a witness against itself. Its relation to the covenant of grace is similar to the relation which Hagar bore to Sarah; and in the one case, as in the other, the son of the bondwoman must give place to the "children of the free" (iv. 21-31).

The freedom we have thus acquired we must preserve. Such is the natural opening of

PART III.—Practical (chapter v. to end).

1. The Apostle beseeches the Galatians to stand fast in this freedom, and not to be led astray by false teachers (v. 1-12).

2. Always remembering that freedom must not degenerate into license (v. 13-16).

3. The works of the flesh, however, are easily to be distinguished from the works of the Spirit (v. 17-26).

4. Charity towards an erring brother is a necessary condition on the part of those who are themselves so liable to temptation (vi. 1-5).

5. And not less needful is liberality towards all men, and especially towards those who are of the household of faith (vi. 6-10).

6. The Apostle concludes with a final warning against Judaism, a reassertion of the truths of the gospel, and a promise of peace to those who live up to and in them (vi. 11-16).

7. The Apostle briefly insists on his peculiar authority (vi. 17); and,

8. Bestows his benediction on the brethren (vi. 18).

It is worth remembering, that when Luther began his holy war against the corruptions of the Roman Church, this Epistle to the Galatians was one of the most effective weapons in his armoury. His Commentary upon it he wrote, and re-wrote, and he preferred it to any of his other works. "The Epistle to the Galatians," he said, "is *my* epistle; I have betrothed myself to it; it is my wife."

There exists a certain resemblance between it and the Second Epistle to the Corinthians, as might be expected from their identity of topics. In both, says Professor Jowett,* may be observed the same sensitiveness in the Apostle to the behaviour of his converts to himself, the same earnestness about the points of difference, the same remembrance of his "infirmity" while he was yet with them, the same consciousness of the precarious basis on which his own authority rested in the existing state of the two Churches. In both there is a greater display of his own feelings than in any other portion of his writings, a deeper contrast of inward exultation and outward suffering, more of personal entreaty, a greater readiness to impart himself.

But, according to Professor Lightfoot,† the affinity which the Epistle to the Galatians bears to the Epistle to the Romans is still more striking. Setting aside the purely personal portion, and a few digressive illustrations, connected with the time at, and circumstances under, which it was written, "almost every thought and argument in the Epistle to the Galatians may be matched from the other Epistle." Our limits will only permit us to give a few parallel passages :—

GALATIANS.	ROMANS.
Gal. iii. 6.—Even as Abraham believed God, and it was accounted to him for righteousness.	Rom. iv. 3.—Abraham believed God, and it was accounted to him for righteousness.
Gal. iii. 10.—For as many as are of the works of the law are under the curse.	Rom. iv. 15.—Because the law worketh wrath.
Gal. iii. 11.—But that no man is justified by the law in the sight of God, it	Rom. iii. 21.—But now the righteousness of God without the law is

---

* Jowett, "Epistles of St. Paul," *in loco.*
† Lightfoot, "On the Galatians," p. 45.

is evident: for, The just shall live by faith.

Gal. iii. 22.—The Scripture hath concluded all under sin, that the promise by faith of Jesus Christ might be given to them that believe.

Gal. iii. 27.—For as many of you as have been baptized into Christ have put on Christ.

Gal. iv. 5–7.—That we might receive the adoption of sons. And because ye are sons, God hath sent forth the Spirit of his Son into your hearts, crying, Abba, Father. Wherefore thou art no more a servant, but a son; and if a son, then an heir of God through Christ.

Gal. ii. 16.—For by the works of the law shall no flesh be justified (Ps. cxliii. 2).

manifested, being witnessed by the law and the prophets.
Rom. i. 17.—As it is written, The just shall live by faith.

Rom. xi. 32.—God hath concluded them all in unbelief, that he might have mercy upon all.

Rom. vi. 3.—As many of us as have been baptized into Christ.
Rom. xiii. 14.—Put ye on the Lord Jesus Christ.

Rom. viii. 14–17.—For as many as are led by the Spirit of God, they are the sons of God. For ye have not received the Spirit of bondage again to fear; but ye have received the Spirit of adoption, whereby we cry, Abba, Father. The Spirit itself beareth witness with our spirit, that we are the children of God: and if children, then heirs, heirs of God, and joint-heirs with Christ.

Rom. iii. 20.—For by the works of the law shall no flesh be justified before him.

It is generally supposed that on this occasion the Apostle remained three months at Corinth. Probably he employed himself in vindicating his authority against those who had denied it, in his usual missionary labours, in visiting the various Churches scattered over Achaia, and in urging forward the great collection he had instituted for the poorer Christians at Jerusalem. As soon as it was completed, certain persons were named by the Church to act as treasurers, and carry it to Jerusalem on the occasion of Paul's approaching journey to the Holy City (1 Cor. xvi. 3).

But he accomplished yet another work. A Christian

deaconess, named Phœbe, belonging to the sea-port of Cenchreæ, was bound on a journey to Rome,—in reference, we may suppose, to some private affairs. Paul determined to make her the bearer of an Apostolic Letter to the Church in that city, which he intended shortly to visit, but with many of whose members, though they had not seen his face in the flesh, he was acquainted, through common friends or frequent correspondence. We may well marvel at the fulness of the mind which, in the space of some three months, could pour out so much forcible argument and eloquent appeal as is embodied in the two great epistles written by Paul at Corinth! Written, too, by no secluded bookworm, or leisure-gifted student, but by an Apostle pressed with the cares, anxieties, and business of numerous infant Churches.

That the Epistle to the Romans was written at Corinth is distinctly stated in its fifteenth chapter. The Apostle is on his way to Jerusalem, "ministering to the saints" (xv. 25), and carrying thither the contributions of Macedonia and Achaia for the relief of their poorer brethren. Having completed his missionary labours in Greece and Asia Minor, he purposes, after a pilgrimage to Jerusalem, to visit the converts at Rome on his way to Spain (xv. 24),—the latter intention, we may add, being one which, so far as we know, he was never able to carry out. The allusion to Cenchreæ, the port of Corinth (xvi. 1), agrees with the other circumstances, in indicating his second sojourn at Corinth as the time and place of writing the Epistle to the Romans.

There were some peculiarities in the condition of the Roman Church which need illustration, in order to explain Paul's object in writing this epistle;—one, says Professor Jowett, that has ever been regarded as first in importance among the Apostle's writings, as the corner-stone of that gospel which he preached among the Gentiles. The Roman Church seems to have been at once Jewish and Gentile; Gentile in origin, but Jewish in feeling. Jewish, because St. Paul everywhere argues with its members as Jews; Gentile, because as such he expressly addresses them by name (i. 14). In this double fact, says Professor Jowett, we now perceive there is nothing strange or anomalous: it represents the general condition of the early Christian Churches, whether Jewish or Gentile; whether founded by St. Paul, or by the Apostles of the Circumcision. It was not only in idea, he adds, that the Old Testament prepared the way for the New, by holding up the truth of the unity of the Godhead; but the spread of truth among the Gentiles, and the influence of the Jewish Scriptures, were themselves actual preparatives for the gospel.

Thus, then, we may take the Roman Church to have consisted originally of Gentiles, who had been converted to Judaism, but had afterwards embraced Christianity. We can hardly doubt but that in course of time it would receive within its fold accessions both of Jews and Gentiles, as they heard and embraced the gospel of Christ; and that thus a constant struggle would be maintained between one party ever clinging closely to their Judaic observances, and another party ever desirous of a fuller liberty.

These circumstances will account for the style and subject of the Epistle to the Romans. "The condemnation of the Jew first, and afterwards of the Gentile,—the justification of the Jew first, and afterwards of the Gentile,—the actual fact of the rejection of the Jews, and the hope of their restoration,—are all of them topics appropriate to what we may conceive to have been the feeling of the Roman converts, in whom a Jewish education had not obliterated a Gentile origin, and whom a Gentile origin did not deprive of the hope of Jewish promises. The Apostle no longer appears to be speaking to the winds of heaven what, after being borne to and fro upon the earth, might return to the profit of the Church after many days, but what had an immediate interest for it, and arose naturally out of its actual state."*

The *Epistle to the Romans* is not the product of Nature. It is the plain result of grace. Nothing but grace, the grace of the Lord Jesus, who liveth, and was dead, and is alive for evermore, could have produced it. And when these living words become themselves the source of eternal life to others; when, spiritually,

> "They from thick films shall purge the visual ray,
> And on the sightless eyeball pour the day"

of a new and regenerate existence, the brightness of a heavenly and divine light, and open the eyes to behold glories before unknown in worlds as yet not realized, then we may learn who it is whose Spirit of life and light yet breathes and flutters, yet quivers and palpitates in them; then we may confess the mission of Paul to be verily and indeed from God; then we may feel and know that the revelation is, beyond all doubt, the revelation of one who, being "an Apostle, not of men, neither by man, but an Apostle sent by Jesus Christ and God the Father, who raised Him from the dead," was empowered to say, "Though we, or an angel from heaven, preach any

* Jowett, "Epistles of St. Paul," ii. 27.

other gospel unto you than that which we have preached unto you, let him be accursed." For then, assuredly, we can understand that it was a revelation once for all given to the saints, which time itself shall have no right, no power to disannul, but which, from age to age, shall live on unchanged, till it is merged in, and superseded by, the final unveiling of the Son of man in glory.*

We proceed to an analysis of its contents:— †

PART I.—Personal (chapter i., verses 1 to 15).

A brief allusion to his intended visit to Rome, prefaced by the usual salutation (i. 1-15).

PART II.—DOCTRINAL (chapter i. 16 to xi. 36).

1. The Apostle explains the true principle of his teaching,—the gospel is the power of God unto salvation to every one that believeth; to the Jew first, and also to the Greek. "For therein is the righteousness of God revealed from faith to faith: as it is written, 'The just shall live by faith'" (i. 16, 17).

2. Prior to the declaration of Christ's gospel, all men were alike under the Divine condemnation:—

(a) The Heathen, whose leading sins are enumerated (i. 18-32).

(b) The Jew, whose self-sufficiency is severely censured (ii. 1-29).

3. The Jew, it is true, enjoys a certain privilege, but he is not the less guilty because he has sinned in the law; and the general condemnation of both Jew and Gentile is proved by reference to Scripture (iii. 1-20).

4. Now, under the gospel, a mode of justification ("righteousness") is revealed to all; to all, because it is not of the Jewish Law, but of faith, and therefore universal (iii. 21-26).

5. By this law of faith all boasting is excluded (iii. 27-31).

6. As an example of its working, Abraham is quoted, whose faith

---

* Stanley Leathes, "Witness of St. Paul to Christ" (Boyle Lectures, 1869), pp. 233, 234.

† Founded, mainly, on Professor Lightfoot's, in Smith's "Bible Dictionary," iii. 1057, 1058.

in God was counted unto him for righteousness before he was circumcised, and who is thus the father of all believers (iv.).

7. In the same way we are justified by faith through the blood of Christ; as sin and death came by Adam, all now being justified by the Saviour's obedience (v.).

8. Having died to the law, we have died to sin (vi. 1-14); but this putting away of the law does not accord to us any moral license (vi. 15-23). "On the contrary, as the law has passed away, so must sin, for sin and the law are correlative; at the same time this is no disparagement of the law, but rather a proof of human weakness (vii. 1-25). So, henceforth, in Christ we are free from sin, we have the Spirit, and look forward in hope, triumphing over our present afflictions" (viii. 1-39).

9. While grieving over the rejection of the Jews, we must remember that the promise was not to the whole people, but to a select seed (ix. 1-13); and mysterious as this ordinance of God may seem to us, we may not presume to criticise it (ix. 13-31).

10. Both the calling of the Gentiles and rejection of the Jews were foretold; the reason why the Jews rejected the gospel explained (ix. 32, 33).

11. Justification was offered to all men by faith,—to all men, including the Gentiles,—and this truth was clearly known to the Jews (x.).

12. Though they would not believe, their rejection is not final; through that rejection the Gentiles were gathered in, and through the Gentiles the Jews, in due time, will be brought to Christ (xi. 1-32), whence Paul is led to enlarge on God's unsearchable judgments (xi. 33-36).

PART III.—Practical (chapter xii. to xv. 15).

1. As a corollary from these premises, Paul exhorts the Roman Christians, in glowing language, to the daily practice of all Christian virtues (xii., xiii.).

2. He warns them against insisting upon comparatively trivial observances, and thereby offending weaker brethren; and enlarges on the example of Christ as an encouragement to tolerance and charity (xiv.; xv. 1-15).

PART IV.—Conclusion (chapter xv. 16 to end).

1. Paul, in conclusion, explains his motive ("as the minister of Jesus Christ to the Gentiles") in writing this epistle, and announces his intention of visiting them (xv. 16–33).
2. He greets by name certain members of the Roman Church.
3. Finally exhorts them against divisions and differences, and pronounces his apostolic benediction.

Before the Apostle sailed from Jerusalem, where he had every reason to apprehend the hostility of the Judaizing portion of the Church, a plot against his life was hatched among the Corinthian Jews (Acts xx. 3). He therefore departed at once, by land, for Macedonia; and thence by Berea, Thessalonica, and Philippi, he proceeded to Troas. His companions on this occasion were Sopater of Berea; Aristarchus and Secundus of Thessalonica; Gaius of Derbe; and Timotheus and Tychicus and Trophimus, from proconsular Asia. But they did not all cross over to Asia with St. Paul. While he and Luke remained at Philippi, during the Passover, they preceded him to Troas, where Luke and the Apostle joined them, after a tedious voyage of five days (Acts xx. 6).

At Troas the little missionary band remained a week. And on the Sabbath evening before their departure, they were assembled, along with the Christians of Troas, in an upper room,—a room lighted by many lamps,—celebrating that breaking of the bread, in the Holy Communion, which was at this time an invariable custom in those religious assemblies known as ἀγάπαι. And as Paul, in view of his approaching departure, addressed the brethren at more than ordinary length, a certain young man, named

Eutychus, who sat in the window-seat,* overpowered by the heat of the crowded room, fell asleep, and in his slumber dropped from his elevated position on to the floor beneath. He was taken up dead, greatly to the grief of all the congregation. But Paul went down, and embracing the body,—as we read of Elijah (1 Kings xvii. 21) and Elisha (2 Kings iv. 34), on similar occasions, —he bade them not be troubled, for his life was in him. And, accordingly, Eutychus again took his place in the assembly, who broke bread, with infinite joy and gratitude, and having partaken, as was usual in the Agapē, of their ordinary meal, remained conversing until dawn of day (Acts xx. 8–12).

The ship was now ready to sail, and the Apostle's companions went on board, he himself staying to complete some arrangements, and joining them at Assus, a port about twenty miles distant.

Assus, now *Beiram Kalesi*, is a sea-port on the northern shore of the Gulf of Adramyttium, about seven miles from the opposite coast of the Island of Lesbos; or somewhat in the same position as Ardrossan is to Arran, or Hayling to the Isle of Wight. It was connected with the inland towns of the province by a good Roman road, which extended to Troas, and was situated on a high and remarkably precipitous cliff, commanding a marine prospect of exquisite and diversified beauty. A thoroughly Greek town, its remains are of more than ordinary interest; and being of granite, are in an unusually perfect condition. The citadel, the theatre, and the Street of Tombs, are the leading features.†

The sea-voyage to Assus, round Cape Lectum, was

---

* The Eastern windows have neither glass nor shutters.
† Leake, "Travels in Asia Minor," p. 128.

longer than the overland route, and we do not suppose that Paul kept his companions waiting. Having embarked on board the ship, they sailed across the narrow strait to Mitylene, the capital of the Island of Lesbos, where they stayed the night.

The beauty of the Lesbian capital was the theme of the poets and architects of Rome. It is the "fair Mitylene" of Ovid; Cicero speaks of it "as eminently noble by nature, and by the superior character of its edifices." Now-a-days we usually connect it with the memory of the celebrated Greek poetess; we think of it as the place

" Where burning Sappho lived and sung."

In its rear rises a range of mountains, singularly remarkable for the boldness and picturesqueness of their outline.

Slowly navigating the blue unruffled sea, with lovely natural prospects on either hand, which we cannot doubt were fully appreciated by the imaginative and enthusiastic mind of Paul, they came, next day, to Chios,* an island rich in orange-gardens, groves of citron, almonds, and pomegranates, in mountain-shadows and leafy valleys. Afterwards, they put in at Samos, famous for its purple vineyards,—

" Fill high the cup with Samian wine,"—

for its historic memories, and its ceramic manufacture; and then lay-to for the night at Trogyllium,† a mountainous promontory and a celebrated town on the Ionian coast, separated from Samos by a strait scarcely one mile in breadth. Here was fought the great battle between

---

* The modern Scio—in Turkish, *Saki Adassi*—32 miles in length, and 18 miles in breadth.

† An anchorage here is still called *St. Paul's Port*.

the Greeks and Persians in B.C. 479, in which the latter were totally defeated.

The night of Tuesday was spent in this little port, because the moon set early, and it was desirable to wait for daylight to make the harbour of Miletus.

MILETUS, though in Paul's time inferior in wealth and importance to Ephesus, was of far greater antiquity. The capital of Ionia, it had sent forth eighty colonies to plant themselves on the shores of the Black Sea, eastward, and westward along the Mediterranean to the Pillars of Hercules. Once it had four harbours; not a trace of them is now extant; and even the river Meander has wrought for itself new channels in the low alluvial plain which was once the scene of so much prosperity. For though it had suffered severely in the Persian war, and afterwards in Alexander the Great's invasion, its ruin was mainly due to natural causes—to the deposit of alluvial soil at the river's mouth, which gradually removed it further and further from the sea. Its site is now fully ten miles from the coast. But in the history of philosophy it will be celebrated as the city of Thales and Hecatæus; in that of Christianity, from the visit of St. Paul.

At Miletus, Paul and his companions landed; and the Apostle sent a message to Ephesus, which was about twenty-seven miles distant, desiring the presence of the elders (presbyters) of its Church. On their arrival, which probably took place next day, he addressed them in very pathetic and impressive terms.

"Ye know," he said, "from the first day that I came into Asia, after what manner I have been with you at all seasons, serving the Lord with all humility of mind, and with many tears and with temptations [trials] which befell me by the lying in wait of the Jews; and how I kept back nothing that could be profitable unto you, but have showed you, and have taught you publicly, and from house to house, testifying both to the Jews, and also to the Greeks, repentance toward God, and faith toward our Lord Jesus Christ.

"And now, behold, I go bound in my spirit unto Jerusalem, not knowing what things may befall me there, save that the Holy Ghost witnesseth in every city, saying, that bonds and afflictions abide me.

"But none of these things move me; I hold my life of no account, nor is it so precious to me, so that I may finish my course with joy, and the ministry which I have received from the Lord Jesus, to testify the glad tidings of the grace of God.

"And now, behold, I know that ye all among whom I have gone from city to city, proclaiming the kingdom of God, shall see my face no more. Wherefore I take you to witness this day that I am free from the blood of all men. For I have not shunned to declare unto you all the counsel of God.

"Take heed, therefore, unto yourselves, and to all the flock in which the Holy Spirit has made you overseers, that ye feed the Church of God, which He hath purchased with His own blood. For this I know, that after my departure grievous wolves shall enter in among you, not sparing the flock. And from your own selves shall men arise, speaking perverted words, that they may draw away the disciples after them. Therefore, watch, and remember that for the space of three years I ceased not to warn every one of you, night and day, with tears.

"And now, brethren, I commend you to God, and to the word of His grace; even to Him who is able to build you up, and to give you an inheritance among all them that are sanctified. I have coveted no man's silver, or gold, or apparel. Yea, ye yourselves know that these hands ministered to my necessities, and to those who were with me. And all this I did for your example, that ye, so labouring, ought to support the weak, and to remember the words of the Lord Jesus, how He said, 'It is more blessed to give than to receive.'"

After this tenderly eloquent address, the brethren joined in a united act of solemn leave-taking, and weeping bitterly, they fell upon Paul's neck, and kissed him. And most they sorrowed because of his own prophetic words, that they should see his face no more. How often in after-years must they have thought, with infinite rejoicing, of the intercourse they had been privileged to hold with the great Apostle! How often must their hearts have burned within them as they remembered the words of truth and wisdom he had so often poured into their ears! In moments of doubt and discouragement, such memories would surely stir them like the sound of a trumpet, and in their knowledge of Paul's deep earnest faith their own would be rekindled into a living flame! But when they recalled the tenderness which inspired that heroic nature,—the overflowing love which lent angelic light to that rugged countenance,—the consciousness of a Divine commission which gave dignity to that mean presence,—the fiery eloquence which by turns startled, and terrified, and won, and persuaded, and overawed its hearers,—it would be with a deeper, more pathetic, and fonder feeling, they would think of the great Apostle!

Then softer emotions will have possessed them, and, in their deep sense of an irreparable loss, they may well have longed

"For the touch of a vanished hand,
And the sound of a voice that was still!"

The wind blew fair, and the Apostle could no longer delay. Followed, as we may well imagine, by the wistful looks of the brethren, he and his companions embarked on board their hired vessel, which, running before the auspicious breeze, soon vanished from their sight. With a straight course they made for Cos,—an island in the Myrtoan Sea, famous for its wines, and its purple stuffs, and its precious unguents,—where they cast anchor in the sheltered and commodious harbour of its chief town, which bore the same name.

Cos [*] is an island about twenty-three miles long, from south-west to north-east, and separated from the mainland by a narrow strait. Groups of small verdant isles stud, like emeralds, the sapphire sea which spreads and shines around it. Its capital, before Paul's visit, had been shattered by an earthquake, but the fortifications erected by Alcibiades remained to some extent uninjured, and pilgrims could still repair to its famous Temple of Æsculapius, and worship at the opulent shrine of the god of healing. It was the birthplace, we may add, of Apelles the painter, and Hippocrates the physician.

Next day the voyage was resumed, and the Apostle's ship held her way through the channel which lies between southern Cos and that projection of the Asiatic mainland anciently known as the Point of Cnidus, now *Cape*

---

[*] Now called *Stanchio.—See* Ross, "Reisen nach Kos, Halicarnassos" (Halle, 1852), and "Reisen auf den Griechen Inseln," ii. 87, *sqq.*; and iii. 125, *sqq.*

Crio. The extremity of this remarkable headland descends sheer into the sea, and is separated by a level space, or neck, from the main; so that at a distance it may be taken for an island. It has been truly remarked that its history, no less than its appearance, was well impressed on the mind of the Greek navigator of old; for it was the scene of Conon's victory, and the memory of their great admiral made the south-western angle of the Asiatic peninsula as dear to the Athenians, as the memories of Jervis and Nelson—St. Vincent and Trafalgar—the south-western corner of Spain to English voyagers.*

Rounding Cape Crio, St. Paul's vessel soon made the Island of Rhodes.

The old proverb said that the sun shone every day on Rhodes; and it is not too fanciful, perhaps, to assert that it is always lit up with the glory of the past. Certainly, no other island in the Mediterranean—not even Candia, or Cyprus—is so rich in those memories of art and literature and warfare, of glorious thoughts and glorious deeds, which are the richest inheritance of nations.

Its annals begin about 400 B.C., with the foundation of its capital, at the north-eastern extremity of the island. After the death of Alexander, this capital rose into a position of great power and influence; and in its vigilant suppression of piracy, its wise mercantile laws, and its provision for the support of the poor, anticipated the safest polity of the most civilized of modern nations. Simultaneously with its increase in wealth, and the development of its material supremacy, it fostered the arts; at the mouth of its harbour stood the gigantic pharos, vulgarly called the Colossus; and on the high ground in the central quarter of the city was situated its magnificent Temple of the Sun. All around it were gardens, fragrant with roses, and bright with the most beautiful statuary; and the public

---

* Conybeare and Howson, ii. 228.

buildings were all designed on a scale of magnificence commensurate with the dignity of the state.

Rhodes became the faithful ally of Rome, and its fleets largely assisted the Roman armies in the conquest of the East. As a reward, it was endowed with special privileges, and permitted for many years to enjoy a considerable amount of independence. It was not reduced to a province until the reign of Vespasian.

Its Byzantine period was scarcely less fortunate. Under Constantine it became the metropolis of the "Province of the Islands" (*Provincia Insularum*); it was the last position held by the Christians of the East against the encroaching flood of Mohammedanism; it was the fortress of the Knights of St. John, whose memorials are everywhere visible in its walls, and streets, and harbour, and who here acquired a deathless renown for their Order by the chivalry with which they defended it against Soliman the Magnificent.

After staying one night in the harbour of Rhodes,—fourteen centuries later to be the scene of so fierce a struggle between the Cross and the Crescent,—St. Paul's ship, next morning, proceeded to Patara, across a sea as blue as the sky that shines upon and is reflected in it.

PATARA is the sea-port of Xanthus, of whose past splendour the antiquities discovered by Sir Charles Fellows, and preserved in the British Museum, have afforded the student a striking conception. Here the river Xanthus, after winding through a fertile valley, poured its bright waters into a sheltered bay; but the bay is now filled up with the "blown sand," which has rolled inland in destroying billows, and buried the ruins of the city once famous for its worship and oracle of Apollo.*

Of Patara the remains are not extensive; but as they include a triple archway, the public baths, and a vast theatre hewn out of the

---

* Sir C. Fellows, "Travels in Lycia," p. 222, *et sqq.*

side of a hill, it cannot be said that they are without archæological interest.

At Patara St. Paul's vessel completed her voyage, else she was bound for some port on the southern coast of Asia Minor. But in the harbour, fortunately, lay a vessel about to sail for Phœnicia,—the Apostle's destination,—on board of which he and his companions immediately embarked, and leaving Patara the same day,* sailed across the open sea in a south-easterly direction, the canvas swelling before a prosperous breeze.

The distance between Patara and Tyre, the great Phœnician port, is 340 geographical miles, and with a strong north-easterly wind would be accomplished in about forty-eight hours. The course lies outside the rich island of Cyprus, whose western shore the Apostle's ship would run very near, passing the notorious city of Paphos, the seat of the licentious worship of Aphrodite. He reached Tyre, therefore, in two days. Here his ship had to unload, and he accordingly remained in the Phœnician capital for seven days.

TYRE, as every reader knows, has a history of its own, so pregnant with mournful interest, that no summary can do justice to it. Once it was the great commercial centre of the world's activity, whose "merchants were princes, and its traffickers the honourable of the earth." It was built partly on an island, and partly on the mainland, which was separated from the island by a narrow passage of sea, and dedicated to Melkarth, or Hercules, whose temple was reported to be the most ancient of all the temples of the world. In Solomon's time its artificers were as famous for their skill, as its merchants for their opulence: the great Hebrew monarch sent to

* So we may conclude, from the mode of expression used by the historian.

Hiram, king of Tyre, for cedar-trees out of Lebanon, to be hewn by Hiram's subjects, since "there is not among us that can hew timber like the Sidonians." And they were also renowned as cunning workmen in brass and copper, gold and silver.

But Tyre was cursed with an excessive greed of gain; a greed of gain which induced its merchants to buy Hebrew captives from their enemies, and sell them as slaves to the Greeks and Edomites. By so doing, however, they drew upon themselves and their descendants the denunciations of the Hebrew prophets. We can well believe that the wealthy and powerful Tyrians regarded their predictions with contemptuous indifference; and this indifference would scarcely be shaken by the result of their protracted war with Shalmaneser, king of Assyria, for after a five years' siege they beat off his army, and rejoiced in a considerable increase of military reputation (B.C. 721–715).

From the prophecies of Ezekiel we gather some particulars of its prosperous condition at that epoch. We learn that it enlisted mercenary soldiers in its armies—Phœnicians, Æthiopians, and Persians. Its trade was extensive, especially in the precious metals: it imported gold from Arabia by the Persian Gulf; silver, iron, lead, and tin from Tarshish, or Tartessus, in the south of Spain; and copper from Cyprus, and the districts between the Black Sea and the Caspian. With wheat it was supplied from Palestine; the reason, as has been acutely remarked, why no war ever occurred between Tyre and the Israelites. From Palestine it also obtained oil, honey, and balm; wine from the country round about Damascus; linen from Egypt; and from the Peloponnesus those shell-fish dyes* which were long so famous as the Tyrian purple.

When at the climax of material prosperity, a new and formidable enemy appeared against the island-city, and threatened it with the fate foretold by the Hebrew prophets. This was Nebuchadnezzar, who, at the head of his Chaldean army, laid siege to it, and with relentless perseverance continued the siege for thirteen years.† Whether he captured it or not is still a historical puzzle; but it

---

* The species of shell-fish from which the dye was extracted is now recognized to have been the *Murex trunculus*.

† Josephus, cit. Apion, i. 21.

seems certain, at all events, that it became a tributary of the Assyrian empire. Afterwards, it occupied the same position with respect to Persia, and furnished a quota of ships of war to the vast expedition which Xerxes led against Greece. Mapên, the son of Serim the Tyrian, is mentioned by Herodotus as one of the ablest seamen in the Persian armada.

History now loses sight of Tyre for a considerable period. When it emerges again into the light of day, it is as the coveted spoil of Alexander the Great (B.C. 332). · The possession of its fleet was of absolute necessity to the success of his grand schemes of conquest, and when Tyre rejected his demands, he prepared to avenge himself on the haughty city. Its capture was no common achievement, for it stood on an island, half a mile from the mainland, and was surrounded by massive walls, reaching on one side to an elevation of a hundred and fifty feet. All the military resources of the great conqueror were brought to bear against it; but he only succeeded by constructing a huge causeway across the channel between the city and the mainland, for the advance of his troops and their military engines; and in this work he would have failed had not the labours of his artisans been covered by the fleets of the Cyprians and Sidonians.

On the capture of the city, its garrison was put to the sword, and 30,000 of its inhabitants were sold into slavery.

Even after this terrible blow, it recovered somewhat of its ancient prosperity through the activity of immigrants attracted by its favourable position. The Seleucidæ, who succeeded to the Syrian portion of Alexander's dominions, favoured it with many special immunities; and though of most of these it was deprived by Augustus, their loss may have affected the pride, but did not affect the material prosperity, of its inhabitants. It was famous in the Roman period for its purple dyes, but no longer imported its shell-fish from Lacedæmon, having a more valuable species of *murex* on its own shores. At this time,—that is, when Christ visited it (Matt. xv. 21; Mark vii. 24),—its circumference was not less than nineteen Roman miles, and it was crowded with houses of many stories.

It continued to preserve its opulence down to the time of Jerome, who, about A.D. 415, wrote of it as "the noblest and fairest city in Phœnicia;" and probably it had decayed but little when the prophecies of Ezekiel were partially fulfilled in the ruin inflicted upon it by the Arabs, under Khalif Omar (A.D. 638). It was then compelled to pay a poll-tax to its conquerors; was bound to provide every Moslem traveller with three days' board and lodging free; to admit the Moslems into its churches; to remove every cross, and silence every bell: while its inhabitants bound themselves to wear a peculiar dress; to build no new churches, and never to ride on horseback. In this condition of abject slavery it dragged on its existence for several centuries. It was captured by the Crusaders in 1124, and William, a Frenchman, was appointed its Archbishop. It was then famous for its glass and sugar manufactures, and maritime enterprise. In 1291, however, on the approach of the Moslem army, under the Sultan of Egypt and Damascus, its inhabitants, aware that they could offer no successful resistance, embarked on board their vessels, and abandoned the little island, which for three thousand years had been the site of a wealthy and important city. From this last blow it has never recovered. Sandys, in 1611, writes: "The once famous Tyre is now no other than a heap of ruins; yet have they a reverent aspect, and do instruct the reverent beholder with their exemplary frailty." * Nor is its present condition much more grateful to the traveller's eye. Among the shattered remains of the ancient city dwell some 3000 to 4000 Syrians, in mean and squalid huts, who know nothing of the glories of the once famous and wealthy Tyre.

There is some reason to suppose that a Christian Church had been established at Tyre soon after the death of Stephen (Acts xi. 19), which may have been visited by St. Paul on the occasion of his missionary tour through the regions of Syria and Cilicia (Gal. i. 21). If such were the case, it would account for the extraordinary affection with which he was received by the Tyrians.

* Sandys, in "Purchas's Pilgrims," ii., p. 1393.

ARRIVAL AT PTOLEMAIS.

He remained a week among them, and some, who possessed the gift of prophecy,* endeavoured to dissuade him from his journey to Jerusalem, by foretelling the perils that there awaited him. This trial of his faith and earnestness Paul easily resisted; and on the day of his departure, he was accompanied out of the city by a strange and affecting procession of the brethren, their wives and children: and all kneeling down on the shore, Paul offered up prayer on their and his own behalf, to the solemn accompaniment of the waves ceaselessly beating upon the rocks (Acts xxi. 5).

On the same day, before sunset, Paul and his companions arrived at Ptolemais, where they bade farewell to the sea, the rest of their expedition falling to be accomplished by land. They stayed a day with the Christians of Ptolemais, and then set out for Cæsarea.

PTOLEMAIS is the *Accho*† of which we read in Judges i. 31, as one of the towns of the tribe of Asher. During the prolonged contests between Persia and Egypt, its excellent harbour made it a place of very considerable importance. Between the headland on which it stands, and the promontory of Carmel on the north, spreads the

---

* Acts xxi. 4. "The notice here is very important, that these Tyrian disciples said to Paul, 'by the Spirit,' that he should not go to Jerusalem, and yet he went thither, and, as he himself declares, bound in Spirit by the leading of God. We thus have an instance of that which Paul asserts in 1 Cor. xiv. 32, that the spirits of the prophets are 'subject to the prophets;' that is, that the revelation made by the Holy Spirit to each man's spirit was under the influence of that man's will and temperament, moulded by and taking the form of his own capacities and resolves. So here: these Tyrian *prophets* knew by the Spirit, which testified this in every city (xx. 23), that bonds and imprisonment awaited Paul. But he paid no regard to the prohibition, being himself under a leading of the same Spirit too plain for him to mistake it."—Dean Alford, "New Testament," *in loc.*

† The meaning of the Hebrew word is said to be "hot sand." It is now called *Acca*.

only bay which is found along the whole extent of the Syrian coast. The range of hills which, from Tyre southwards, seem to hug the shore, here retires for a few miles inland, and at their base lies extended a rich and smiling plain, watered by the Nahr Namûn (the ancient *Belus*),* whose waters flow into the sea close under the walls of the time-honoured town.

During the Macedonian period, Ptolemais became a place of note, from its position on the frontier of Syria. Eventually, it was included within the Egyptian territories, and from one of the Ptolemies received the name of Ptolemais. It was afterwards captured by Antiochus the Great, and attached to the Syrian kingdom; but when the latter fell into ruin, it established its independence, and this independence it enjoyed until it was captured by Cleopatra, who reattached it to the Syrian monarchy. Shortly afterwards it was taken by Tigranes, king of Armenia; and again, by the Romans, who elevated it to the rank of a colony, with the title *Colonia Claudii Cæsaris*.

Passing over many centuries, we find it in the possession of the Turks, and remember that when Napoleon invaded Egypt, he endeavoured to secure this valuable sea-port,—which bore the name of St. Jean d'Acre,†—but was defeated by the courage and energy of Sir Sidney Smith. When Mehemet Ali made his daring effort to establish an Egyptian kingdom, it was seized and garrisoned by Egyptian soldiers; but was recovered for the Turks by the English fleet, under Sir Robert Stopford and Sir Charles Napier. We need only add that the modern town contains no memorials of the ancient Ptolemais; but is a centre of commercial enterprise, and the most prosperous sea-port on the Syrian coast.

At Cæsarea St. Paul was gladly welcomed by the family of Philip the Evangelist, who appears to have resided here during the intervals between his missionary excursions. His family consisted of four daughters, who were an example, as it has been pointed out, of the fulfilment

---

* Dr. Thomson, "The Land and the Book."

† A corruption of " St. John of Akha," the name given to it by the Crusaders.

of Joel's prediction, quoted by St. Peter, that, at the opening of the new dispensation, God's Spirit should descend upon His "handmaidens" as well as His bondsmen, and that the "daughters," as well as the sons, should prophesy (Joel ii. 28, 29; Acts ii. 17, 18; 1 Cor. xiv. 34; 1 Tim. ii. 12). The prophetic power was enjoyed by these four women of Cæsarea, who were living that life of pious virginity* commended by St. Paul as "good for the present distress" (1 Cor. vii.), and were exercising their gift in concert for the benefit of the Church.

The Apostle remained at Cæsarea for some days. Having arrived in Judea some time before the great festival, he had no longer any occasion to hurry his movements. Intelligence of his arrival, however, reached the Holy City, and came to the ears of the prophet Agabus; the same who had predicted a famine in the reign of the Emperor Claudius (Acts xi. 28). He immediately hastened to Cæsarea, entered Philip's house, and taking St. Paul's girdle, he bound with it his own hands and feet,† declaring, in the name of the Holy Spirit, that the Jews in like manner should bind the owner of that girdle, and deliver him into the hands of the Gentiles (Acts xxi. 11).

And when we heard these things, says St. Luke, both we—that is, the Apostle's companions—and the brethren of Cæsarea, besought him not to go up to Jerusalem. Who cannot fancy the little band, gathering around their revered and beloved master, kneeling at his feet, and with tears and sobs, it may be, imploring him not to venture

---

* According to tradition, two of them were afterwards married.
† For similar symbolical actions, see Isa. xx., Jer. xiv., Ezek. iv.

into assured peril ? But the courageous spirit of Paul was not to be shaken. He was much moved by the evidences of the deep affection borne to him, and gently remonstrated with his friends for making so trying an appeal to his sympathies. "Why will you weep," he said, "and break my heart? Cease, cease your supplications: for I am ready, not to be bound only,—not only to suffer the burden of chains and the weariness of captivity,— but, if need be, to die at Jerusalem for the name of the Lord Jesus."

So when the sorrowing company found that he was not to be moved from the path of duty, they desisted from their tearful entreaties, and echoing our Lord's prayer, exclaimed, Thy will, O Father, be done* (Acts xxi. 10-14).

But the great Pentecostal festival was rapidly approaching, and from all parts of the world where the Jewish race had planted its offshoots, pilgrims were hastening to the Holy City. It was time for Paul and his companions to take their departure; and accordingly they went on their way, attended by some of the disciples from Cæsarea, and by one Mnason, a native of Cyprus,† who had undertaken to lodge them in his house. At Jerusalem they received that cordial welcome which Christians should ever accord to Christians, and which was the especial due of the Apostle of the Gentiles, the founder of so many Christian Churches. On the day after their arrival, they repaired to the house of James the Just— "the Lord's brother," and the overseer, bishop, or presi-

* This is one of the passages, says Dean Alford, from which we may not unfairly infer that the Lord's Prayer was used by the Christians of the Apostolic Age.

† He is supposed to have been one of our Saviour's earliest disciples.

dent of the Jerusalem community—where all the elders (presbyters) had assembled to receive them. Mutual salutations were exchanged, and Paul then proceeded to relate in detail the wonders which God, through his ministry, had wrought in the Gentile world, and how the banner of the Cross of Christ had been planted in Greece, and along the shores of the Mediterranean.

This striking narrative produced a great effect on its hearers, who, at its close, broke forth into solemn and united thanksgiving.

In the course of his address, it is possible that Paul alluded to the difficulties with which he had been called to contend in Galatia and at Corinth through the hostility of the Judaizing faction; and after the first emotions excited by his fervid eloquence had subsided, the strong feeling entertained on this subject by the Christians of Jerusalem began to show itself. Many of his hearers recollected that he was supposed to regard the Mosaic customs with indifference, and, under this impression, they addressed him:—" Thou seest, brother, how many thousands of Jews there are which believe; and they are all zealous of the law: and they are informed of thee, that thou teachest all the Jews which are among the Gentiles to forsake Moses, saying that they ought not to circumcise their children, nor walk after the Jewish customs" (Acts xxi. 20, 21). James and the elders professed to disbelieve the correctness of these statements; but in order to give them a public denial, suggested that he should perform some act of homage to the law and its observances. There were four disciples who had taken the Nazarite vow; a vow whose completion involved a considerable outlay for offerings to be presented to the Temple. Let the Apostle join himself with them for the seven days of the vow which remained unexpired, and defray their expenses. By so doing, he would silence the calumnies of his enemies (Acts xxi. 23–25).*

Paul readily agreed to a proposal which involved no sacrifice of principle, and, on the following day, having performed the preliminary purifications, went with the Christian Nazarites to the Temple, and informed the priests that the due offerings would be presented on the completion of the period of the vow.

But before the seventh day arrived, certain Jews from Asia Minor, who had come up to the Pentecostal feast, recognized the bold and eloquent Apostle of the Gentiles, while walking in the streets of Jerusalem with his companion, Trophimus the Ephesian. On one occasion they saw him in the Temple, and seizing the opportunity of gratifying their lust of vengeance, they set upon him, shouting: "Men of Israel, help! This is he who everywhere teaches all men to scorn the people, the law, and this holy place; yea, who hath also brought Gentiles into the Temple!" This latter charge was as false as the first, and was only suggested by the circumstance that they had seen Trophimus in Paul's company, not in the Temple, but in the city.

A violent mob, however, was quickly assembled: Paul was dragged down from the Court of the Women into the Outer Court, and the Levitical Guard immediately shut behind him the Corinthian Gates, that the Temple

---

* *See* Conybeare and Howson, ii. 248, 249.

might not be profaned by tumult or bloodshed. With their victim in their hands, the Jews would quickly have proceeded to murder; but the Roman sentinels in the Antonia tower had sent information of the riot to their commander, Claudius Lysias (Acts xxi. 31), who, with some centurions and a strong force of soldiers, immediately hastened to the spot. On the approach of the Roman eagles, the multitude desisted from their ill-usage of the Apostle, whom Lysias arrested as his own prisoner, ordering him to be chained to a soldier on either hand. He then inquired of what crime he had been guilty, but could gain no intelligible reply from the confused and angry crowd. Suspecting him to be a certain Egyptian pretender, who had assumed the character of a prophet —attracted to his standard four thousand Sicarii, or "assassins"—and given out that the walls of Jerusalem would fall at his command,* he ordered him to be conveyed to the barracks within the fortress. So great, however, was the pressure of the mob, that, to execute this order, the soldiers had to take him up in their arms. When they had reached the top of the staircase, Paul, with characteristic presence of mind, turned to the Roman commander, and inquired of him, in Greek, "May I speak with thee?" Claudius Lysias, surprised at the language of the prisoner, asked him whether he was mistaken in supposing him to be the Egyptian rebel. "Nay," replied the Apostle, "I am no Egyptian, but a Jew—a native of Tarsus—a citizen of no mean city; wherefore, I request permission to speak unto this people." Impressed, perhaps, by his "aspect and manner," the Roman officer

* Josephus, "Wars of the Jews," ii. 13, 3.

consented. And standing on the stairs, beckoning with his chained hands, and looking forward with that steadfast gaze which was peculiar to him, the Apostle silenced the noisy sea beneath him, and, in the Hebrew tongue, spake as follows :—*

* In reference to St. Paul's speech, a recent writer remarks:—"It is described by St. Paul himself, in his opening words, as his 'defence,' addressed to his brethren and fathers. It is in this light that it ought to be regarded. As we have seen, the desire which occupied the Apostle's mind at this time, was that of vindicating his message and work as those of a faithful Jew. The discourse spoken to the angry people at Jerusalem is his own justification of himself. He adopts the historical method, after which all the recorded appeals to Jewish audiences are framed. He is a servant of facts. He had been from the first a zealous Israelite, like his hearers. He had changed his course because the God of his fathers had turned him from one path into another. It is thus that he is led into a narrative of his conversion. We have already noticed (and endeavoured to reconcile) the differences, in the statement of bare facts, between this narrative and that of the ninth chapter. The business of the student, in this place, is to see how far the purpose of the Apostle will account for whatever is special in this address. That purpose explains the detailed reference to his rigorously Jewish education, and to his history before his conversion. It gives point to the announcement that it was by a direct operation from without upon his spirit, and not by the gradual influence of other minds upon his, that his course was changed. Incidentally, we may see a reason for the admission that his companions 'heard not the voice of Him that spake to me' in the fact that some of them, not believing in Jesus with their former leader, may have been living at Jerusalem, and possibly present amongst the audience. In this speech the Apostle is glad to mention, what we were not told before, that the Ananias who interpreted the will of the Lord to him more fully at Damascus, was 'a devout man according to the law, having a good report of all the Jews which dwelt there,' and that he made his communication in the name of Jehovah, the God of Israel, saying, 'The God of our fathers hath chosen thee, that thou shouldest know His will, and see the Righteous One, and hear a voice out of His mouth; for thou shalt be a witness for Him unto all men of what thou hast seen and heard.' Having thus claimed, according to his wont, the character of a simple instrument and witness, St. Paul goes on to describe another revelation of which we read nothing elsewhere. He had been accused of being an enemy to the Temple. He relates that after the visit to Damascus he went up again to Jerusalem, and was praying once in the Temple itself, till he fell into a trance. Then he saw the Lord, and was bidden to leave Jerusalem quickly, because the people there would not receive his testimony concerning Jesus. His own impulse was to stay at Jerusalem, and he pleaded with the Lord that there it was well known how he had

" Brethren and fathers, hear me, and let me now defend myself before you. I am myself an Israelite, born in Tarsus, a city of Cilicia, yet brought up in this city,* at the feet of Gamaliel, and taught in the strictest doctrine of the law of our fathers; and was zealous in the cause of God, as ye all are this day.

"And I persecuted this sect [of the Christians] unto the death, binding with chains, and casting into prison, both men and women. And of this the high priest can bear witness, and all the Sanhedrim; from whom, moreover, I received letters to the brethren, and went to Damascus, to bring those who were there bound to Jerusalem, that they might be punished.

"But it came to pass that as I journeyed, when I drew near to Damascus about noon, suddenly there shone from heaven a great light round about me. And I fell to the ground, and heard a voice saying unto me, 'Saul, Saul, why persecutest thou me?' And I answered, 'Who art thou, Lord?' And He said unto me, 'I am Jesus of Nazareth,† whom thou persecutest.'

---

persecuted those of whom he was now one, implying, it would appear, that at Jerusalem his testimony was likely to be more impressive and irresistible than elsewhere; but the Lord answered with a simple command, 'Depart; for I will send thee far hence unto the Gentiles.'"—Rev. J. Llewellyn Davies, M.A., in Dr. Smith's "Dictionary of the Bible," ii. 753, 754. (Compare also Rev. E. Liddon, M.A., in Dr. Fairbairn's "Dictionary of the Bible;" Meyer, "Commentary on Acts," xxii. 1-21; and Dr. Vaughan, "The Church of the First Days," iii. 195-200.)

* The Apostle here uses the very words he had just addressed to Lysias, but, with wonderful tact, gives them a new application. To the Roman commander he had laid stress on his birth at Tarsus, "no contemptible city;" to the Jews, he enlarges on his education at Jerusalem.—*See* Dean Howson, "Character of St. Paul," p. 30.

† Saul was going to Damascus to persecute the *Nazarenes*, as the Christians were commonly called, when he was stopped by the Lord, announcing Himself

"And the men who were with me saw the light, and were terrified; but they heard not the voice of Him that spake unto me. And I said, 'What shall I do, Lord?' And the Lord said, 'Arise, and go into Damascus, and there thou shalt be told of all things which are appointed for thee to do.'

"And when I could not see, for the glory of that light, I was led by the hands of my companions, and entered into Damascus.

"And a certain Ananias, a devout man according to the law, having a good report of all the Jews who dwelt there, came, and stood beside me, and said unto me, 'Brother Saul, receive thy sight.' And the same hour, with recovered sight, I looked upon him. And he said, 'The God of our fathers hath chosen thee to know His will, and to see the Just One, and to hear the word of His mouth. For thou shalt be His witness to all men of what thou hast seen and heard. And, now, why tarriest thou? Arise, and be baptized, and wash away thy sins, and call upon His name.'

"And it came to pass, after I had returned to Jerusalem, and while I was praying in the Temple, that I fell into a trance, and saw Him saying unto me, 'Make haste, and get thee quickly out of Jerusalem, for they will not receive thy testimony concerning me.' And I said, 'Lord, they themselves know that I imprisoned and

---

from heaven as *Jesus the Nazarene.*—Conybeare and Howson, ii. 264. An able analysis of this defence, bringing out its adroitness and its felicitous adaptation to the feelings of a Jewish audience, will be found in Dean Howson's "Character of St. Paul," pp. 27-35. The German student should also turn to Dr. Meyer's elaborate Commentary; to which if we do not more frequently refer, it is not because we are insensible to its value.

scourged in every synagogue the believers in Thee. And when the blood of Thy witness Stephen was shed, I myself also was standing by, and consenting gladly to his death, and keeping the raiment of them who slew him.' And He said unto me, ' Depart; for I will send thee far hence unto the Gentiles.' "*

Hitherto the multitude had listened in silence, perhaps with interest; but at Paul's mention of the abhorred word "Gentiles," the national pride was aroused; they broke out into a storm of rage and fury. Away, they cried, away with such a wretch from the face of the earth; he was not worthy to have lived! In their madness they shook their upper garments, as if to free themselves from the pollution of the words he had uttered, and they cast dust into the air.

This tempestuous violence astonished the Roman commander, and thinking that it must arise from some circumstance which Paul had refused to confess, he ordered him to be carried into the tower, and tortured with the scourge. But as the soldiers appointed for this purpose were binding him with thongs to the scourging-post, he addressed the centurion, who superintended the operations, with the startling question, "Is it lawful for you to scourge a man who is a Roman citizen, and uncondemned?" From that moment the ægis of the Roman law protected the prisoner. The centurion immediately hastened to Claudius Lysias, with the warning: "Take heed what thou doest: for this man is a Roman citizen."

---

* Paul's object in relating this vision seems to have been to show that he had longed and prayed to preach the gospel to his own people, and that it was by the Lord's special command he went to the Gentiles.—Dean Alford.

Astonished and alarmed, the commander repaired to Paul. "Art thou indeed a Roman citizen?" "I am," answered Paul. "It was with a great sum," continued Lysias, "that *I* purchased the privileges of citizenship." "Then am I more of a Roman citizen than thou art, for I was born free" (Acts xxii. 24–28).

The commander ordered Paul to be unbound in all haste, and dismissed the lictors; much troubled in his mind that he had committed an offence against the "majesty of Rome" in binding one of her citizens. He was compelled still to keep him in custody, for he knew not what was his offence; and, moreover, it was the sole means of preserving him from the fury of his enemies. But on the morrow he summoned a meeting of the Sanhedrim, or Jewish Council; and when they were assembled in the hall Gapith, placed Paul before them. The Apostle, having examined the faces of his judges with a searching look (Acts xxiii. 1), began with a fearless assertion of his innocence,—"Men and brethren, up to this very day have I lived in all good conscience a true and faithful Jew." Before he could utter another word, Ananias, the high priest,* bade those who stood near him strike him in the mouth. Paul had a fiery temperament; and, moreover, there is such a thing as righteous wrath. To this atrocious violation of all principles of law and justice, he replied vehemently: "God shall smite *thee*, thou whited wall;† for sittest thou to judge me after the law, and commandest me to be smitten contrary to

---

* He was the son of Nebedæus, and appointed high priest by Herod, king of Chalcis, in A.D. 48. He was succeeded by Ismael.

† A whited wall; that is, a wall of clay or mud, made fair externally with plaster and whitewash.

the law?" The bystanders rejoined: "Revilest thou God's high priest?" St. Paul, subduing his anger, answered: "I knew not that he *was* the high priest,* or I would not so have spoken; since we are ordered not to speak evil of the ruler of our people" (Ex. xxii. 28).†

From the temper of the Court it was evident that the Apostle could not hope for a fair hearing or an impartial decision. But he knew that his judges belonged to two violently hostile parties, the Sadducees and the Pharisees; the former denying, the latter affirming, the great doctrine of the Resurrection of the Dead, and the existence of spiritual creatures. Of their dissensions he felt it allowable to avail himself, and he therefore exclaimed: "Men and brethren, I am a Pharisee, and the son of a Pharisee; and I am brought here this day because I have borne witness to the hope and resurrection of the dead" (Acts xxiii. 6). Immediately, as Paul had expected, the two factions came into violent collision; and while the Sadducees raged against him, the Pharisees asserted that he had done no wrong: if, indeed, as he had said, a spirit or angel had spoken to him, let them not fight against God.

The tumult that ensued was so furious that Lysias feared Paul would be torn to pieces, and having in his mind the responsibility of a Roman citizen's life, he sent his soldiers to rescue him from the crowd, and carry him

---

* Some authorities (as Milman and Lightfoot) look upon Ananias as a usurper, and understand St. Paul to mean that he did not know there was any one then lawfully exercising the sacred office. But the text will hardly bear this interpretation.

† It may here be noted that Ananias, a few years later, was murdered by the Sicarii.—Josephus, "Wars of the Jews," ii. 17, 9.

safely into the Antonia Tower (Acts xxiii. 10). There he rested in peace, and in the night his Master appeared to him in a vision, with comforting and inspiring words —" Be of good cheer, Paul; for as thou hast testified of me in Jerusalem, so must thou testify of me in Rome."

By these few words, says Dean Alford, the Lord assured him of a safe issue from his present troubles; of an accomplishment of his desire to visit Rome; and of the certainty that he would there be permitted to preach Christ's gospel. So that they upheld and consoled him, first, in the uncertainty of his life from the Jews; second, in the uncertainty, hereafter, of his imprisonment at Cæsarea; third, in the uncertainty of the great tempest in the Mediterranean; fourth, in the uncertainty of his fate on arriving at Rome. "So may one crumb of Divine grace and help be multiplied to feed five thousand wants and anxieties."*

The morning came, and brought with it a new danger. Wroth at the disappointment which had befallen their evil intentions, more than forty of the Jews engaged themselves by a solemn oath neither to eat nor drink until they had put the Apostle to death (Acts xxiii. 12). They then repaired to the leading members of the Sanhedrim with a proposal that they should request the Roman commandant to bring him a second time before them, in order to resume the investigation interrupted by the riot; in which case they would lie in wait for him on his way, and kill him. Fortunately their nefarious scheme was overheard by the Apostle's nephew,

* Dean Alford, "New Testament," *in loc.*

—who had probably accompanied him to Jerusalem,—and immediately hastening to the tower, he informed his uncle of what he had to fear. St. Paul then summoned one of the centurions, and desired him to take the young man to Claudius Lysias, because he had some important intelligence to communicate.

By the Roman commandant he was courteously received, and having told his tale, was dismissed with an injunction to keep the matter secret. Then Lysias directed two centurions to draw out an escort of two hundred legionaries, seventy cavalry, and two hundred spearmen or light-armed infantry, and at nine in the evening to start with St. Paul for Cæsarea. Then he wrote a despatch to the governor Felix in the following terms :—

"*Claudius Lysias unto the most excellent governor Felix, greeting:*

"This man was captured by the Jews, and would have been killed by them, had I not arrived with a detachment, and rescued him, on understanding that he was a Roman.* And when I would have known on what ground he was accused, I brought him before their Council. Then I discovered that he was charged with certain breaches of the Jewish law, but that he had nothing laid to his charge worthy of imprisonment or death. So, hearing that the Jews laid in wait for him, I sent him straightway to thee, and ordered his accusers also to say before thee of what they accused him. Farewell."

* This is said that Lysias may conceal from his superior the mistake he had actually committed.

At the appointed hour the escort set out,—Paul riding on horseback between the two soldiers to whom he was chained,—and in due time, without any hindrance from the Jews, arrived at Antipatris.* Here they halted for awhile, and the cavalry resumed their journey to Cæsarea; while the infantry, as there was no longer any fear of a surprise, returned to headquarters at Jerusalem (Acts xxiii. 32). Paul and his guard probably reached Cæsarea in the afternoon, where the prisoner was immediately carried into the presence of Felix. The governor read the letter of Claudius Lysias, and then, turning to the Apostle, inquired to what province he belonged. On hearing that he was a Cilician, he replied that he would hear his case as soon as his accusers arrived, and ordered that, in the meantime, he should be confined in Herod's *Prætorium;* an old royal palace built by Herod, which was doubtlessly furnished with a due number of prison-cells.

* Antipatris was forty-two Roman miles from Jerusalem, and twenty-six from Cæsarea. Its ancient name was Capharsaba (retained in the Arab *Kefr-Saba*), but when it was rebuilt by Herod the Great, he christened it Antipatris, in honour of his father Antipater. Josephus describes it as situated in a richly-wooded and well-watered plain, in the shadow of a range of hills. He speaks of a military canal or trench as having been dug from Antipatris to the sea, near Joppa, by one of the Asmonean sovereigns (Josephus, "Antiquities," book xiii. 15, sect. 1; "Wars of the Jews," book i. sect. 4). No remains of the ancient city have yet been discovered.

CHAPTER VI.

PAUL'S IMPRISONMENT AT CÆSAREA, AND VOYAGE TO ROME.

A.D. 58–61.

Cæsarea—Myra of Lycia—Cnidus—The Fair Havens—Phœnix—Clauda—Melita—Syracuse—Rhegium—Puteoli—Appii Forum—Tres Tabernas—Rome.

BEFORE we proceed to describe the circumstances of Paul's trial before Felix, and his imprisonment at Cæsarea, it will be desirable to ascertain, as best we may, what manner of man he was on whose word the Apostle's fate apparently depended.

On the death of Herod the Great (Agrippa I.), the Roman emperors had not allowed any successor to mount the throne of Judea, but handed over its entire government to a procurator. The first who held this position was Cuspius Fadus (A.D. 44), succeeded by Tiberius Alexander (A.D. 48), after whom came Ventidius Cumanus (A.D. 48), and, in A.D. 52, Antonius Felix.*

---

* Suidas calls him Claudius. According to Tacitus, he was joint-procurator with Cumanus, the latter having Galilee for his province, and the former Samaria ("Annales," xii. 54).

Felix was the brother of Pallas, the powerful freedman of the Emperor Claudius, and owed his procuratorship to this connection. Through the same fortunate circumstance he retained it on the accession of Nero; Pallas preserving under the new Cæsar much of the influence he had enjoyed under the old. He ruled his province, according to Tacitus, in a profligate, ferocious, and shameful manner.* Josephus fully confirms this unfavourable testimony, and shows that he crucified by hundreds the Jewish patriots and zealots.

His procuratorship was a period of tumult and sedition. False Messiahs started up, inciting the Jews to revolt; an Egyptian magician and his followers disturbed the peace of Jerusalem, whose citizens, moreover, broke out into frequent contentions with their priests. It was obvious that he was wanting in firmness, in equity, and in the capacity to govern men. Conscious, perhaps, of his weakness, he endeavoured to terrify his subjects into submission by the most odious cruelties;† but the only result was, that he accelerated the ruin of the rapidly decaying commonwealth.‡

Before the tribunal§ of this weak and wicked ruler St.

---

* "Per omnem sævitiam et libidinem jus regium servili ingenio exercuit."— Tacitus, "Hist.," v. 9; and "Annales," xii. 54.

† *See* Josephus, "Antiquities," book ii., chap. 8; and "Wars of the Jews," book ii., chap. 13.

‡ According to Tacitus ("Ann.," v. 9), he imitated the worst actions of his colleague, Cumanus.

§ The tribunal (βῆμα) was portable, and stood upon a tesselated pavement, in front, it is probable, of the procurator's residence.

Paul was summoned, five days after his arrival at Cæsarea. The high priest, Ananias, had come down from Jerusalem, accompanied by some of the elders, and by an orator, Tertullus—probably an Italian—whose services as an advocate had been specially engaged. He opened the case of his employers with more skill than honesty, by praising Felix for the tranquillity the land had enjoyed under his provident rule, though his hearers must have known that never was praise less deserved. He then proceeded to accuse Paul "as a pestilent mover of sedition among all the Jews throughout the world" —a charge amounting to high treason; as a ringleader of the sect of Nazarenes; and a profaner of the Temple (Acts xxiv. 5, 6). This disturber of the public peace, he said, had therefore been arrested, and the Jews were about to put him on his trial according to their usages, when he was forcibly rescued from their hands by the chief captain Lysias, and hurried off to Cæsarea.

The high priest and elders here testified to the truth of their advocate's statement, probably hoping that Felix would be induced to remand the prisoner for trial before their own courts; but the procurator does not seem to have held the Jewish authorities in high esteem, and turning to Paul, he made a sign that he would hear what he had to say in his defence.

The Apostle began by an expression of satisfaction that he had to plead before a judge so long acquainted with the manners and customs of his nation; and, in reply to Tertullus, pointed out that he could not certainly have been a mover of sedition, inasmuch as on his visit to Jerusalem, twelve days before,* he had disputed with no one, nor caused any excitement in the synagogues or throughout the city. But, he continued, the true reason of the hostility against him was, that though he fully believed in the Law and the Prophets, and, like his accusers, cherished a firm hope of the resurrection both of the just and unjust, yet he worshipped God after a way which *they* stigmatized as heretical. Not the less did he endeavour to keep always a conscience void of offence toward God and man. As to the charge that he had profaned the Temple, he had visited it in all reverence to deposit alms and offerings for his nation.† Certain Asiatic Jews, who had found him there after his purification, had raised an accusation against him; but why were they not present if they had really a specific charge to make? As for his present accusers, let them say if they had found any fault in him when he stood before the Sanhedrim, other than that he had proclaimed the resurrection of the dead (Acts xxiv. 10–21).

Felix was not ignorant of the character and tendencies, if he knew nothing of the doctrines, of Christianity, and he must therefore have fully appreciated the force of the Apostle's defence. He did not dismiss him at once, however, because he hoped to extort from him or his friends

---

* Dean Alford thus makes out the twelve days :—1. Paul's arrival in Jerusalem (Acts xxi. 15–17); 2. His interview with James (xxi. 18); 3. His taking on him the vow (xxi. 26); 3–7. The time of the vow, interrupted by—7. His apprehension (xxi. 27); 8. His appearance before the Sanhedrim (xxii. 30); 9. His departure from Jerusalem at night; and so to the thirteenth, the day now current, which was the fifth inclusive from his leaving Jerusalem.

† *See* Paley, "Horæ Paulinæ," Romans, No. 1; and compare 1 Cor. xvi. 1–4; 2 Cor. viii. 9; and Romans xv. 25–33.

a gift of money; and accordingly, on the pretence that he would defer judgment until he had seen Lysias, he consigned him to the custody of the centurion who had escorted him to Cæsarea, with instructions to keep him in safety, but to allow his friends free access to him. For this indulgence, however, the Apostle may have been indebted, as Dean Milman remarks, to the rapacity rather than to the virtue of Felix: "knowing probably the profuse liberality of the Christians, and their zealous attachment to their teacher, he expected that the liberty of Paul would be purchased at any price he might demand."*

A few days afterwards he caused the Apostle to be brought before him and his wife Drusilla, evidently being anxious to know more of the doctrines of this strange sect of Nazarenes or Christians, one of whose foremost men he recognized in Paul. Drusilla was a daughter of Herod Agrippa I. and of Cyprus. At the age of six she had been betrothed to Epiphanes, son of Antiochus, king of Commagene; but he declining the marriage, from unwillingness to be circumcised and adopt the Jewish creed, she was married to the more accommodating Azizus, king of Emesa. Having been seen by Felix, he grew so enamoured of her beauty, which all the authorities agree in speaking of as extraordinary, that he employed Simon, the Cyprian magician (Acts viii. 9), to entice her from her husband, and openly recognized her as his paramour. Probably he espoused her according to the Roman law, but this, of course, would not be recognized by the Jews. She bore to Felix a son named

* Dean Milman, "History of Christianity," i. 404.

Agrippa, who, together with his mother, perished in the eruption of Vesuvius in the reign of Titus.*

Before the Roman governor and his Jewish princess, Paul, with his wonted force, energy, and eloquence, spoke of the faith of Christ, developing that beautiful moral code which his Lord had laid down in the Sermon on the Mount. And as he reasoned concerning righteousness, and moderation, and the judgment which surely awaited the evil-doer, the heart of Felix trembled within him: the Apostle's words struck home like a two-edged sword, and, in an access of temporary remorse, he bade the bold and faithful preacher leave him for awhile. "Go thy way," he said; "and when [*or* if] I have a fitting opportunity, I will hear thee again." And again, and again, he *did* hear, communing with him often: partly in the hope of extorting a bribe for his release, and partly, it may be, out of a desire to listen to the eloquent teaching of the Apostle; teaching which his intellect must have appreciated, though his conscience remained untouched. For upwards of two years Paul underwent this modified imprisonment; and when, in A.D. 60, Felix was removed from his procuratorship, he left him still in bonds, as a gratification to the Jews, some of whom, as he knew, had accused him to the emperor.†

The new procurator was Porcius Festus, who had been in all probability a slave, and was one of Nero's freedmen. During his government Judea continued in a state of turmoil and revolt, but he ruled with a firm hand, and showed no mercy to the Sicarii, robbers, and magi-

---

* Josephus, "Antiquities," book xx., chap. 7, sections 1, 2.
† He only escaped punishment through the influence of his brother Pallas.

cians. He became involved in a dispute with the Jews at Jerusalem, in reference to a lofty wall which they had erected to prevent King Agrippa, in his palace, from looking down into the Temple Court. As the same obstruction concealed the proceedings in the Temple from the Roman guard posted in the Tower of Antonia, Festus strongly supported Agrippa, but permitted the Jews to refer the matter to the decision of the emperor. The decision proved in their favour, through the influence of Poppæa, who was a Jewish proselyte. Soon afterwards, or in the summer of A.D. 62, Festus died, leaving behind him the reputation of a sagacious, firm, and equitable magistrate.

Three days after the arrival of Festus at Cæsarea, he repaired to Jerusalem, and had an interview with the high priest and the principal Jews, who took advantage of his visit to represent to him, from their own point of view, the case of the notorious heretic, Paul, and to beg that he might be sent up for trial before the Sanhedrim. This they did with the view of waylaying their victim on the road, and killing him. But Festus knew that the Roman law did not allow an uncondemned person to be handed over to the tender mercies of his accusers; and we can well believe that he suspected the motives which prompted the unusual request of the Jewish leaders. He replied that Paul must remain in custody at Cæsarea; that he himself was on the point of repairing thither; and that it would be well for some of them to accompany him, and openly prefer their charges against the accused.

After a stay of eight or ten days at Jerusalem, Festus

returned to his seat of government; and some of the Jews having followed him, Paul was immediately brought to trial. His enemies repeated their old charges, but adduced no proofs of their truth; so that nothing remained for the Apostle but to deny, in simple language, that he had either offended against the Jewish law, profaned the Temple, or been guilty of treason towards the emperor (Acts xxv. 8). His sincerity and frankness favourably impressed the procurator, but as Festus had only just assumed the reins of government, he was loath to adjudicate summarily in a matter which had evidently so great an importance for the Jewish rulers. He therefore suggested to Paul that he should go up to Jerusalem and be formally tried before the tribunal of his own nation, but in the presence and under the sanction of the Roman governor. It is impossible that Festus can have supposed his proposition would be accepted, and he put it forward obviously to gratify the Jews.

Paul, however, in firm and independent language, claimed his rights as a Roman citizen. "I stand," he exclaimed, "at Cæsar's judgment seat, where I ought to be judged: to the Jews I have done no wrong, as thou very well knowest. If, indeed, I could be proved guilty, I would willingly die; but if my accusers cannot prove the charges they have brought against me, thou canst not deliver me into their hands. As a Roman citizen, I appeal unto Cæsar" (Acts xxv. 10, 11).

Having heard this appeal, Festus consulted with his assessors, and knowing that it could not be disallowed,[*]

---

[*] The imperial tribunal was the supreme court of appeal from all inferior courts either in Rome or the provinces.

he replied: "Hast thou appealed unto Cæsar? then to Cæsar thou shalt go."

But now the Roman governor found himself in a far greater difficulty than his prisoner. If he sent Paul to Rome, he must send with him a report of the crimes imputed to him by his accusers; and how was he to embody such flimsy charges in any language that would be intelligible to a Roman court of judicature? An opportune event relieved him of his perplexity. The younger Agrippa (Herod II.) had just returned from Rome, where, under the eye of the emperor, he had spent his minority. He had succeeded to a portion only of his father's dominions; but he possessed the Asmonean palace at Jerusalem, and retained the right of appointing the high priest—a right which he exercised apparently "with all the capricious despotism of a Roman governor." He appeared in royal magnificence at Cæsarea, with his sister Bernice, on a visit of ceremony to Festus. The Roman governor seems to have gladly availed himself of the opportunity of consulting him—as a man acquainted with the Jewish law—on the case of Paul.

"There is a certain man left here in prison by Felix," he said, "whom, when I was at Jerusalem, the chief priests and elders of the Jews accused of certain crimes, desiring to have judgment against him. I answered them that it was not usual for the Romans to give up an uncondemned man to destruction before he had been confronted with his accusers, and permitted to defend himself. And, therefore, when they came down hither, after my return, without any delay, but on the very next morning, I took my place on the tribunal, and commanded Paul to be brought before me. Then, indeed, I found that his accusers did not charge him with any such crimes as I had supposed, but with certain matters relating to their own law, and specially in reference to one Jesus, who was dead, but whom Paul declared to be alive. Now, as I was ignorant of the manner in which these things should be dealt with, I asked him whether he would go to Jerusalem and be tried before the judges of his own nation. Whereupon he appealed unto Cæsar, and therefore I have commanded him to be kept in prison until I can despatch him to Rome" (Acts xxv. 14-21).

There can be little doubt that Agrippa must have heard of the new sect of Nazarenes, and of Paul, their eloquent and indefatigable teacher. His curiosity was aroused by the story which Festus told him, and he expressed a great desire to see the prisoner. Festus readily assented, and on the following day Paul was summoned to bear his Master's name "before Gentiles and kings."

The morrow came; and Agrippa and Bernice, in royal pomp, attended by the chief captains, or tribunes, and principal men of the city,* took their seats in the audience-chamber of the Roman procurator. Paul was then brought forth, and Festus, turning to the Jewish monarch, said:—

"King Agrippa, and all men who are here present

* "Yet more and more complete must the giving of the testimony in these parts be, before the witness departs for Rome. In Jerusalem, the long-suffering of the Lord towards the rejectors of the gospel was now exhausted. In Antioch, the new mother Church of Gentiles and Christians was flourishing; here, in Cæsarea, the residence of the procurator, the testimony which had begun in the house of Cornelius the centurion had now risen upward, till it comes before this brilliant assembly of all the local authorities, in the presence of the last King of the Jews."—Stier.

with us, ye see this man, about whom the Jews have petitioned me both at Jerusalem and in this city, declaring that he ought to be put to death. But I have not found that he hath committed any crime deserving to be so punished; and since he hath himself appealed to Cæsar, I have resolved to send him to Rome. Yet as I have no definite charges to place before my lord,* I have caused Paul to be brought specially before thee, O King Agrippa, that after thou hast examined him I may have somewhat to write. For it seemeth to me unreasonable to send a prisoner, and not at the same time to signify the crimes of which he is accused" (Acts xxv. 24-27).

The Jewish king then intimated to Paul that he was at liberty to speak in his own defence. And the Apostle, stretching forth his manacled hand, commenced a long and elaborate oration, on the general purport and bearing of which it seems desirable to offer here a few remarks.

It contains St. Paul's *second* explanation of the way in which he, the persecutor, had been brought to serve his Lord and Saviour, and the *third* narrative in the New Testament of the circumstances which attended his conversion. In some minor details this narrative differs from the others, by way both of omitting and adding, but not more so than might be expected from the circumstances under which it was delivered. In no way does it contradict them. In all three the same principal points are found: the wonderful outburst of light from heaven, the prostration, the Divine voice, the instructions from Jesus.

---

* It is worth while to notice the title "my lord," as an incidental corroboration of the authenticity of the apostolic narrative. Augustus and Tiberius had refused this title when offered by the Senate, but Caligula and his successors accepted it.

But in the present account the words, "I am Jesus whom thou persecutest," are followed by a fuller explanation—as if then spoken by the Lord—of the Apostle's future work. In the other narratives this explanation is deferred to a subsequent occasion.

"But when," says Mr. Davies, "we consider how fully the mysterious communication made at the moment of the conversion *included* what was afterwards conveyed, through Ananias and in other ways, to the mind of Paul, and how needless it was for Paul, in his present address before Agrippa, to mark the stages by which the whole lesson was taught, it seems merely captious to base upon the method of this account a charge of disagreement between the different parts of this history. They bear, on the contrary, a striking mark of genuineness in the degree in which they approach contradiction without reaching it. It is most natural that a story told on different occasions should be told differently; and if in such a case we find no contradiction as to the facts, we gain all the firmer impression of the substantial truth of the story.

"The particulars added to the former account of the present narrative are, that the words of Jesus were spoken in Hebrew, and that the first question to Saul was followed by the saying, 'It is hard for thee to kick against the goad.' (This saying is omitted by the best authorities in the ninth chapter.) The language of the commission which St. Paul says he received from Jesus deserves close study, and will be found to bear a striking resemblance to a passage in Colossians (i. 12-14). The ideas of light, redemption, forgiveness, inheritance, and faith in Christ, belong characteristically to the gospel which Paul preached amongst the Gentiles. Not less striking is it to observe the older terms in which he describes to Agrippa his obedience to the heavenly vision. He had made it his business, he says, to proclaim to all men 'that they should repent and turn to God, and do works meet for repentance.' Words such as John the Baptist uttered, but not less truly Pauline. And he finally reiterates that the testimony on account of which the Jews sought to kill him was in exact agreement with Moses and the prophets. They had taught men to expect that Christ should suffer, and ·that he should be the first that should rise from the dead, and should show light unto the people and to the Gentiles. Of such a Messiah Paul was the servant and preacher."*

With these remarks in his mind, the reader may turn to a consideration of Paul's defence (ἀπολόγια), Acts xxvi. 2–23:—†

"I think myself happy, King Agrippa, that I shall defend myself to-day before *thee* against all the charges of my Jewish accusers; especially because thou art well versed in all Jewish customs and questions. Wherefore I pray thee to hear me patiently.

"My life and conduct from my youth, as it was at first among my own people at Jerusalem, is known to all the Jews. They knew me of old [I say] from the beginning, and can testify [if they would] that, following the strictest

---

* Rev. J. Ll. Davies, in Smith's "Bible Dictionary," iii. 756, 757.
† We adopt the paraphrase given by Conybeare and Howson, ii. 302-305.

sect of our religion, I lived a Pharisee.* And now I stand here to be judged for the hope of the promise† made by God unto our fathers. Which promise is the end whereto, in all their zealous worship,‡ night and day, our twelve tribes hope to come.§ Yet this hope, O Agrippa, is charged against me as a crime, and that by Jews. What, is it judged among you a thing incredible that God should raise the dead?‖

"Now I determined, in my own mind, that I ought exceedingly to oppose the name of Jesus of Nazareth. And this I did in Jerusalem, and many of the holy people [πολλούς τε τῶν ἁγίων]¶ I myself shut up in prison, having received from the chief priests authority to do so; and when they were condemned to death I gave my vote against them. And in every synagogue I continually punished them, and endeavoured to compel

---

* "A strong personal and religious feeling in regard to the old constitution of the chosen people seems to be shown in St. Paul's emphatic references to his own tribe."—Dean Howson, "Character of St. Paul," p. 45.

† That is, the promise of the Messiah.

‡ Λατρεύω strictly signifies, to perform the external rites of worship (as in Rom. i. 19).

§ "There was a difference between Paul and the Jews, which lies beneath the surface of this verse, but is yet not brought out: *he* had already arrived at the accomplishment of this hope, to which *they*, with all their sacrifices and zeal, were as yet only earnestly *tending*, having it yet in the future only."—Alford, *in loc.*

‖ "This is an *argumentum ad hominem* to the Jews, whose own scriptures furnished them with cases where the dead had been raised; as, for example, by Elisha."—Conybeare and Howson, ii. 303.

¶ "This speech should be carefully compared with that in chap. xxii., with the view of observing St. Paul's judicious adaptation of his statements to his audience. Thus, here he calls the Christians ἅγιοι, which the Jews in the Temple would not have tolerated."—Conybeare and Howson, ii. 303. As Stier remarks, Paul speaks as one before a friendly audience, rather than before his judges.

them to blaspheme; and being exceedingly furious against them, I went even to foreign cities to persecute them.

"With this purpose I was on my road to Damascus, bearing my authority and commission from the chief priests,* when I saw in the way, O king, at noon, a light from heaven, surpassing the brightness of the sun, shining round about me and those who journeyed with me. And when we all were fallen to the earth, I heard a voice speaking to me, and saying in the Hebrew tongue, *Saul, Saul, why persecutest thou me? it is hard for thee to kick against the goad.*† And I said, *Who art thou, Lord?* And the Lord said, *I am Jesus whom thou persecutest. But rise and stand upon thy feet; for to this end I have appeared unto thee, to ordain thee a minister and a witness both of those things which thou hast seen, and of those things wherein I shall appear unto thee. And thee have I chosen from the house of Israel, and from among the Gentiles; unto whom now I send thee, to open their eyes, that they may turn from darkness unto light, and from the power of Satan unto God; that by faith in me they may receive forgiveness of sins, and an inheritance among the sanctified.*‡

---

* The presidents of the twenty-four classes into which the priests were divided.

† That is, to resist your internal compunctions and convictions.

‡ "There can be no question that Paul here condenses into one various sayings of our Lord to him at different times, in visions, and by Ananias. Nor can this, on the strictest view, be considered any deviation from truth. It is what all must more or less do who are abridging a narrative, or giving the general sense of things said at various times. There were reasons for his being minute and particular in the *details of his conversion;* that once related, the commission which he thereupon received is not followed into *its* details, but summed up as committed to him by the Lord himself."—Dean Alford, *in loc.* *See* Professor Birks, "Horæ Apostolicæ" (app. to edit. of "Horæ Paulinæ"), pp. 324-330.

"Whereupon, O King Agrippa, I was not disobedient to the heavenly vision. But first to those at Damascus and Jerusalem, and throughout all the land of Judea, and also to the Gentiles, I proclaimed the tidings that they should repent and turn to God, and do works worthy of their repentance.

"For these causes the Jews, when they caught me in the Temple, endeavoured to kill me.

"Therefore, through the succour which I have received from God, I stand firm unto this day, and bear my testimony both to small and great; but I declare nothing else than what the prophets and Moses foretold; that the Messiah should suffer, and that He should be the first to rise from the dead, and should be the messenger of light to the house of Israel, and also to the Gentiles." *

"If we were to search all Scripture through, we could not find any words better calculated to exhibit the reality of the conversion we have been considering than these are. They contain a direct and explicit denial of all the sentiments he had most fondly cherished. They set forth the Man whom he had perhaps spent months, or even years, in persecuting, as the one channel of forgiveness, and the one ordained means of righteousness before God. They are full of the ardent zeal and the irrepres-

* "As to *doctrine* (besides the great belief in the Resurrection, with all its logical results as regards the whole question of miracles), the following fundamental truths will be found in the sentences of this short address:—The existence and power of Satan, the reality of conversion, the necessity of the sufferings of Christ, the remission of sins, faith, repentance, good works the proof of repentance, the fulfilment of Old Testament prophecy, the enlightening of the mind and the supporting of the life by grace from above. A creed or a catechism might be constructed from this speech at Cæsarea."—Dean Howson, "Character of St. Paul," pp. 48, 49.

sible enthusiasm of a new convert, who, not content with advancing the truth he has embraced, will expose also the error he has renounced which once enthralled him—who will destroy in order that he may build. There can be no doubt that the man who spoke these words, or words like them, had renounced all dependence on the Mosaic law. He was no longer a Jew as opposed to a Christian, however much of Judaism his Christianity had imbibed. He may have believed, indeed, in the Divine mission of Moses, but he did not believe in the worth of reliance on Mosaic institutions, and compliance with Mosaic ordinances, as a means to righteousness."*

Hitherto Festus had listened, if with incredulity, still in polite silence, though to the sceptical mind of a Roman, who, like most of his rank and culture, had learned to disbelieve in his own gods, the Apostle's enthusiasm must-have seemed an absurd delusion. But when he came to speak of the Messiah as rising from the dead, he could no longer hold his peace, and, remembering, perhaps, the books and writings which Paul may have received and studied in prison, he exclaimed, in a loud voice, " Paul, Paul, thou art mad ; thy incessant study † [τὰ πολλὰ γράμματα] hath driven thee mad."

Earnest but courteous was the Apostle's reply :

" I am not mad, most noble Festus, but speak forth the words of truth and soberness. For the king hath knowledge of these matters ; and, moreover, I speak to him

---

* Stanley Leathes, "Witness of St. Paul to Christ" (Boyle Lectures, 1869), p. 63.

† Or the Greek may mean, as in our Authorized Version, "thy much learning."

with boldness, because I am persuaded that none of these things is unknown to him, for this hath not been done in a corner."

Then, turning to the last of the Jewish kings, as he reclined by the side of the Roman governor, he inquired: "King Agrippa, believest thou the prophets? I know that thou believest."

The king answered, scoffingly, or with easy indifference: "Thou wilt soon persuade me to become a Christian."*

In solemn and dignified tones, but with true courtesy, the Apostle replied: "I would to God that, whether soon or late, not only thou, but all who hear me to-day, might become such as I am, excepting only these bonds" (Acts xxvi. 29).

Agrippa wished to hear no more; it is probable that Paul's words had impressed him more deeply than he was willing to avow; and with Bernice his sister, and their suite, he hastily withdrew from the audience-chamber. He then entered into conversation with the procurator respecting the Apostle, and both agreed that Paul had done nothing deserving either of death or imprisonment. "In truth," remarked Agrippa, "he might have been set at liberty, had he not appealed to Rome."

This appeal was irrevocable by an inferior authority. Whether Paul would have preferred remaining in Judea,

---

* The Greek is, 'Ἐν ὀλίγῳ με πείθεις Χριστιανὸν γενέσθαι. In our Authorized Version, 'Ἐν ὀλίγῳ is mistranslated "almost," a meaning which the words cannot possibly bear. They may signify either "in few words," "with little difficulty," "lightly," or "in a short time:" the last appears the most appropriate in the passage before us. "Preach but a short time longer," says the king, ironically, "and lo! you will change me into a Christian."

after an acquittal from Festus, and under the liberal protection of Agrippa; or whether (as is more likely) Rome seemed to offer him a nobler and more promising field for his Christian zeal,—Paul (as Dean Milman remarks), in setting forth on his voyage, left probably for ever the land of his forefathers—that land beyond all others inhospitable to the religion of Christ—that land which Paul, perhaps almost alone of Jewish descent, had ceased to consider the one narrow portion of the habitable world sanctified by the Universal Father as the chosen dwelling of His people—the future seat of bliss, glory, and boundless dominion.*

Before we proceed to accompany the Apostle in his voyage to Rome, it is necessary we should remind the reader of some of the difficulties which beset navigation and crippled maritime enterprise in the first century of our era. Mr. Smith, in his valuable work on the "Voyage and Shipwreck of St. Paul," very justly observes, that we are apt to consider the ancients as timid and unskilful sailors, afraid to venture out of sight of land, or to make long voyages in the winter. But no evidence exists that this was the case. The reason they made no voyages after the end of summer was, in the main, the comparative obscurity of the sky in winter, and not the gales which prevail at that season. With no means of directing their course, except by observation of the celestial bodies, they were necessarily prevented from putting to sea when they could not depend upon their being visible. The Greeks and Romans knew nothing of the

* Dean Milman, "History of Christianity," i. 405, 406.

compass; their astronomical instruments must have been of the rudest description; they were unprovided with nautical charts: how, then, without sun or star to guide them, could they venture out into the open? But they were thoroughly acquainted with the waters of the Levant, its currents, and its shifting winds; and his vessel, if somewhat heavy in build and rude in equipment, was handled with dexterity and promptitude.

The ship of the Greek and Roman mariner was double-bowed—that is, both ends were alike. Take (says Mr. Smith) a full-built merchant-ship of the present day, cut it in two, and replace the stern half by one exactly the same as that of the bow, and you will have a tolerably accurate idea of an ancient merchantman. There were two rudders (paddles), one on each quarter; *undergirders* (ὑποζώματα), or ropes to pass round the hull, and so prevent the planks from starting; the average burthen was from four to five hundred tons; and the propelling apparatus consisted of one large mast (in some cases, two), with stout ropes rove through a block at the mast-head, and a single sail* of immense size, fastened to an enormous yard. Such a vessel was unable to tack with any great readiness, nor could she be kept nearer the wind than within seven points; but with a fair breeze she probably made seven knots an hour.

It was on board a vessel of this description—a vessel of Adramyttium †—that St. Paul embarked, with other

---

* Top-sails were sometimes carried, but there was only one main-sail.

† A sea-port of Mysia, opposite Lesbos. Probably she had been on a voyage to Alexandria, and touched at Cæsarea on her return.

AT SIDON.

prisoners, under charge of a centurion, named Julius, belonging to the "Augustine cohort," or imperial bodyguard. He was accompanied by the Evangelist Luke and Aristarchus of Thessalonica.

With a fair wind—for that the wind was fair we may infer from the distance accomplished, sixty-seven geographical miles—they reached, next day, the sea-port of Sidon, where the centurion, who throughout the voyage behaved with the most generous courtesy, permitted the Apostle to land and visit his friends.

SIDON is the last city on the Phœnician coast in which we can trace the footsteps of St. Paul. It was a city of stirring memories and many impressive associations: the limit of "the border of the Canaanites," in the description of the peopling of the earth after the Great Flood (Gen. x. 19); "the haven of the sea, an haven of ships," in the fleeting vision of the holy patriarch (Gen. xlix. 13); the "great Sidon" of the wars of Joshua (Josh. xi. 8); the city that never submitted to the Israelites (Judges i. 31); the home of the adventurous merchants who crossed the seas (Isa. xiii.) The poet of the "Iliad" and the "Odyssey" has celebrated it.[*] Herodotus speaks of its sailors as the most expert of all the Phœnicians.[†] At a later epoch it was conquered by the Persians, but it retained much of its commercial prosperity. Still more recently it was occupied by Fakrid-din, the Prince of the Druses, who blocked up its port to prevent the entrance of the Turkish fleet, and threw in such vast masses of earth and stone that houses are now standing on the spot where, in the Last Crusade, King Louis of France anchored his warships.

On leaving Sidon, the voyagers found the wind unfavourable; and instead of sailing to the south of Cyprus, which would have been their direct course, they were

---

[*] Homer, "Iliad," vi. 290; "Odyssey," iv. 84.
[†] Herodotus, book vii., chap. 89, 96.

compelled to keep to the north and north-east of it. This route brought them within the influence of the current that sets to the north-west past the eastern extremity of Cyprus, and to the west along the southern coast of Asia Minor.

Hence the Apostle's ship, in the smooth waters near the shore, easily worked to windward, under the green mountains of Cilicia, and through the bay of Pamphylia, to Lycia, the first district in the province of Asia. "Thus we follow the Apostle once more across the sea over which he had first sailed with Barnabas from Antioch to Salamis; and within sight of the summits of Taurus, which rise above his native city; and close by Perga and Attaleia; till he came to Myra, a Lycian harbour, not far from Patara, the last point at which he had touched on his return from his second (?) missionary journey."*

MYRA was an important city of Lycia. Its port, or harbour, was properly called *Andriæa*, and was three miles distant from it; but the river Andriaki was navigable for some miles above its mouth.

The city itself (the *Dembre* of the Greeks) was situated at the entrance of a tremendous gorge, which penetrated deep into the mountain masses of Lycia.† Between it and the sea extended a wide and fertile plain, covered with handsome buildings. The theatre, of which some ruins are extant, lies at the base of the cliffs, facing westward. Of greater interest, however, is the large Byzantine church, planted in the solitude of the ravine,—the head-church or cathedral of the diocese, when Lycia was a province, and Myra its capital. Numerous tombs, embellished with much ornament, are scattered among the ruins.

In medieval times Myra was strangely called "the Port of the Adriatic," and visited by Anglo-Saxon travellers. St. Nicholas,

* Conybeare and Howson, ii. 393.
† Sir C. Fellows, "Asia Minor," p. 190, *et sqq.*

the patron of Greek sailors, was born at Patara, and buried at Myra. His supposed relics were removed to St. Petersburg during the Greek Revolution.

In the harbour of Andriæa the centurion Julius found an Alexandrian corn-ship bound for Italy (Acts xxvii. 6), and he availed himself immediately of so favourable a chance for shortening the voyage to Rome. This corn-ship, as she had on board upwards of 270 sailors and passengers, must have been a large vessel; but from the misfortunes she met with, one would suppose that, according to the old classic superstition, she was launched under an "inauspicious star."

From the first the weather proved unfavourable. Paul and his companions were "many days" before reaching Cnidus, which is only 130 miles distant from Myra. The cause of their delay was, undoubtedly, the north-westerly winds. "We learn," says Mr. Smith, "from the sailing-directions for the Mediterranean, that throughout the whole of that sea, but mostly in the eastern half, including the Adriatic and Archipelago, north-westerly winds prevail in the summer months." It was, therefore, with difficulty our voyagers reached Cnidus (Cape Crio); nor could they make good their course any further, "the wind not suffering them" (Acts xxvii. 7).

Though St. Paul's ship did not put into the harbour of CNIDUS, we may be allowed a brief digression in connection with so celebrated a city.

And first, as to its situation. The extreme south-western point of the peninsula of Asia Minor is formed by a bold, steep, and sea-washed promontory, which was formerly isolated, but is now connected with the mainland by an artificial causeway. On either side of this causeway lies a commodious and sheltered harbour, the southern one being the larger, and enclosed by two massive moles. On the headland we speak of (*Cape Crio*), the Dorians erected a temple to the sun-god; and on the mainland to the east of it, lining the two harbours, and stretching over the rising ground, they founded the city of Cnidus.

Owing to its advantageous position, it became the seat of an extensive commerce, and its inhabitants were distinguished by their luxurious habits and love of art. It was for Cnidus Praxiteles executed his celebrated Venus, to compass whose loveliness he blended the charms of five of the most beautiful women in the city. This famous statue was extant in the days of Paul; for reference is made to it by the Latin writer Lucian, who flourished about A.D. 120–190. At one time the Cnidians dared to dispute the supremacy of the sea with Athens; but their navy was crushed by Conon, in the great naval battle which he won within sight of their city walls. It continued, however, a prosperous and wealthy town until long after the Roman period; and in return for the services it rendered in the war between Rome and the East, was rewarded with many privileges.

Few places (says Admiral Beaufort) bear more incontestable proofs of former magnificence, and fewer still of the ruffian industry of their destroyers. The whole area of the city is one promiscuous mass of ruins, among which may be traced streets and gateways, porticoes and theatres.

The remains of the harbours are interesting. The northern has a narrow entrance between two piers, which are of considerable height and solidity; the southern, and larger, is formed by two transverse moles, carried out into the sea to the depth of nearly one hundred feet. One of these is almost perfect; the other, which is more exposed to the swell from the south-west, can only be seen under water.

It is impossible to conjecture the reasons which prevented the Alexandrian ship from putting into Cnidus. She continued her voyage, however, under the lee of the island of Crete, and ran down as far as Cape Salmone. From the course thus adopted, nautical authorities have deduced that the wind still blew from the north-west,[*] which enabled Paul and his companions to weather the cape, and make for a comparatively sheltered roadstead, now, as then, known by the name of " Fair Havens" (Λιμέονες Κάλους). Near it was a town called Lasæa,[†] which St. Luke mentions,—not on account of its importance, but probably because, during the vessel's stay in the roadstead, an intercourse was established between its inhabitants and the wind-bound voyagers. For a favourable change of the wind they waited some time—until, indeed, the Fast of the Atonement or Expiation[‡] being past, and the autumnal equinox at hand, when open-sea navigation became very dangerous, the captain hesitated whether he should winter at Fair Havens, or seek some more convenient harbour. It is a proof of the influence and consideration which St. Paul must have enjoyed on board, though, as yet, his full value as an inspired counsellor was not realized,[§] that, in this conjuncture, he was allowed to offer an opinion on what would seem to have been a purely nautical question. This opinion—whether the result of his own prudent foresight, or of a prophetic power—was, that they should not attempt to pursue their voyage; and he declared that the attempt, if made, would lead to the loss of the ship and her cargo, and to the peril of the lives of her crew and passengers.

Such was not the decision, however, of the owner and master of the vessel, nor, it would seem, of the majority of those on board; and the centurion, therefore, de-

[*] Smith, "Voyage and Shipwreck of St. Paul."
[†] About two hours to the eastward of " Fair Havens."
[‡] This was celebrated about the close of September or beginning of October.
[§] Dr. Vaughan, "The Church of the First Days," iii. 345

termined that, when the wind changed, they would make for the more commodious harbour of Phœnix,*—identified with the modern *Lutro*,—which lay further to the west.

After a further delay, the long looked for change occurred; and a light breeze springing up from the south, the mariners "thought that their purpose was already accomplished" (Acts xxvii. 13). They weighed anchor, and the vessel bore round the green headland of Cape Matala, four or five miles west by south from Fair Havens. With a gentle southerly wind she could not fail to weather the cape; and thence to Phœnix, thirty-five miles, their course would be almost direct. Already the high land above that sea-port rose on the horizon; and with fair weather, sails set, and the boat towing astern (Acts xxvii. 16), they continued their voyage, rejoicing and forgetful,—forgetful of past dangers, rejoicing in the repose which awaited them.

But, without a moment's warning, the scene was changed. They had weathered Cape Matala, and were sailing close in-shore, when suddenly a high wind came down from the pine-clad sides of Mount Ida, struck the unfortunate vessel, and drove her out of her course, in spite of all the exertions of the helmsman. The gale was a kind of typhoon or cyclone, coming from the east-northeast, and known to the mariners of old by the name of Euroclydon (Εὐρακύλων); and while it covered the sky with angry clouds, it raised the sea in mountainous billows and columns of spray and foam, which buffeted

* *Phenice* in the Authorized Version (Acts xxvii. 12). It was a town and harbour on the south coast of Greece, and derived its name, in all probability, from the Greek word for the palm-tree, which Theophrastus describes as indigenous to the island.

the ship to and fro with ceaseless fury. All her crew could do was to keep her head before the wind, to hoist the boat on board,* lest she should be shattered by the rushing waters, to undergird the ship with the stout ropes provided for that purpose, and to set as much sail as she could carry, lest they should be driven upon the sandbanks and shallows of the Syrtis.

At this time they were drifting under the lee of the little island of Clauda.† From thence they continued their course in a westerly by northerly direction, the violence of the storm in no wise abating. On the following day they lightened their vessel by throwing overboard whatever could be spared,—probably because, in spite of the undergirding, the straining ship, labouring constantly in a heavy sea, had already sprung a leak. On the third day, both crew and passengers disembarrassed her of all her spare gear. Then followed several days of anxiety and apprehension; the sky obscured, the wind howling; the waves, crested with foam, chasing one another like ravenous monsters seeking whom they might devour. Hard was the labour to keep the vessel before the wind, to bale out the water, to repair the riven shrouds; and great was the suffering induced by want of provisions, and the impossibility of preparing any regular meal. The discomfort, too, must have been terrible, considering the crowded state of the ship. As day deepened into night, and night gave place to day,—the change being marked by a partial brightening of the sky, but not by any hopeful gleams of sunshine, or dis-

---

* Smith, "Voyage and Shipwreck of St. Paul," p. 64.
† The modern Gozzo.

persal of the dim, dense clouds; as, in spite of every exertion, the water poured in through the straining timbers, until there seemed every probability that the ship would founder; as the tremendous gale still continued to rage, and drove its victim whithersoever it willed, until neither captain nor crew could conjecture in what direction they were drifting,—the minds of those on board sank into the very darkness of despair, and all hope was abandoned (λοιπὸν περιῃρεῖτο ἐλπὶς πᾶσα τοῦ σώζεσθαι ἡμᾶς).

At this crisis—on the fourteenth day of the voyage—the only one of all that crowded ship who preserved his calm composure and intrepid courage, the Apostle Paul,[*] rose up among the exhausted sailors and the tearful passengers, and addressed them in words of encouragement, which must have sounded in their ears like a direct message from heaven. And so, indeed, it was :—

"Sirs," he said, "ye should have hearkened to my counsel, and not have set sail from Crete : thus would you have escaped this harm [to your persons] and loss [of property].

"But now I exhort you to be of good cheer : for there shall be no loss of any man's life among you, but only of the ship.

"For there stood by me this night an angel of God, whose I am, and whom I serve, saying, *Fear not, Paul;*

---

[*] "There was among them now but one person capable of command. It was the Christian prisoner, unheeded till danger pressed, but now the one leading and sustaining and animating spirit. He reminds them, yet without reproaches, of their disregard of his warning. The remembrance might make them listen now—too late to avoid, but not too late to mitigate, the evil."—Dr. Vaughan, "The Church of the First Days," iii. 347.

thou must stand before Cæsar: and, lo! God hath given thee all who sail with thee.

"Wherefore, sirs, be of good cheer: for I believe God, that what hath been declared unto me shall come to pass. Nevertheless, we must be cast upon a certain island." (Acts xxvii. 21–26.)

We are not told what effect the words of Paul produced upon the minds of those who heard him, but we cannot doubt that they were greatly consoled and cheered; that "they were nerved for the toil and difficulty which was immediately before them, and prepared thenceforward to listen to the Jewish prisoner as a teacher sent with a Divine commission."

About the middle of the fourteenth night the sailors began to suspect that they were approaching land. The terrible sound of waves clashing and beating upon a rocky coast could not be mistaken,—can *never* be mistaken by any whose senses have been sharpened by experience of the sea. Accordingly, orders were given to heave the lead, and the depth of water was found to be twenty fathoms. A pause, and again they sounded; the depth was only fifteen fathoms. Through the deep darkness they were evidently drifting on an unknown shore. What was to be done? The vicinity of land was not altogether an evil, since it offered a prospect of saving the lives of those on board by running the leaking and shattered ship ashore, but to do so before it was day would be to rush on certain destruction. They must, if possible, bring the vessel to anchor, and hold on till daybreak; and, with this view, they let go four anchors by the stern.* Happily, these caught the ground; the vessel's dangerous course was arrested; and crew and passengers waited anxiously for the cheering light of morning.

> * The following explanation why Paul's ship was anchored by the *stern* will interest the reader:—" Her way would be more easily arrested, and she would be in a better position for being run ashore next day. Since this mode of anchoring, however, has raised some questions, it may be desirable, in passing, to make a remark on the subject. That a vessel *can* anchor by the stern is sufficiently proved (if proof were needed) by the history of some of our own naval engagements. So it was at the battle of the Nile. And when ships are about to attack batteries, it is customary for them to go into action prepared to anchor in this way. This was the case at Algiers. There is still greater interest in quoting the instance of Copenhagen, not only from the accounts we have of the precision with which each ship let go her anchors astern, as she arrived nearly opposite her appointed station, but because it is said that Nelson stated after the battle, that he had that morning been reading the twenty-seventh chapter of the Acts of the Apostles.
>
> "But though it will be granted that this manœuvre is possible with due preparation, it may be doubted whether it could be accomplished in a gale of wind on a lee-shore, without any previous notice. The question in fact is, whether ancient ships in the Mediterranean were always *prepared* to anchor in this way. Some answer to this doubt is supplied by the present practice of the Levantine caiques, which preserve in great measure the traditionary build and rig of ancient merchantmen. These modern Greek vessels may still be seen anchoring by the stern in the Golden Horn at Constantinople, or on the coast of Patmos. But the best illustration is afforded by one of the paintings of Herculaneum, which represents, as Mr. Smith observes, 'a ship so strictly contemporaneous with that of St. Paul, that there is nothing impossible in the supposition, that the artist had taken his subject from that very ship, on loosing from the pier at Puteoli.'

There is this additional advantage to be obtained from an inspection of this rude drawing, that we see very clearly how the rudders would be in danger of interfering with this mode of anchoring. Our supposed objector, if he had a keen sense of practical difficulties, might still insist that to have anchored in this way (or, indeed, in the ordinary way) would have been of little avail in St. Paul's

The rain, however, was falling in torrents; the gale still blew; in every interval of its fury the roar of the breakers fell upon the alarmed ear; the ship still leaked heavily; and there was every reason to fear that she would founder before daybreak. Under such appalling circumstances the Egyptian seamen again lost heart; and making a pretext that they were carrying out some anchors from the bow, they prepared to lower the boat, and, at all hazards, to attempt to save themselves. The Apostle penetrated their design, and "either from some Divine intimation of the instruments which were to be providentially employed for the safety of all on board, or from an intuitive judgment, which showed him that those who would be thus left behind—the passengers and soldiers—would not be able to work the ship in any emergency that might arise,"—he proceeded to baffle it by giving information to the Roman soldiers and his friend the centurion. They solved the difficulty with military promptitude. With their short swords they severed the ropes, and the boat fell off into the sea, either to be instantly swamped, or dashed to pieces against the rocks.

It is evident that by this time Paul's prudence and coolness had secured him a commanding influence on board; and we now find him, as the first streaks of dawn appeared in the eastern sky, exercising that in-

---

ship: since it could not be supposed that the anchors would have held in such a gale of wind. To this we can only reply, that this course was adopted to meet a dangerous emergency. The sailors could not have been certain of the result. They might, indeed, have had confidence in their cables; but they could not be sure of their holding ground."—Conybeare and Howson, ii. 345, 346. (See also James Smith, "Voyage and Shipwreck of St. Paul," pp. 92-94.)

fluence to make the crew and passengers adopt the needful means of recruiting both their physical and mental energies. He reminded them that for fourteen days they had eaten and drank but little,* and that it was actually necessary to their safety they should now partake of a hearty meal. And he encouraged them to do so with the assurance that not a hair should fall from the head of any one of them † (Acts xxvii. 34). Thus speaking, he took bread,‡ and in the presence of the motley assemblage—Greeks, Romans, Egyptians, Asiatics, seamen, soldiers, merchants, traders—he returned thanks unto God for the preservation He had hitherto accorded them, and for the mercies with which He continually surrounded their path.

Two hundred and seventy-six in number, they sat down to a hastily prepared repast; and having satisfied their appetites, and renewed their strength,§ they set to work actively to lighten the ship still further, by casting overboard its cargo of wheat.

* The Greek ἄσιτοι διατελεῖτε μηθὲν προσλαβόμενοι is a hyperbolical expression, and not to be taken literally. It cannot mean literally that Paul and his fellow-voyagers had abstained entirely from food for a whole fortnight.

† A proverbial expression,—also used by our Saviour.

‡ St. Paul does not celebrate an ἀγάπη, says De Wette, nor does he act as the father of a family, but simply as a devout Jew, who, before he eats, gives thanks to God.

§ "After this, in the prospect of a speedy end, for good or evil, of their present suffering, they threw overboard the remaining (and probably damaged) wheat, that the vessel might be lightened for its last grounding. Morning dawned upon an unknown shore. But it was their one chance: and presently they could discern, through the early twilight, an opening in the cliffs, disclosing a sandy or pebbly beach, upon which it might be possible to run the vessel aground. They took up the anchors, loosed the rudders from their fastenings, hoisted the main or (more probably) the fore-sail to the wind, and made towards the shore."—Dr. Vaughan, "The Church of the First Days," iii. 350, 351.

The day had dawned, and the shore was clearly visible, but the mariners were unable to recognize it. There was no landmark by which they could identify it. They saw, however, a narrow creek or inlet, with a smooth beach, and immediately resolved on steering their vessel so as to take the ground, if possible, at this favourable point. Accordingly, they cut away the stern anchors, unloosed the bands with which the rudder-paddles had been secured, and hoisting up the fore-sail * (ἀρτεμών), they made toward the beach. At a place "where two seas met" the vessel grounded, the bow driving fast into a bottom of mud and clay,† and remaining immovable, while the stern remained exposed to the fury of the waves, and was soon broken up.

The lives of all on board, so far, were safe. But now it occurred to the Roman soldiery as possible that the prisoners might take advantage of the wreck to swim on shore, and effect their escape. To prevent this, they proposed, with the characteristic cruelty of the Romans, to kill them at once. They were rescued from this peril by the ascendency which Paul had established over the centurion's mind. For he, in his anxiety to save the Apostle, prevented his soldiers from carrying out their brutal design; and then gave orders that those who could swim should cast themselves into the sea first,

---

* Smith, "Voyage of St. Paul," p. 101. The Greek is incorrectly translated "main-sail" in the Authorized Version.

† In St. Paul's Bay, Malta, the bottom is composed of singularly tenacious clay. "A ship, therefore, impelled by the force of the gale into a creek with such a bottom, would strike a bottom of mud, graduating into tenacious clay, into which the fore part would fix itself and be held fast, while the stern was exposed to the force of the waves."—J. Smith, "Voyage and Shipwreck of St. Paul," p. 103.

while the others made use of spars, and broken fragments of the wreck. Thus it came to pass that the whole two hundred and seventy-six reached the shore in safety.

And when they were escaped, then they knew that the island on which they were wrecked was Melita.

As *two* islands were anciently called by this name, the reference in the narrative in the Acts would not in itself be a sufficient proof that the one where Paul landed is our modern Malta. But the following reasons are adduced by the best accredited authorities in confirmation of the generally received opinion,

1st. In the twenty-seventh verse, the ship is said to have been "driven up and down in Adria," and it has been argued that "Adria" must mean the Adriatic, and that the Melita of the text is, therefore, the small island called Meleda, which lies off the Illyrian coast;* but the truth is, that Adria, in the wider sense, embraced not only the Venetian Gulf, but the whole sea to the south of Greece.

2nd. The entire course of St. Luke's narrative shows that Paul's ship could not have been driven so far to the northward.

3rd. The objection made that the inhabitants of Malta, at this time, were civilized and refined, and could not therefore have been called βάρβαροι, is frivolous. They were Phœnicians, and spoke a Phœnician dialect, and, in this sense were, to the Greeks and Romans, "barbarians." See Romans i. 14, where the word is used evidently as a synonym for peoples dwelling outside the Greek and Latin world.

4th. Another objection frequently urged is, that no

* Coleridge, "Table Talk," p. 185.

vipers are now found in Malta, and but little wood. But are not these changes the natural result of increasing population and advancing civilization? Mr. Smith justly observes that no person who has studied the modifications which the operations of man have produced on the animals of any country, will be surprised that a particular species of reptile should have become extinct in Malta. And he refers to the gradual disappearance of the viper from the island of Arran, off the coast of Scotland, since it has become more frequented. Perhaps, he says,[*] there is nowhere a surface of equal extent in so artificial a state as that of Malta is at the present day, and nowhere has the aboriginal forest been more completely cleared. We need not therefore be surprised that, with the disappearance of the woods, the noxious reptiles which infested them should also have disappeared.

5th. Considering the direction and rate of drift of the vessel after she left Clauda, it is impossible to conceive that she would reach any other island than Malta; and there are satisfactory indications, besides the not to be despised evidence of ancient tradition, that the part of the island where she ran ashore was that very bay—"St. Paul's," or *Cala di San Paola*—which has always been pointed out as the scene of the wreck.

These indications are summed up, very clearly and concisely, by Conybeare and Howson:—[†]

In the first place we are told that they became aware of land *by the presence of breakers, and yet without striking.* Now, an inspection of the chart will show the reader that

---

[*] Smith, "Voyage of St. Paul," pp. 111, 112.
[†] Conybeare and Howson, ii. 351, 352. See also Smith, pp. 80-91.

a ship drifting west by north might approach *Koura Point*, the eastern extremity of St. Paul's Bay, without having fallen in previously with any other part of the coast; for, towards the neighbourhood of Valetta, the

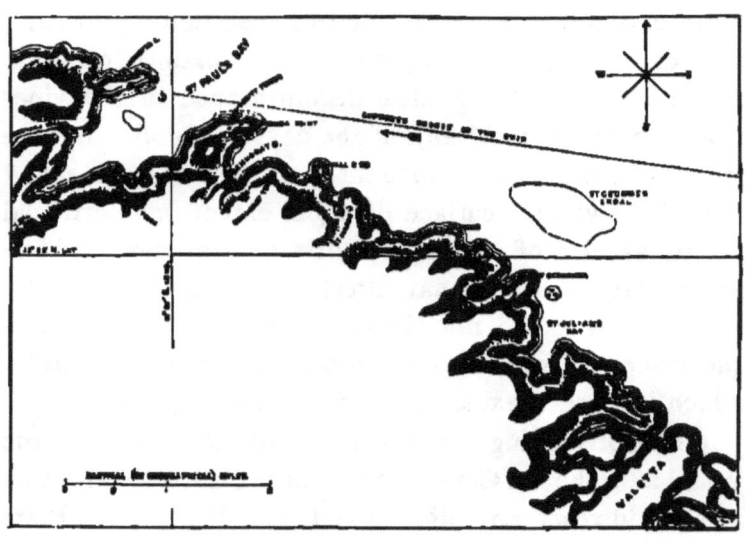

shore trends rapidly to the southward. Again, the character of this point, as described in the Sailing Directions (used by British ships), is such, that, with north-easterly gales, there must infallibly have been heavy breakers upon it. Yet a vessel drifting west by north might pass it, within a quarter of a mile, without striking on the rocks. But what are the soundings at this point? They are now *twenty fathoms*. If we proceed a little further we find *fifteen fathoms*. It may be said that this, in itself, is nothing remarkable. But if we add, that the fifteen fathom depth is *in the direction of the vessel's drift* (west by north) from the twenty fathom depth, the coincidence is startling. But at this point we observe, on looking at the chart, that now there would be *breakers ahead*,—and yet at such a distance ahead that there would be *time for the vessel to anchor* before actually striking on the rocks. All these conditions must necessarily be fulfilled; and we see that they are fulfilled without any attempt at ingenious explanation. But we may proceed further. The character of the coast on the western side of the bay is such, though the greater part of it bristles with precipices, that there are three or four indentations (as at the opening of the Mestara Valley), which exhibit the appearance of "a creek with a sandy beach." * And again, it is to be observed that the small island of Salmonetta is so situated that the sailors, looking from the deck of the vessel at anchor, could not possibly have perceived that it was no continuous part of the mainland; while, on the other hand, when running her ashore, they must plainly have observed the opening of the channel, which would thus appear, like the Bosphorus, "a place between two seas." And, lastly, to revert to the fact that the anchors held through the night (a result which could not confidently have been predicted), we find it stated, in our English Sailing Directions, that the ground in St. Paul's Bay is so good, that "while the cables hold there is no danger, as the anchors will never start."

For these reasons we have come to the conclusion, after a careful examination of the subject, that Paul's ship was wrecked on the north-western shore of Malta, at the place long known as *St. Paul's Bay.*

* Κόλπον....ἔχοντα αἰγιαλόν.—Acts xxvii. 39.

Few islands in the Mediterranean possess a more stirring history than MALTA. At an early period it was a Phœnician settlement, and a corrupt form of the Phœnician language was spoken here as late as the days of St. Paul. During the Second Punic War it passed into the hands of the Romans, and grew famous for the fertility of its soil, the wealth of its inhabitants, its manufacture of cotton, its excellent quarries, its honey, and its fruits.* The Maltese orange is noted for its luscious blood-red pulp. After the fall of the Roman colonies, Malta became a possession of the Vandals, and its harbours the resort of the boldest pirates of the Mediterranean. It was next captured by the Moors; but, in spite of all these changes, the germ of Christianity planted by St. Paul was never wholly crushed out.

When the Knights of St. John were driven from Rhodes they retired to this island, which under their beneficent sway attained the climax of its medieval prosperity. They surrounded Valetta with impregnable fortifications, which defied the fleets and armies of the Turks; and crowded the city with splendid buildings, which to this day command the admiration of the stranger. As, however, the spirit and tendencies of civilization overcame the old feudal element, the knights declined in power and prosperity; and in 1798 they surrendered, without striking a blow, to Napoleon Buonaparte. In the following year the island was captured by the English fleet, under Nelson, and being strongly garrisoned, was held, *vi et armis*, throughout the long struggle between England and the French Empire, furnishing our fleets with a most valuable rendezvous. By the Treaty of Vienna, it was formally handed over to England; and it still remains one of the principal stages on our route to India, and a centre of the greatest importance both to our military and commercial fleets. Its population and wealth have largely increased under English rule, and its fortifications have been so carefully strengthened, restored, and enlarged, that while Britain retains the command of the seas, it can never be captured.

The weary voyagers who landed under such untoward

* It was a dependency of the Roman province of Sicily, and its chief officer appears, from inscriptions, to have borne the title of Πρῶτος Μελιταίων (Primus Melitensium), the very title applied to him by St. Luke (Acts xxviii. 7).

circumstances on the shore of Malta, were received most hospitably by the inhabitants. A fire was immediately kindled to warm them, and each received the friendliest attention. With his usual activity, Paul collected a bundle of faggots to feed the welcome flame,—an act which led to a very remarkable illustration of the miraculous powers he had received from God. Aroused by the heat, a viper sprang from the burning fuel, and fastened upon the Apostle's hand; which, when the natives observed, they exclaimed: "No doubt this man is a murderer, and though he has escaped from the sea, vengeance will not suffer him to live." But when they saw him shake off the beast into the fire, without having sustained any injury, they underwent a sudden revulsion of feeling, and from denouncing him as a murderer would fain have worshipped him as a god.

It was owing to this incident, perhaps, and to the esteem in which he was held by the centurion Julius, that Paul was invited to take up his residence in the house of Publius, the "Primus Melitensium," or ruler of the island. Here he stayed three days, and was most courteously entertained. The illness of the father of Publius—he was suffering from fever and dysentery—furnished him with an opportunity of repaying this hospitality. He obtained admission to his chamber, and having prayed, and laid his hands upon him, the old man was healed. The miracle he had wrought was soon noised over the whole island, and many other sick persons hastened to solicit and receive his assistance. We can well believe that the Apostle, while thus healing the body, was not forgetful of his mission, and that none who repaired to him on account of their physical maladies were allowed to depart without a knowledge of their soul's danger.

For three months Paul and his companions remained in the island, receiving every mark of gratitude and honour from its inhabitants. And when on board another Alexandrian corn-ship they prepared to resume their voyage to Italy, every necessary was most liberally supplied to them.

The *Castor and Pollux*, as Paul's third vessel was called,—after the two twin-deities, the "lucida sidera," or Dioscuri, who were supposed to be the patrons of sailors,—proceeded from Malta to Syracuse, in whose noble harbour she remained for three days. It is probable that St. Paul was allowed to land and visit the famous city associated with so many impressive historic memories, —with the defeat of the great Athenian fleet, under Nicias, —a defeat which foreshadowed the approaching fall of Athens,—and the long Punic wars, so changeful in their fortunes, which resulted in the subjugation of Carthage to Rome. We do not think, however, that so brief a visit justifies the tradition which represents St. Paul as the founder of the Sicilian Church.

Sailing out of Syracuse, and past Ortygia,—once an island, but afterwards connected in a continuous line with the buildings under the ridge of Epipolæ,—the *Castor and Pollux* shaped her course northwards for the Straits of Messina; but the wind blowing from the west, she was obliged to bear up for Rhegium, a city whose patron divinities were, by a singular coincidence, those "Great Twin-Brethren" whose carved images St. Paul's vessel carried at her prow.

On the following morning, the wind veered round to the south, and the *Castor and Pollux* made her course direct for Puetoli (one hundred and eighty-two miles from Rhegium), which she reached in about four and twenty hours. No part of their voyage can have more deeply interested St. Paul and his companions.

Before the close of the first day, we read,* they would see on the left the volcanic cone and smoke of Stromboli, the nearest of the Liparian Islands. In the course of the night they would have neared that projecting part of the mainland which forms the southern limit of the Bay of Salome. Sailing across the wide opening of this noble gulf, they would, in a few hours, enter that other bay, the Bay of Naples, in whose northern part Puteoli was situated. No long description need be given of a scene which has been so often sung and painted, and rendered familiar by every kind of illustration, even to those who have never seen it. Its south-eastern limit is the promontory of Minerva, with the island of Capreæ opposite, which is so associated with the memory of Tiberius,† that its cliffs still seem to rise from the blue waters as a monument of license and debauchery in the midst of the comeliest scenes of nature. The opposite boundary was the promontory of Misenum, where the Imperial fleet of the "Lower Sea" lay at anchor in the

---

* Conybeare and Howson, ii. 359, 360.
†   "From Rome retired
   To Capreæ—an island small, but strong,
   On the Campanian shore—with purpose there
   His horrid lusts in private to enjoy."—Milton.

blue shadows of the lovely islands of Ischia and Procida. Between these two famous headlands the Campanian coast exhibits a succession of the most exquisite pictures, with a grace of outline and a warmth of colouring such as could never have been dreamed of even by the brain of Shelley. And prominent above them, with its vine-clad slopes rich in enduring greenness, rose the huge mass of the mighty Vesuvius, which had not yet revealed the terrors of its volcanic fire, and whose luxuriant gardens lent no unimportant attraction to this strange, this fascinating, this impressive spectacle.

On the following day, towards the hush of twilight, the great ship, with its cargo of wheat on board,—and *that one* passenger, who was destined by his proclamation of Christ to shake the very foundations of the Roman world,—sailed into the harbour of Puteoli, whose quays were crowded with idlers awaiting her arrival. She was easily recognized, for all other vessels were compelled to strike their top-sail as they rounded into the bay.* She alone, on account of her valuable freight of corn, was exempted from this sign of inferiority. As soon as she reached her moorings, Paul and his companions, still in charge of the Roman soldiers, disembarked, and finding certain of the brethren in the city, they abode with them seven days (Acts xxviii. 14).

PUTEOLI, the modern *Pozzuoli*, was so called from its strong mineral springs.† Its earlier name was *Dicæarchia*, and the city was of Greek foundation. Its importance, however, does not seem to have dated earlier than the era of the Second Punic War, when its

---
* Seneca, "Epistolæ," 77.
† From the Latin *a puteis*.

harbour was found a valuable rendezvous for the Roman fleets. Ambassadors from Carthage landed, and troops for Spain embarked here. As the corn trade with Egypt developed, it gained in wealth and influence, and its privileges as a "colony" were enlarged and renewed by Nero. The beauty of the surrounding country induced many of the wealthy Roman patricians to build their villas in its environs; and especially around Baiæ, where Nero plotted the murder of his mother. The Lucrine lake, close at hand, furnished an abundant supply of oysters, and the orchards and gardens inland of vegetables and fruit. In the fifth century the luxurious city was ravaged, first by Alaric and his Goths, next by Genseric and his Vandals; and from these two fearful calamities it never recovered.

Its ruins are considerable. They include sixteen piers of the ancient mole, which was built of the concrete called *Pozsolana*, so remarkable for its durability; the baths, the reservoirs, the aqueduct; and the so-called Temple of Serapis, whose sea-worn columns bear curious testimony to the changes of level which this part of the Italian coast has undergone.

At Puteoli terminated St. Paul's "perils of the sea." He proceeded from thence to Rome by land; following the line of the great *Via Appia*, or Appian Way,* the oldest and most celebrated of the Roman roads, the most crowded approach to the metropolis of the world, the great thoroughfare which, year after year, exhibited the striking spectacle so picturesquely described by Milton:—

> "Prætors, proconsuls, to their provinces
> Hasting, or on return, in robes of state;
> Lictors and rods, the ensigns of their power,
> Legions and cohorts, turms of horse and wings;
> Or embassies from regions far remote."

It is probable that the first stage of the Apostle's journey would terminate at Capua; the luxurious city

---

* Constructed by the censor Appius Claudius, A.U.C. 442.

which enervated the troops of Hannibal, and which had bitter occasion to rue the friendship it had shown the Carthaginian Jew. But being raised by Julius Cæsar to the rank of a "colony," it regained its former splendour, and returned, as we know from many passages in the Latin writers, to its former vices. It was the most important city on the Appian Way between Rome and Brundusium, and the country round it was not less celebrated for its fertility than for its rich pastoral beauty.

The next stage would be from Capua to Terracina; the road for nearly the whole distance skirting the beautiful shore of the Mediterranean, and traversing a district rich in classic associations.

At the third milestone it crossed, at Casilinum, the river Vulturnus. Casilinum was then falling into decay, but in the ninth century the old bones became filled with new life, and under the name of Casilino, or "New Capua," the town enjoyed a fresh lease of prosperity.

Crossing the river Savo (15 miles) by what was then called the Campanian Bridge (*Campanus Pons*), the travellers arrived at Sinuessa,—a bright and lively town on the sea-coast, where, in the famous journey described by Horace (in the fifth satire of the First Book), he and his friends met Plotius, Varius, and Virgil:—

"Plotius et Varius Sinuessæ Virgiliusque occurrunt."

St. Paul now entered on a region of gardens and vineyards, bounded inland by the verdurous hills of the Falernian and Massic range, once so famous for their vines, and offering at every step some lovely glimpses of a scenery which may almost be characterized as Arcadian.

At Minturnæ he came to a "country-side" celebrated

in the annals of Rome as the scene of the last desperate struggles of Marius; at Formiæ, he may have gazed on the villa once inhabited by Cicero, where the great orator was overtaken by Antony's hired murderers, and cruelly put to death. Soon afterwards the road turned aside from the sea, and wound through the stony passes of the Cæcuban hills. At Fundi it turned to the south, and again reached the coast, where on its limestone cliffs, proud of its massive walls, and temples, and houses, stood the lofty Anxur, the modern Terracina.

After leaving Anxur, the Appia Via proceeded to Rome in a direct line from south-west to north-east, crossing the Pontine marshes, and the southern spurs of the Alban hills.

A few miles beyond Terracina,*—where a fountain, in whose waters Horace washed his hands on the occasion of the journey already referred to,—

"Ora manusque tuâ lavimus, Feronia, lymphâ;
Milia tum pransi tria repimus,"—

rose near the sanctuary of Feronia,—the traveller reaches the termination of a canal, excavated by Augustus for the purpose of draining the marshes, and continued for twenty miles along the side of the road. Over this distance travellers could take their choice, either to float along the tranquil stream in barges drawn by mules, or to keep to the pavement of the Way itself.

We may again refer to Horace for his experience of the canal voyage; premising that *he* started from Forum Appî, "thronged with sailors and greedy innkeepers,"

* Conybeare and Howson, ii. 367.

while the centurion and his prisoners would necessarily disembark there:—

"Inde Forum Appî,
Differtum nautis, cauponibus atque malignis.
Hoc iter ignavi divisimus, altius ac nos
Praecinctis unum: minus est gravis Appia tardis.....
            Jam nox inducere terris
Umbras et coelo diffundere signa parabat.
Tum pueri nautis, pueris convicia nautae.
Ingerere: *Huc appelle! Trecentos inseris! Ohe
Jam satis est!* Dum aes exigitur, dum mula ligatur,
Tota abit hora. Mali culices ranaeque palustres
Avertunt somnos, absentem ut cantat amicam
Multâ prolutus vappâ nauta atque viator
Certatim. Tandem fessus dormire viator
Incipit, ac missae pastum retinacula mulae
Nauta piger saxo religat stertitque supinus.
Jamque dies aderat, nil quum procedere lintrem
Sentimus, donec cerebrosus prosilit unus
Ac mulae nautaeque caput lumbosque saligno
Fuste dolat; quartâ vix demum exponimur horâ."*

[We proceeded to Forum Appî, a place thronged with sailors and greedy innkeepers. This stage, generally made as one by persons more hurried than ourselves, we, being indolent, divided into two; the Appian Way, however, is better for leisurely travellers....The night was now preparing to spread her shadows over the earth, and to display the constellations in the heavens. Then our slaves began to lavish their banter on the watermen, and the watermen retorted on our slaves. "Here, bring to, I tell you." "You are overcrowding the boat; hold, it is surely full enough." Thus, while the fare was paid, and the mule harnessed, a whole hour was wasted. The horrible gnats and the croaking frogs drove off repose. While the boatman, who was well drenched with heavy wine, and one of the passengers vied with each other in chanting the praises of their absent lady-loves, until the wearied traveller began to sleep, and the lazy boatman, tying the halter of his grazing mule to a stone, lay down on his back and snored. When day dawned, we saw that the boat was making no progress; and a choleric fellow, leaping ashore, poured a volley of

* Horace, "Satires," book i. 5, lines 3-23.

blows on the head and ribs of both mule and boatman with a willow cudgel. At last we reached our destination about the fourth hour (10 A.M.).]

We may be sure that St. Paul and his companions, under the charge of a Roman centurion, would meet with no such delay, nor see such characteristic scenes, as the satirist has described so pleasantly. Still he must have been no less glad than Horace to reach the termination of his voyage (if he went by the canal), for at Forum Appi he was met by a company of Christians, who, having heard of the Apostle's arrival at Puteoli, had come forth from Rome, a distance of forty-three miles, to bid him welcome. This proof of their devotion touched him deeply; it showed him how the spirit of the gospel united in one indissoluble bond all who believed in it; and he thanked God, and took courage (Acts xxviii. 15).

About ten miles nearer Rome, at a place called "The Three Taverns,"* he was met by a second company of the brethren; and thus attended, he continued his journey along the southern slope of the Alban Mount,—then gay with foliage and gardens, and crowded with the handsome villas of the wealthy. After passing Lanuvium, the road crossed "a crater-like valley on immense substructions,† which still remain." Next came Aricia,—now *Laricia*,—whose hill-side, in the days of Juvenal and Persius, swarmed with beggars, soliciting the travellers as they left or entered Rome. And on the summit of the next high ground St. Paul obtained his first view of

---

* Mentioned by Cicero in his "Epist. ad Atticum," ii. 12.
† These consist of a magnificent viaduct, built of squared blocks of peperino, 700 feet in length, and in some places 70 feet in height.

the Great City, the metropolis of the world, the mistress of the nations, which even now, in the nineteenth century, possesses an influence over the mind and imagination of men such as no other city exercises.

"There is no doubt," as one of our authorities remarks, "that the prospect was, in many respects, very different from the view which is now obtained from the same spot. It is true that the natural features of the scene are unaltered. The long wall of blue Sabine mountains, with Soracte in the distance, closed in the Campagna, which stretched far across to the sea and round the base of the Alban hills. But ancient Rome was not, like modern Rome, impressive from its solitude, standing alone, with its one conspicuous cupola, in the midst of a desolate though beautiful waste. St. Paul would see a vast city, covering the Campagna, and almost continuously connected by its suburbs with the villas on the hill where he stood, and with the bright towns which clustered on the sides of the mountains opposite. Over all the intermediate space were the houses and gardens, through which aqueducts and roads might be traced in converging lines towards the confused mass of edifices which formed the city of Rome. Here no conspicuous building, elevated above the rest, attracted the eye or the imagination. Ancient Rome had neither cupola* nor campanile. Still less had it any of those spires which give life to all the landscapes of northern Christendom. It was a wide-spread aggregate of buildings, which, though separated

---

* It is true that Agrippa had built his Pantheon (or rather baths), with its domed roof: but as yet the world had seen no elevated dome like that of St. Peter's or St. Paul's.

by narrow streets and open squares, appeared, when seen from near Aricia, blended into one indiscriminate mass: for distance concealed the contrasts which divided the crowded habitations of the poor, and the dark haunts of filth and misery, from the theatres and colonnades, the baths, the temples and palaces with gilded roofs, flashing back the sun."*

At Bovillæ, six miles from Aricia,—the scene of the murder of Clodius,—the Via Appia descended into the plain; and thence it proceeded to the city in a straight line, between two rows of the tombs and monuments of the patrician dead,—of the Scipios, and the Servilii, and the Metelli,—and many others whose names had figured splendidly in the long annals of the Roman commonwealth. As the travellers neared the metropolis, the road became more crowded; carriages of every description increased in number; magistrates, preceded by the insignia of their official authority, made their appearance; the stately tramp of the Roman soldiery occasionally fell upon the ear; long trains of vehicles, loaded with precious wares, slowly wound their way among the ever augmenting throng; and, now and then, some Roman beauty, flashing with gold and gems, was carried by in her sumptuous *lectica*. The goal of St. Paul's journey was reached. The Christian Apostle was in Pagan Rome; entering as a prisoner,—all unknown and unheeded, except by a very few,—the great city, whose future fortunes were to be so largely influenced by the power of that gospel he was specially commissioned to preach.

Either at the *Prætorium*, or barrack, attached to the

* Conybeare and Howson, ii. 371, 372.

Imperial Palace, or in the *Prætorian camp*, outside the city walls, the centurion surrendered his prisoner to Burrus, the prætorian prefect, whose duty it was to take charge of all accused persons who were to be tried before the emperor.*

Paul, then, was at last in ROME,—in the mighty city which had become the metropolis of the civilized world; had reached the long-fixed goal of his hopes and desires, where he was to accomplish his witness to the truth. He had reached Rome; but not, perhaps, as he had expected to reach it,—free and unfettered, and in a position, while doing his Master's work, to examine its architectural wonders and survey its famous scenes, which, for a man of culture, like the Apostle, must have possessed a peculiar interest. It is well to remember that he was a scholar; and there is no need to suppose that he eschewed the pleasure which every cultivated intellect discovers in the contemplation of the monuments of art and science. We know that he would keep feeling, and imagination, and sentiment ever subordinate to the study and practice of religious duties; but we do not think he was an ascetic, or that he denied himself those pure and wholesome gratifications which depend upon intellectual exercise.

Rome, however, in Paul's day, was not the Rome which we are now so fond of picturing to ourselves; and many of those mighty edifices which our memories immediately associate with the "Eternal City" when it is named in our hearing—edifices consecrated by time, and hallowed by poetry—did not then exist. To most of us Rome is the city of the Coliseum, of the Arch of Titus, of Trajan's Column; but none of these proud memorials of imperial magnificence and military glory were as yet conceived of. There was enough, however, to gratify the artistic sense of any refined mind; and chained though he was to a Roman soldier, the Apostle, if permitted to walk abroad, cannot but have admired the grand achievements of human labour which rose in every direction, while bitterly deploring the sin and folly and madness connected with too many of them. How

---

* See Smith, "Dictionary of Antiquities," art. *Praefectus Praetorio*, p. 952.

he would long that the Sun of Righteousness might rise, and pour His purifying light upon the dark places of the famous city!

Then as now the stranger in Rome would first direct his steps to the *Forum Romanum*, where, as the poet sings,

> "A thousand years of silenced factions sleep—
> The Forum, where the immortal accents glow,
> And still the eloquent air breathes—burns with Cicero."

This was the gathering-place of the Roman plebeians, and the scene of the struggles and contests which had marked the later years of the Republic. Here the great orators of Rome, Cicero and Cato, Hortensius and Cæsar, swayed the passions of men by their varying eloquence. Down to the assumption of supreme power by Augustus, the Forum had been the "safety-valve" of Rome, and had provided an escape for the prejudices and frenzies of a haughty, a vigorous, but a semi-barbarous race. It had been the centre, the focus (as it were), of Roman political life, where citizen met citizen, and discussed the position of the state, the affairs of the commonwealth, the pretensions of the patricians, the rights of the plebeians.

> "The field of freedom, faction, fame, and blood:
> Here a proud people's passions were exhaled,
> From the first hour of empire in the bud,
> To that when further worlds to conquer failed."

Under the Cæsars it lost much of its political importance, but it still remained the principal rendezvous in Rome, and the great mart of trade, commerce, and scandal. Here were held the Courts of Justice, plaintiff and defendant arguing their causes in public. Here were suspended the Twelve Tables, that he who ran might read; and the Fasti, written on white tablets, which made known the days and hours when the magistrates sat at their tribunals. Here the vigorous heart of Rome throbbed in all the fulness of its vitality, and across the crowded area streamed long lines of representatives of the numerous nations of the earth who were in alliance with, or under subjection to, the Empire.

As the Acropolis was the central point of Athens, so was the

Capitoline hill of Rome, and it was at the base of the Capitoline that the Forum was situated. It is now known by the name of the *Campo Vaccino*, or Cattle Market; the greater part of its area, as early as the fifteenth century, having become the resort of cattle-dealers and their herds,—"a kind of Roman Smithfield." The latest authorities represent it as having extended (at a later date than that of Paul's imprisonment) from the Arch of Septimus Severus to the Temple of the Dioscuri in its longer diameter, and from the front of the church of San Adriano to the steps of the Basilica Julia in its shorter; an area, in all, of about seven *jugera*, or nearly four and a half English acres, closely hemmed in by streets and houses. Roughly speaking, it was 670 feet long and 202 feet broad. In Paul's time it included the temple and *hostia* of Julius Cæsar, the noble Basilica of Paulus, the supposed site of the Lacus Curtius, the Rostra, and other memorable edifices and places to which we shall presently allude.

On the east and north it was bounded by the *Sacra Via*, or "Sacred Way," of which the side near the Forum was left open, while on the other stood corridors and halls, such as those of the *argentarii*, or money-changers, which, at a later period, gradually gave place to temples and basilicas.

Why was it called *Sacra Via?*

Most probably from the sacred purposes for which it was used. Certain sacred offerings—namely, a white sheep or lamb sacrificed on the ides of every month to Jupiter—were borne along this road to the *Arx*, or citadel, on the Capitoline hill; and along this road, moreover, the augurs descended from the Arx, and, having inspected the entrails of the sacrificial victims, proceeded to consecrate any edifice or enterprise in the city below. For nothing was done in Rome until the wishes of the gods had been consulted.

The Sacred Way extended in a straight line from the beautiful Arch of Fabius to a point afterwards occupied by the imposing monument which the Roman Senate raised in honour of the conqueror of Jerusalem. At its highest point, the Summa Sacra Via, stood the temple of Venus and Rome; and in its vicinity, the temple of Peace, afterwards destroyed by fire. The classical student will remember that the Sacred Way was a favourite resort with the poet Horace:—

> "Ibam forte Viâ Sacrâ, sicut meus est mos,
> Nescio quid meditans nugarum, et totus in illis."

[I chanced to be strolling in the Sacred Way, as is my wont, meditating on all sorts of trifles, and entirely absorbed in them.]

The lover of English poetry and of the romance of history will also recollect the vigorous passage in Lord Macaulay's "Prophecy of Capys":—*

> "Blest and thrice blest the Roman
> Who sees Rome's brightest day,
> Who sees that long victorious pomp
> Wind down the *Sacred Way*,
> And through the bellowing Forum,
> And round the Suppliant's Grove,
> Up to the everlasting gates
> Of Capitolian Jove."

It was in one of the *Veteres Tabernæ*, or Shops, which Tarquinius Priscus had allowed to be erected along the Sacred Way, that Virginius bought the knife with which he saved his daughter's honour—a beautiful, yet a terrible deed, which moves alike our awe and our admiration. Here we may again quote Macaulay:—

> "'Thy father hath in his despair one fearful refuge left.
> ....In this hand I clutch what still can save
> Thy gentle youth from taunts and blows, the portion of the slave;
> Yea, and from nameless evil, that passeth taunt and blow,—
> Foul outrage which thou knowest not, which thou shalt never know.
> Then clasp me round the neck once more, and give me one more kiss;
> And now, mine own dear little girl, there is no way but this.'
> With that he lifted high the steel, and smote her in the side,
> And in her blood she sank to earth, and with one sob she died."

On entering the Forum, the stranger now sees before him, on the Capitoline hill, the *Tabularium*, the *Archivium*, or Office of Public Records, erected by Quintus Lutatius Catulus, B.C. 78, where the bronze plates, or *tabulæ*, which recorded the decrees of the Senate, and other public acts, were preserved. Connected with it was the *Ærarium*, or State Treasury, which, indeed, was contained within

* Lord Macaulay, "Lays of Ancient Rome."

its massive walls, and was also united with the temple of Saturn.*
Above it towers the glorious Capitol; the fortress built by Romulus,
and the temple begun by Tarquin, reconstructed by Sulla, and repaired by the Emperor Augustus. Other temples were dedicated
to Jupiter under different surnames, descriptive of his various attributes; and around were grouped, to watch over the Roman destinies, a crowd of protecting deities. The Capitol,—cradle of an
empire which endured for twelve hundred years,—is now a bare
and commonplace hill covered with modern houses of insignificant
aspect; its very elevation has diminished, owing to the debris and
ruin piled about its base, and accumulated on its declivities; and
even in the Forum it has been found necessary to excavate the soil,
to restore to the half-buried edifices the original elegance of their
proportions.

Place yourself now at the foot of the three Corinthian columns of
the *Græcostasis*,—the hall in which the ambassadors from allied
nations were received by the Senate,†—and you see, on your left,
below the long monotonous range of buildings erected on the basis
of the Tabularium, the graceful Ionic portico of the temple of Saturn.
On the same level, but towards the right, you seek in vain, in the
brick façades of the church of San Adriano, for any vestiges of the
Basilica Pauli Æmilii, which, some thirty years before the visit of St.
Paul, had been erected and enriched by Paulus Æmilius; and which
has since contributed to the church of St. John Lateran a superb
gate of brass, and to that of St. Paul (*fuori le mura*, without the
walls) several columns of violet-coloured marble. Thus the shapely
pillars on which it is possible the Apostle may have looked, now
serve, in part, to commemorate the site of his martyrdom. Further
to the right you may survey the lofty façade of the temple of An-
toninus and Faustina—erected, of course, long after Paul's mission
was accomplished—now converted into the church of San Lorenzo
in Miranda. Close by this spot, in the days of the Apostle,

---

* An excellent description of the ruins now extant occurs in the *Athenæum*
for September 20, 1873, p. 375. It is written by Mr. Charles Hemans.
† Some authorities regard them as the remains of the temple of Minerva Chal-
cidice.

stood the triumphal Arch of Fabius, the conqueror of the Allobroges.

Observe, too, as one of the monuments which the Apostle may have seen, the *Rostra*, or ancient Tribunal, now represented by a semicircular wall faced with coloured marbles. It does not seem to have been raised much above the level of the *Comitium*, or public place of assembly.

Another celebrated monument extant in the days of the Apostle was the Duilian Column, or *Columna Rostrata;* so called from the beaks of ships sculptured upon it. It commemorated the naval victory gained over the Carthaginians by the Roman fleet, under Caius Duilius, B.C. 260.

In front of the rostra stood the statue of Marsyas, with uplifted hand, as the emblem of civic liberty. This was the favourite haunt of the Roman pleaders, who too often mistook *license* for liberty.

Of more than ordinary interest to the stranger who now visits Rome, are the remains of its *basilicas*, because they furnished the models of the early Christian churches, and in some cases were themselves adapted to the purposes of Christian worship. That such would be their employment, could not have been anticipated by the Apostle when he traversed the Roman Forum.

A *basilica* was then a building which served a double purpose; it was both a court of law and an exchange. The first edifice of this description was erected by Marcus Porcius Cato in B.C. 184. Twenty others were raised at different periods within the city, of which the most famous seem to have been the *Basilica Sempronia*, constructed by Titus Sempronius, B.C. 171; the *Basilica Pauli Æmilii*, in the Forum, built by Paulus Æmilius; the *Basilica Opimia*, also in the Forum; the *Basilica Pompeii*, called also the *Regia*, near the theatre of Pompey; the *Basilica Julia*, in the Forum, erected by Julius Cæsar; the *Basilica Caii et Lucii*, the grandsons of Augustus, by whom it was founded; and the *Basilica Trajani* and *Basilica Constantini*, both, as their names indicate, of later erection.

The ground-plan of every basilica was rectangular, and the width was not more than one-half, nor less than one-third, of the whole length.

This area was divided internally into three parts, consisting of a central nave, and two side aisles, each separated from the centre by a single row of pillars. At one end of the nave stood the judge's tribunal, in form either rectangular or circular; and sometimes cut off from the length of the nave,—sometimes projecting beyond the building as a hemicycle. Add to these details a gallery running round the entire inside of the building, and you obtain a general idea of the arrangements of a basilica.

You will also see at once how excellently it was adapted to the uses of a Christian church. In the Christian basilica were four parts: first, the vestibule of entrance, or πρόναος; next the nave, ναός, or centre aisle; the choir, or ἄμβον, a part of the extremity of the nave raised by a flight of steps; and fourth, the *sanctuarium*, or sanctuary, ἱερατεῖον, which corresponded to the tribune of the ancient basilica. Here, under a baldacchino or canopy, was placed the high altar, with seats for the bishop and officiating clergy.

But let us quit the Forum, and bestow a passing glance on some other celebrated edifices which adorned the Rome of Nero and St. Paul. At the mention of the PANTHEON, the eloquent apostrophe of the poet immediately occurs to us:—

> "Simple, erect, severe, austere, sublime—
> Shrine of all saints and temple of all gods,
> From Jove to Jesus: spared and blest by Time;
> Looking tranquillity, while falls or nods
> Arch, empire, each thing round thee, and man plods
> His way through thorns to ashes—glorious dome!
> Shalt thou not last? Time's scythe and tyrants' rods
> Shiver upon thee—sanctuary and home
> Of art and piety!—Pantheon!—pride of Rome!"

This "temple of all gods," converted in 608 into a Christian church, under the name of *Sancta Maria ad Martyres*, or *Della Rotonda*—to which circumstance it undoubtedly owes its preservation—stood in the centre of the Campus Martius. The harmony of its outlines, the regularity and loftiness of the rotunda which supports its mighty dome, and the accuracy and rhythmical character of its proportions, justly entitle it to universal admiration.

From an inscription on the façade of its portico, we learn that it was erected by Marcus Agrippa, son-in-law of Augustus, in his third consulate, or B.C. 17. He dedicated it to Jupiter Ultor,* in honour of the victory which Augustus had gained over Antony and Cleopatra; the victory which placed on his shoulders the burden of the empire of the world. It then contained the statues of Mars and Venus, and, according to tradition, images, in gold and silver, of all the deities supposed to be connected with the Julian race. Hence the name of *Pantheon*, which signifies "an assemblage of all the gods."

Architecturally speaking, it consists of two entirely distinct portions, which have seldom been brought into such immediate relation; namely, a circular body and a rectilinear portico. An opinion has been put forward that Agrippa constructed only the portico. The facts alleged in support are, that the façade of the rotunda is entirely detached from the portico, that the entablatures of the portico and the temple do not correspond, and that the architecture of the former is superior to that of the latter; facts which seem to prove, not that the portico was not erected by Agrippa, but that it was an after-thought, and an addition to the original building.

At all events, the portico is certainly the finest portion of the Pantheon. Forsyth, a competent critic, pronounces it "more than faultless; it is positively," he says, "the most sublime result ever produced by so little architecture."

Its length is 110 feet, and it is 44 feet in depth. It consists of sixteen granite columns, with capitals and bases of white marble: eight in front, and the remaining eight arranged behind these in four lines. Each column is composed of a single block, 46 feet 6 inches in height, and 5 feet in diameter: seven of those in front are of gray, the others are of Egyptian red granite.

The vestibule is supported by fluted pilasters of white marble, corresponding with the columns. On the frieze of the entablature runs the inscription: "M. Agrippa L. F. Cos. Tertivm Fecit ;" and the whole is surmounted by a pediment still retaining the marks of its original bas-reliefs.

* Such is the common, but very doubtful account.

The bronze roof which anciently adorned the portico was melted by Pope Urban VIII. into columns for the decoration of the high altar in the Vatican, and into cannons for the battlements of the Castle of San Angelo.

The second part of the building we are considering is a rotunda, covered by a dome. Happily it has escaped the change of years and the greed of men to a considerable extent, and no monument of equal antiquity is so well preserved. "It passed with little alteration," says Forsyth, "from the pagan into the present worship; and so convenient were its niches for the Christian altar, that Michael Angelo, ever studious of ancient beauty, introduced their design as a model in the Catholic Church."

It is 142 feet in diameter, exclusive of the walls, which in some places are said to be twenty feet thick. The height from the pavement to the summit is 143 feet, of which the dome occupies one-half, or 71½ feet. In the upright wall are placed seven large recesses, four of them embellished with Corinthian fluted columns of *giallo antico*, and two with similar columns of *pavonazzetto* marble. Between the larger recesses stand eight *ædicula*, which have been converted into modern altars; and above these runs a finely sculptured marble cornice, supporting an attic with fourteen niches, surmounted by a second cornice. From the latter springs the majestic dome, divided into square panels, which are supposed to have been originally plated with bronze. In the centre a circular aperture, 28 feet in diameter, supplies the only light which the building receives or needs.

Such is the Pantheon in its modern state. To the lover of art it bears an almost sacred character, apart from its religious dedication, as the burial-place of many famous masters: Baldassari Peruzzi, Giovanni da Udine, Taddeo Zucchero, Annibale Caracci, and, above all, Raphael.

We now turn to the Capitoline hill: not, indeed, to enumerate *all* the buildings which crowned its two summits and thronged its declivities, but to direct attention to some of the more remarkable. Here, on the north-eastern crest, stood the great *Temple of the Capi-*

tolian Jove. It was raised upon a high basis or platform, nearly 800 feet square, and measured about 200 feet in length by 175 feet in breadth. Originally erected by the last kings of Rome, it was burned down in 83 B.C., but rebuilt on a grander scale, and of much richer materials. The front, facing the south, had a portico of three rows of columns; on the sides were only two rows; the interior contained three *cellæ*, of which the central was dedicated to Jove, and the two lateral to Juno and Minerva.

Other temples and sacellæ were erected on the north-eastern summit,—as that of *Jupiter Feretrius*, which dated from the days of Romulus, but was restored by Augustus; that of *Fides*, restored by M. Æmilius Scaurus; and those of *Mars* and *Venus Erycina*.

On the south-western eminence were the temple to *Honor et Virtus*, built by Caius Marius; that to *Jupiter Tonans*, one of the foundations of Augustus; and that of *Juno Moneta*, erected by Camillus. "The name of *Moneta* seems, however," says Dr. Dyer,* "to have been conferred upon the goddess some time after the dedication of the temple, since it was occasioned by a voice heard from it after an earthquake, advising (*monens*) that expiation should be made with a pregnant sow." The temple was rebuilt in B.C. 173. Close by it stood a temple to *Concord*, also erected by Camillus, and restored by Tiberius.

Of the *Forum Julium*, near the Æmilian Basilica, with its splendid temple to *Venus Genitrix* (B.C. 45), and the *Forum Augusti*, with its temple to *Mars Ultor*, we have no space to speak. We pass on to the *Palatine hill*, which, as the residence of the emperor, was necessarily an object familiar to the eyes of Paul. It was, as Tacitus, said, *ipsa imperii arx*, the very seat and stronghold of the imperial power, and hence has given name to the residences of all subsequent monarchs and princes. On this celebrated hill stood the *Lupercal*, or grove sacred to Pan; the *Ficus Ruminalis*, or sacred fig-tree, in whose shadow the she-wolf suckled the twin-sons of the Vestal; the *Casa Romuli*, or palace† of the first king of Rome; the *Sanctuary of Victoria*; the *Ædes Matris Deûm*, rebuilt by

---

* Dr. Dyer, "Ancient Rome," *in loc.*
† Or rather, the thatched hut, for it was nothing better

Nero; and the temples to *Jupiter Victor* and *Jupiter Stator*. Here too were the House of Cicero, the House of Scaurus (so celebrated for its magnificence), and the House of Catilina, which Augustus annexed to his imperial residence. Adjoining the latter rose the splendid *Temple of Apollo*, dedicated by the great emperor in B.C. 27. It was surrounded by a portico containing the *Bibliothecæ Græca et Latina* (or Greek and Latin Libraries), the columns of which were of African marble, with the statues of the fifty daughters of Danaus placed in the intervening spaces. The temple itself was of solid white marble.

We must briefly advert to the two palaces raised upon this hill by Nero. The first of these, the *Domus Transitoria*, with its gardens, though inferior in splendour to its successor, the *Domus Aurea*, seems to have occupied quite as considerable an area, and to have reached from the Palatine to the gardens of Mæcenas on the Esquiline. The Aurea Domus, or Golden House, says Dr. Dyer, was a specimen of insane extravagance. Its *atrium* or vestibule was placed on the Velia, on the spot where afterwards rose the temple of Venus and Rome, and contained the gigantic statue of Nero, 120 feet high, whose base is still visible at the north-west side of the Coliseum. We may gain an idea of the magnificent scale of this famous palace from the prose description of Suetonius, and the poetical one of Martial, and we shall find that the poet, bewildered by the reality before him, has found it unnecessary to indulge in any flights of imagination. It was considerably enlarged by Domitian, who embellished it with extraordinary splendour. The anxiety and terror which constantly pressed upon him are vividly shown by a fact recorded in the pages of Suetonius: that he caused the walls of the portico where he was wont to walk to be faced with the stone or crystallized gypsum called *phengites*, so that he might be able to see everything that occurred behind his back. To his perturbed conscience it seemed as if the avenging dagger were ever pursuing him.

We have only to add that the *Domus Aurea* was destroyed by fire in the reign of Trajan.

We have said nothing of the baths of Agrippa, of the theatres and circi, of the bridges and aqueducts, of the gardens and villas on the Esquiline, of the streets which climbed the Aventine and the Cælian, the Quirinal and the Pincian hills, of the splendid quays which lined the banks of the Tiber, of the temples and monuments which everywhere attested the wealth and power of Rome. In truth, we have barely traced the outlines of the picture. Yet have we said enough, we hope, to enable the reader, with the exercise of a little fancy, to summon up before the "mind's eye," a visible presentment of Imperial Rome in the days of the Apostle.

CHAPTER VII.

LAST YEARS OF THE APOSTLE'S LIFE.

A.D. 61-68.

His First Imprisonment at Rome—His Epistles—His Trial and Acquittal—Further Apostolic Labours—The Pastoral Epistles—Second Imprisonment—Martyrdom.

PROBABLY the most important event in the early history of Christianity, apart from the solemn incidents of our Lord's Crucifixion and Resurrection, was the visit of St. Paul to Rome; because it inaugurated the diffusion of the gospel over the civilized world, and that struggle between the new faith and the old creed which resulted in the triumph, so complete and universal, of the former. Hitherto, as we have seen, the progress of the gospel had resembled the course of a small rivulet, which trickles on from point to point almost imperceptibly— now deepening a little, and now broadening a little, refreshing a small belt of herbage on either side, but nowhere visible to the distant gaze. Thenceforth its career was that of a mighty river, which pours onward and onward with ever-increasing force, sweeping down every obstacle it encounters, spreading far and wide its fertilizing waters, and filling the whole world with the thunder of its glorious voice. Hitherto the preacher of the gospel had received to some extent the protection of the Roman law, and when he had come into contact with the Roman authorities, they had shielded him from the malice of his Jewish enemies; but henceforth he was to find himself in direct antagonism with them, as the representatives of that Paganism which Christianity was to overthrow. When St. Paul appealed, says Professor Lightfoot,[*] from the tribunal of the Jewish procurator to the court of Cæsar, he attracted the notice and challenged the hostility of the greatest power which the world had ever seen. The very emperor to whom his appeal was referred bears the ignominy of having inaugurated the first systematic persecution of the Christians; and thus commenced the protracted struggle, the life and death contest, which, after raging for several centuries, terminated in the establishment of the gospel on the ruins of the Roman Empire. We may well believe that it was the impulse given to the progress of Christianity by the presence of its greatest preacher in the metropolis which made the Roman Church conspicuous, and, therefore, a mark for the jealous hatred of Nero. Otherwise it might have remained safe in its obscurity, like the numerous "heresies" which had already borne witness to the decaying influence of the old Roman gods. And thus the preaching of Paul may be regarded as "the necessary antecedent" to the Neronian persecution.

[*] Lightfoot "On the Epistle to the Philippians," introd., 1-28.

Professor Lightfoot argues that it is probable the Apostle foresaw the importance of his decision when he transferred his cause to Cæsar's tribunal. He sees a "significant force" in his declaration at an earlier date that he "*must* see Rome" (Acts xix. 21). He reminds us that it had long been St. Paul's "earnest desire" (Rom. i. 10–16; xv. 22–24; xv. 29, 32) to visit the imperial city, and that he had been strengthened in this purpose by a celestial vision (Acts xxiii. 11). But we prefer to believe that though he went thither in obedience to the Divine command, he was ignorant of the mighty consequences which would result from his journey. Luther, when he launched his fulmination against Tetzel, did not foresee the great issues which depended upon it. The agents of God are not favoured with a full consciousness of the nature of the work they are called upon to do. And we see no reference in St. Paul's later writings which can be interpreted as a sign of any knowledge on his part of the tremendous importance of his labours at Rome. Earnestly and unselfishly he fulfilled his mission, leaving to his God and his Saviour the determination of what that mission should, in the fulness of the ages, accomplish.

It was early in the spring of the year 61[*] that the Apostle of the Gentiles arrived at Rome. The prefect Burrus, who figures so favourably in the pages of Tacitus, seems to have treated him with unusual leniency, influenced perhaps by the letter he had received from Festus, or the good report which the centurion Julius would not fail to give of his prisoner. He allowed him to live

[*] Wieseler, "Chronologie," pp. 66, 67.

apart from the mass of prisoners, in a house which Paul hired at his own expense. But the Apostle was still under surveillance; he lived in bonds (δεσμοί, Phil. i. 7, 13, 14, 16, 17; Eph. vi. 20; Col. iv. 18; 2 Tim. i. 16, &c.)—that is, he was chained by the hand to the soldier who guarded him, and day and night was never alone. As the soldiers would necessarily relieve guard in constant succession, it is probable that a great number of the prætorians would thus be brought into the closest possible intercourse with the Apostle;* and we may be sure that he would avail himself of the opportunity to speak to them the words of good tidings. He himself tells us that his bonds had borne witness to the gospel throughout the prætorian companies.†

Still his imprisonment in all other respects allowed him extraordinary leisure. He saw whom he would; he wrote and conversed without restraint; and he dictated, as we shall see, while thus held in coupling-chains, several important epistles, and, as some authorities assert, many other apostolic letters and commands which have not come down to us.

Various conjectures have been attempted by various authorities as to the locality of St. Paul's Roman residence. Some have supposed that he was confined within the barracks attached to the imperial palace on the Palatine; but such a conjecture seems to ignore the direct mention in the Acts of his own "hired house." More probably it was situated within or near to the great

---

* Dr. Vaughan, "Lectures on St. Paul's Epistle to the Philippians," p. 41.
† Philippians i. 13: "Ὥστε τοὺς δεσμούς μου φανεροὺς ἐν Χριστῷ γενέσθαι ἐν ὅλῳ τῷ πραιτορίῳ.

prætorian camp, outside the walls, to the north-east of the city. Such a position would be convenient for the regular relief of his guards.

With characteristic energy, St. Paul had been but three days in Rome before he begun his work. He found existing in the metropolis a large and important colony of Jews, who, during the earlier part of Nero's reign, had been treated with peculiar favour. They had attained to a degree of influence which alarmed the Roman philosophers; "the vanquished had given laws to the victors." Their literature was a subject of study; even their religion, with its mystical ceremonies, excited curiosity and commanded respect. To the leaders of this important community,—probably to the chiefs of the synagogues,—St. Paul addressed himself, requesting them to meet him at his house. His object in this interview was probably twofold: it carried out his acknowledged rule—" to the Jew first, and afterwards to the Gentile," and it gave him an opportunity of endeavouring to secure the good-will of the most influential of his countrymen. Accordingly he explained to them that, though brought to Rome to answer charges preferred against him by the Jews of Palestine, he had committed no offence against his nation or the law, and the only crime of which he could justly be accused was his maintaining that the "hope of Israel" had been fulfilled.

The Jewish rulers replied, either in ignorance or out of courtesy, that no instructions had been sent to them from Palestine; that they had heard of nothing to his prejudice; that all they knew was, that the sect to which he professed to belong was held everywhere in ill repute.* A day was then fixed for his exposition of his doctrines.

The day came, and the Jews attended in great numbers. At early morning the Apostle began his address; and until evening he continued to urge upon them the acceptance of the truths of the gospel, delivering his testimony concerning the kingdom of God, and showing them, from their own scriptures, how all things were fulfilled in Jesus Christ (Acts xxviii. 23). The result was a division among those who heard him. "Some believed the things which were spoken, and some believed not"

* As some of the German rationalists fix upon this statement in support of their assertion of the unhistorical character of the Acts, it is well we should here bring forward the considerations urged by English critics. The Germans (Baur, Schwegler, and Zeller) assume that the language ascribed to the Jews ignores the existence of a Christian Church at Rome, and that the incident cannot, therefore, be reconciled with the facts recorded in St. Paul's Epistle to the Romans.

But, on the contrary, says Professor Lightfoot, this language seems to be as natural under the circumstances as it was certainly politic. "It is not very likely," he observes, "that the leading Jews would frankly recognize the facts of the case. They had been taught caution by the troubles which the Messianic feuds had brought on their more impetuous fellow-countrymen; and they would do wisely to shield themselves under a prudent reserve. Their best policy was to ignore Christianity; to inquire as little as possible about it; and, when questioned, to understate their knowledge. In a large and populous city like Rome they might, without much difficulty, shut their eyes to its existence." Considering that the population of Imperial Rome was probably three millions, it is possible, indeed, that they were utterly ignorant of the existence of a community which, we suspect, was counted only by hundreds. "When its claims were directly pressed upon them by St. Paul, their character for fairness, perhaps, also, some conscientious scruples, required them to give him at least a formal hearing. At all events, the writer of the Acts is quite aware that there was already a Christian Church in Rome; for he represents the Apostle as met on his way by two deputations from it. Indeed, the two last chapters of the narrative so clearly indicate the presence of an eye-witness, that we can hardly question the incidents, even if we are at a loss how to interpret them."—Professor Lightfoot, "On the Philippians," introd., p. 15.

(Acts xxviii. 24). After a long and stormy debate, the unbelievers departed, the Apostle warning them that they were incurring that awful doom of judicial blindness spoken of by the prophet Isaiah : "Hearing ye shall hear, and shall not understand; and seeing ye shall see, and not perceive: for the heart of this people is waxed gross, and their ears are dull of hearing, and their eyes have they closed; lest they should see with their eyes, and hear with their ears, and understand with their heart, and should be converted, and I should heal them" (Isa. vi. 9, 10).

Thus took place the final separation between the Jews and St. Paul. Henceforward his labours were entirely devoted to the conversion of the Gentile world. That they were not unblessed, we know from his own statement: he begat many children of the Lord even in his bonds (Philemon 10); and he must have been cheered by the intelligence which reached him from all sides of the ever-increasing numbers of the Christian Churches.

Dr. Farrar has a striking description of the residence and work of St. Paul at Rome. "There disembarked," he says,* "at Puteoli a troop of prisoners, whom the Procurator of Judea had sent to Rome under the charge of a centurion. Walking among them, chained and weary, but affectionately tended by two younger companions (Luke and Aristarchus), and treated with profound respect by little deputations of friends who met him at Appî Forum and the Three Taverns, was a man of mean presence and weather-beaten aspect, who was handed over, like the rest, to the charge of Burrus, the

---

* Dr. Farrar, "Seekers after God," pp. 167, 168, *et sqq.*

Præfect of the Prætorian Guards. Learning from the letters of the Jewish procurator that the prisoner had been guilty of no serious offence (Acts xxiv. 23; xxvii. 3), but had used his privilege of Roman citizenship to appeal to Cæsar for protection against the infuriated malice of his co-religionists—possibly also having heard from the centurion Julius some remarkable facts about his behaviour and history—Burrus allowed him, pending the hearing of his appeal, to live in his own hired apartment (Acts xxviii. 30—ἐν ἰδίῳ μισθώματι). This lodging was, in all probability, in that quarter of the city, opposite the island in the Tiber, which corresponds to the modern Trastevere.

"It was the resort," continues Dr. Farrar, "of the very lowest and meanest of the populace—that promiscuous jumble of all nations which makes Tacitus call Rome at this time the 'sewer of the universe.' It was here especially that the Jews exercised some of the meanest trades in Rome,—selling matches, and old clothes, and broken glass, or begging and fortune-telling on the Cestian or Fabrician bridges. In one of these narrow, dark, and dirty streets, thronged by the dregs of the Roman populace, St. Mark and St. Peter had in all probability lived when they founded the little Christian Church at Rome. It was undoubtedly in the same despised locality that St. Paul,—the prisoner who had been consigned to the care of Burrus,—hired a room, sent for the principal Jews, and for two years taught to Jews and Christians, and to any pagans who would listen to him, the doctrines which were destined to regenerate the world.

"Any one entering that mean and dingy room, would have seen a Jew with bent body and furrowed countenance, and with every appearance of age, weakness, and disease, chained by the arm to a Roman soldier. But it is impossible that, had they deigned to look closer, they should not also have seen the gleam of genius and enthusiasm, the fire of inspiration, the serene light of exalted hope and dauntless courage, upon those withered features. And though *he* was chained, 'the word of God was not chained' (2 Tim. ii. 9). Had they listened to the words which he occasionally dictated, or overlooked the large handwriting which alone his weak eyesight and bodily infirmities, as well as the inconvenience of his chains, permitted, they would have heard or read the immortal utterances which strengthened the faith of the nascent and struggling Churches in Ephesus, Philippi, and Colossæ, and which have since been treasured among the most inestimable possessions of a Christian world."

We have seen that, even in Rome, the capital of the pagan world, the Apostle's missionary labours were not unsuccessful. His chains were manifest "in all the palace, and in all other places" (Phil. i. 13); and it may readily be believed that the contagion of his enthusiasm begat a proselytizing spirit in many of his companions. But it is improbable that the "new religion" was embraced by any of the more powerful favourites of the Emperor; and still more improbable that St. Paul, as the mediævalists loved to represent, was allowed to declare its tenets before an applauding and enraptured Senate. The phrase used in the New Testament,—*ἐν*

CERTAIN SPECULATIONS.

ὅλῳ τῷ πραιτωρίῳ,—may, indeed, bear the former interpretation; and we are informed that among the early converts were "they of Cæsar's household" (Phil. iv. 22). But it is more probable that these, or, at all events, most of them, were Jews of the lowest rank, who were then to be found in considerable numbers among the "hundreds of unfortunates of every age and country" composing a Roman *familia*. And it should be remembered, also, that the word "prætorium," according to the most judicious authorities, simply means "the barrack" of that detachment of Roman soldiers which supplied, in due succession, the Apostle's guards.

The interesting and all-important narrative of the writer of "the Acts" takes the Apostle to Rome, and leaves him there. We are compelled, therefore, to compile the history of his later years by means of conjectures more or less probable, and traditions more or less authentic. In terminating so abruptly his chronicle, some critics think that the writer designed to add a second book to the one which has come down to us; in which he would have enlarged his concise allusion to the two years' residence of St. Paul at Rome, and recorded the incidents which preceded his martyrdom. If so, the design was frustrated by want of time or opportunity. Others are of opinion that Theophilus, to whom the historian dedicates his narrative, was personally acquainted with the closing scenes of the Apostle's career, and, therefore, needed no written summary of them. Whether either of these suppositions be correct or not, it is sufficient to remember that, had the details of Paul's final captivity and death been recorded, the account could merely have gratified our curiosity, and not have added to the evidence we already possess of the strength and power of the testimony he bore to Christ. In the sacred book as it is, we have all that is necessary "for edification."

An eloquent French writer has put forward the hypothesis that St. Paul must have appeared before the imperial presence, because such an appearance was the fitting conclusion of his apostolic labours.*

He had boldly confronted, says M. Vidal, every power, intellectual, religious, and political. He had appeared before the most celebrated tribunals of the civilized world, and everywhere had defended the cause of Christ with equal skill and fervour. Armed with the cross of the Saviour, he had dashed down the idols of paganism. He had stood undismayed before the Jewish Sanhedrim; the refined Athenians had listened with admiration to his subtle eloquence. He had measured the standard of all the false gods erected by poets, philosophers, and priests, and revealed their nothingness. He knew the conditions which maintained them yet awhile on their rocking pedestals. He had denounced their useless altars and empty worship. He had spoken to the hearts of proconsuls, governors of provinces, and kings. He had lifted up his voice, and proclaimed the faith of the Christian, in the gorgeous centres of paganism. He had exposed the greed and baseness of the

* Vidal, "St. Paul: sa Vie et ses Œuvres," pp. 240, 241.

mercantile, and the misleading casuistry and heartless scepticism of the philosophical spirit. What work remained for him to do, in order that he might fulfil the prophecy of his Master, "He is a chosen vessel unto me, to bear my name before the Gentiles, and kings, and the children of Israel"? (Acts ix. 15). To stand in chains before the tribunal of Cæsar, to preach his Divine Master to the most formidable power of the age, and to announce to him the judgment of God.

The authority we have quoted * is of opinion that it was unnecessary for the sacred historian to add another word to his picturesque narration. What need had he to say that Paul appeared before Cæsar? His appearance was but the fulfilment of Christ's prophecy to Ananias. After the arrival of the great Apostle at Rome, what *could* the author of "the Acts" have said? That, during the few remaining years of his life, he consolidated his apostolic work by visiting the churches he had founded, and teaching the Word in places of minor importance. But we may assume, says Vidal, that, as soon as the promise of the Saviour had been wrought out, the Holy Spirit ceased to inspire the sacred writer. His task was done.

Proceeding on a literal interpretation of the words of the Saviour,—"Fear not, Paul; thou must be brought before Cæsar" (Acts xxvii. 24),—some writers have conjectured that the Apostle appeared before Nero himself. But the phrase "before Cæsar" scarcely justifies such a rendering. When we speak of carrying a complaint to the foot of the throne, or pleading our cause before the

* Vidal, "St. Paul: sa Vie et ses Œuvres," p. 241.

sovereign, we undoubtedly do not mean that we shall address the sovereign personally, but the court which is the sovereign's legitimate representative.

Accepting, however, for the present, the literal interpretation, we are led to think upon the grandeur of the scene, if the Apostle did in reality obtain admission to the imperial presence.

When the Emperor took his seat upon the tribunal, he was accompanied by the prætorian prefect and one of his ministers or favourites as assessors. In the case of St. Paul these may have been Afranius Burrus and Seneca; the latter fitly representing the decaying philosophy of paganism and its speculative morality.

Alone, without a patron, a friend, or an advocate, St. Paul, we may be sure, would defend his cause with all his customary address, vigour, and force of speech. Had his defence come down to us, none will doubt but that we should find it equal to the famous oration delivered before the Areopagus, or the masterly "apologia" which amazed and confounded King Agrippa; that we should find it skilfully adapted to the men before whom and the circumstances in which he spoke.

It must have been a noble sight,—St. Paul, his arms loaded with chains, clothed in miserable garments, frail and insignificant in person, declaring, before the Emperor and his gorgeous court, the mysteries of the faith of Christ, and the terrors of the final judgment. Who knows but that his speech, sharp as a fiery arrow, may have stricken the heart of the imperial parricide, as it had formerly penetrated the conscience of Felix, and constrained him to dismiss and absolve the prisoner!

Baronius thinks, following Tacitus, that Nero, after the murder of his mother Agrippina, temporarily assumed the mask of a fictitious clemency; and to this passing gust of hypocritical mildness he attributes the Apostle's release. Nero was willing occasionally to figure in the character of a just judge, and to show the world that all who were summoned before his tribunal did not appear as foredoomed and forejudged victims; and, as no legal excuse could be found for the condemnation of the Apostle, he allowed his appeal. Seated on the tribunal, he generally followed the advice of his assessors. Now, Burrus and Seneca, so long as they retained their influence over him, endeavoured to establish the reputation of their imperial master as a judge faithful to the law.

If, says Vidal, St. Paul had not appeared before Nero himself on this momentous occasion, we do not see how his "bonds" could have become famous throughout the entire "prætorium;" and, more particularly, how he could have established friendly relations with some of the officers of Cæsar's household, or gained converts among persons allied to the Emperor. If eminent personages, and Nero's freedmen, and even the slaves of the imperial household, had not heard the subject of St. Paul's imprisonment discussed in the prætorium, and had not observed Nero's unusual clemency towards him, would the thought ever have occurred to them of visiting the "prisoner of Jesus Christ" in his hired house? Would not the followers and courtiers of Nero have dreaded being recognized by the warder, and denounced to the prætorian prefect, if they had visited him in secret?

But after his appearance before Cæsar, and the favourable judgment delivered by the imperial tribunal, there would have been no danger in satisfying their curiosity, their desire to hear the glorious truths it was the Apostle's mission to proclaim.

Such is the line of argument pursued by Vidal and other authorities. As the reader will perceive, it is founded wholly upon conjecture, and upon conjecture which has scarcely the merit of probability. These writers reason from the stand-point of the present. Because Christianity is *now* a mighty power in the world, they attribute to it in its infancy a degree of influence and celebrity which it certainly did not possess. In the eyes of the Roman authorities the Christians were a small and insignificant sect of Jews, who had adopted some doctrines and ceremonies peculiar to themselves, and of no importance so far as the safety of the State was concerned. The security of the early Christians lay in their very want of importance. And, therefore, we have no right to suppose that St. Paul's arrival in Rome became immediately a matter of imperial concern. He was a despised Hebrew prisoner, and nothing more. His appeal would be heard in due course by the proper judicial authorities, and adjudged, in all probability, on its own merits. We may reasonably conclude that, if the Apostle had appeared before Nero, and if his appearance had produced any signal impression on the leaders of the Roman world, authentic testimony to facts of such singular interest would have been bequeathed to posterity.* No such

* It is unnecessary to follow the course of speculation further in this direction. Some writers indulge in the most fanciful guesses respecting the supposed con-

testimony, however, occurs in any pagan writer, nor is there any distinct evidence on the subject in the pages of the fathers or early ecclesiastical historians. It is our impression, therefore, that St. Paul was never confronted personally with the master of Imperial Rome. No doubt, by giving up the ordinary belief in this occurrence we sweep aside some picturesque suppositions, and eliminate from the closing chapters of the Apostle's history a certain dramatic element; but, on the other hand, that history needs no adventitious interest. We now proceed to resume the thread of our narrative.

From the concluding lines of Luke's narrative, we learn that the Apostle resided in Rome for upwards of two years. From the specific manner in which this period is mentioned, we may infer that at its close some great change occurred in his condition. What was this change? It can have been no other, surely, than his trial, acquittal, and release. We know that he must have been set free before July, A.D. 64; for the great fire which then devastated Rome was the signal for a massacre of the Christians, and had St. Paul, their great teacher, been at that time in the metropolis, he would hardly have escaped the fate

verts made in Cæsar's household. Baronius, for instance, includes among them the Empress Sabina Poppæa, Pomponia Græcina, Evellius, and Torpes or Tropes. But there is not the shadow of a justification for regarding any one of these as Christian proselytes, except, perhaps, Pomponia Græcina; and this only on the strength of a passage in Tacitus ("Annales," xiii. 32), which speaks of " Pomponia Græcina, the wife of Acilius Plautius," as having been accused of practising a religion unauthorized by the State. Again: the Epaphroditus mentioned by the Apostle in his " Epistle to the Philippians," is identified with a freedman of the same name enfranchised by Nero, but who afterwards assisted in his master's murder. In the same manner, the Narcissus named in the " Epistle to the Romans" (xvi. 11) is asserted to be the freedman of Claudius.

which overwhelmed so many less prominent individuals. If it be objected that two years was a long interval to elapse between imprisonment and trial, we answer: that, first, the accusers and witnesses had to come from a far-off land; that, second, the accusers had every reason to delay an issue which they must have known would fail before the imperial tribunal; that, third, by keeping St. Paul in prison, they may have hoped to check, or arrest altogether, his proselytizing mission; that St. Paul himself had little reason to hasten his trial, even if he had the power, since he was safe, while "in bonds," from the malice of the Jewish rulers, and able to carry on his work of organization unmolested; and that, lastly, Nero's idleness or caprice may have led him to defer the hearing of a cause which, to a Roman emperor, must have seemed singularly abstruse and uninviting.

There must have been much that was tedious, irksome, and painful in St. Paul's imprisonment; but, nevertheless, it had its alleviations. We have already referred to the comfort he must have derived from the gradual extension of the gospel of Christ. He had also a source of consolation and encouragement in the society of his friends. It is quite allowable to conjecture that he met at Rome with some, or all, of those "old, familiar faces" whom he names in his Epistle to the Romans, —Aquila and Priscilla, who for his life would have laid down their own necks; the mother of Rufus, who, in times past, had treated him with maternal affection (Rom. xvi. 13); his countrymen, Andronicus, Junias, Herodion, Epænetus his well-beloved, Urbanus his helper in Christ, Mary (who, from her name, must have been of Jewish extraction), Amplias, Stachys, and Persis.

An old and constant friend, Luke, the physician and evangelist—hereafter to be his biographer—was constantly by his side; and Timotheus, one of the youngest and the best-beloved of his disciples. He was attended by Epaphroditus (Phil. ii. 25-30), who came from the Church of Philippi with pecuniary aid; by Aristarchus of Thessalonica, who patiently shared his captivity; by Tychicus, a native of the Roman province of Asia, and probably of Ephesus its capital; by Epaphras, the evangelist of Colossæ, who came to consult him on the heresies which threatened the peace of the Colossian Church (Col. i. 7-iv. 12).

We read also of John Mark, who wavered no more, but clung loyally and steadfastly to the banner of Christ (Col. iv. 10); of Demas, as yet among the faithful, but soon to be found a renegade and deserter (Col. iv. 14; Philemon 24); of Jesus "the just," one of the most faithful of the Jewish converts; and, finally, of Onesimus, Philemon's runaway slave, "not now a slave, but above a slave—a brother beloved," whose career has rightly been described as "the most touching episode in the apostolic history, and the noblest monument of the moral power of the gospel."

The mention of this poor slave, whom the truth made free, brings us naturally to a consideration of St. Paul's epistolary labours during his imprisonment. It is now generally admitted that he wrote at this time four epistles —to Philemon, to the Colossians, to the Ephesians, and to the Philippians. It is almost universally admitted that the first three were written and despatched at or about the same time, and the Epistle to the Philippians towards the close of Paul's captivity.*

The Epistle to the Colossians serves as an intermediary between that to Philemon and that to the Ephesians. As regards the former, note that Onesimus accompanies both epistles (Col. iv. 9; Philemon 10–12); that in both greetings are sent to Archippus (Col. iv. 17; Philemon 2); and that the same persons are enumerated as Paul's companions at the time of writing (Col. i. 1–4; Philemon 23, 24). As regards the latter, note that both were intrusted to the same messenger, Tychicus (Col. iv. 7; Eph. vi. 21); and that both exhibit a singular resemblance in style and matter.

We infer that the Epistle to the Philippians was the last written, because it alludes to the extraordinary development of the Christian Church at Rome; because, from the omission of the names of Luke and Aristarchus in the salutation, it may be conjectured that they were no longer among the Apostle's companions;† because the several communications between Philippi and Rome which the epistle implies must have occupied a considerable time after his arrival; and, lastly, because the tone of sadness which prevails in the epistle would seem to be natural to a period of doubt and anxiety, such as the immediate period before the Apostle's trial.‡

---

* *See* Davidson, Conybeare and Howson, Dean Alford, and the Bishop of Gloucester (Dr. Ellicott); also, Wieseler and De Wette.

† Their names occur in the Epistles to Philemon (24) and the Colossians (iv. 10, 14).

‡ We confess these reasons are not very forcible, and Professor Lightfoot does much towards overthrowing them ("On the Philippians," pp. 31–39).

Taking them in the following-chronological order—Colossians, Ephesians, Philemon, Philippians—we proceed to a brief analysis of their contents :—

Epistle to the Colossians.

[It has been conjectured, with much probability, that this epistle was written prior to the death of the prætor Burrus, in A.D. 62, as after that event Paul's imprisonment seems to have become more rigorous. It was called forth by information received from Epaphras and Onesimus—both, it is supposed, natives of Colossæ—and is designed to reprove the half-Judaizing, half-Orientalizing tendencies exhibited by the Colossian Church.]

1. The epistle opens with the usual salutation (i. 1, 2).

2. Paul returns thanks to God for the faith of the Colossians, the love they had shown him, and the success which had attended the preaching of Epaphras (i. 3–8).

3. He prays for their further increase in grace (i. 9–11), and that they may fully comprehend the character of the Saviour, who is the image of the invisible God, the Head of the Church, in whom all things consist, and by whom all things have been reconciled to the Father (i. 12–20).

4. He points out that in their own case this reconciliation had been manifested, and that they are now presented holy and unblamable and unreprovable before God, if they remain constant to the truth of the gospel (i. 21–24), of which gospel Paul declares himself the minister (i. 25–29).

5. For this gospel, moreover, he had greatly suffered—his sufferings being not only for those he had seen, but also for those he had not seen—so that they might arrive at a full acknowledgment of the mystery of the Father and of Christ, and not be led away by "enticing words" (ii. 1–6).

6. Before all things they were to rest upon Jesus, and give no heed to the vain deceits and tradition of men. In Jesus dwells all the fulness of the Godhead; He is the head of all principality and power; and through Him they had triumphed over all the powers of darkness (ii. 7–15).

7. Therefore they are not to confound religion with mere ceremonial observances, or with the worshipping of angels, or with any ascetic practices, which, however they might show like wisdom in will-worship, and pretended humility, and neglect of the body, were of no real value (ii. 16-23).

8. But they were to set their affection on things above; were to mortify, not the body, but carnal desires and passions; were to avoid wrath, malice, blasphemy, obscenity, lying; and, as the elect of God, to assume the Christian graces of humility, meekness, long-suffering, and, above all, charity, which is the bond of perfectness (iii. 1-14).

9. Then, the grace of God dwelling in their hearts, they might teach and admonish one another with "psalms and hymns and spiritual songs" (iii. 15-17).

10. The Apostle is thus led to enumerate the special duties of wives towards their husbands, husbands towards their wives, children and parents, servants and masters, towards one another (iii. 18-25; compare Eph. v. and vi.).

11. He concludes with a fervent exhortation that they should "continue in prayer"—praying too for Paul himself, that he might be successful in preaching the gospel; and informs them that Tychicus and Onesimus, the bearers of the epistle, would bring them acquainted with his present condition (iv. 2-9).

12. After recording the greetings sent to them by Aristarchus, Marcus, Jesus surnamed Justus, Epaphras, Luke, and Demas (iv. 10-13), he desires that his epistle, after being read by the Colossians, shall be read in the Church of Laodicea, and that, in like manner, his Epistle to the Laodiceans shall be read by them (iv. 14-17).

13. The usual salutation concludes an epistle, brief, it is true, but profound, and full of beauty.

Epistle to the Ephesians. *

[This epistle seems to have been suggested by the deep love which the Apostle felt for his converts at Ephesus, and which the mission

---

* Several critics are of opinion that this epistle was addressed, not to the Church at Ephesus, but to the Church at Laodicea.—*See* Conybeare and Howson, ii. 405, 406.

of Tychicus, with an epistle to the Church of Colossæ, afforded him a convenient opportunity of evincing in written teaching and exhortation. The epistle thus contains many thoughts that had pervaded the nearly contemporaneous Epistle to the Colossians, reiterates many of the same practical warnings and exhortations, bears even the tinge of the same diction; but at the same time enlarges upon such profound mysteries of the Divine counsels, displays so fully *the origin and developments of the Church in Christ*, its union, communion, and aggregation in Him, that this majestic epistle can never be deemed otherwise than one of the most sublime and consolatory outpourings of the Spirit of God to the children of men. "To the Christian at Ephesus, dwelling under the shadow of the great temple of Diana, daily seeing its outward grandeur, and almost daily hearing of its pompous ritualism, the allusions in this epistle to this mystic building of which Christ was the cornerstone, the Apostles the foundations, and himself and his fellow-Christians portions of the august superstructure (ii. 19-22), must have spoken with a force, an appropriateness, and a reassuring depth of teaching, that cannot be over-estimated."*]

PART I.—Doctrinal (i.–iii.).

1. The epistle opens with a brief address to the Christian brethren in Ephesus (i. 1-3).

2. Ascribes praise to God the Father, in noble language, for having blessed and redeemed us in Christ, and made known to us His eternal purpose of uniting all in Him (i. 3-14).

3. The Apostle prays that all the brethren may become fully acquainted with the riches of God's grace, and the magnitude of His power in the resurrection and exaltation of our Saviour (i. 15-23);

4. And reminds them of the special mercies they had themselves experienced, inasmuch as God had quickened them, raised them, and enthroned them with Christ (ii. 1-10).

5. They were also to remember that in Christ lay all their peace; that through Him both they and the Jews could approach the

---

* Bishop Ellicott, Smith's "Bible Dictionary," ii. 560.

Father; and that on Him, as on a corner-stone, they had been built into an holy temple in the Lord (ii. 11-22).

6. Wherefore, having heard of the revelation, which had been made known unto him, of the mystery of this call of the Gentiles, and of the part which he filled towards it—even that he should preach among the Gentiles the unsearchable riches of Christ—they were not to grow faint at his tribulations; and for this cause he prayed to the Universal Father that He would strengthen them with His Spirit, so that they might attain to a full knowledge of the love of the Redeemer (iii. 1-19).

7. The prayer concludes with "a sublime doxology," which is ever on the lips and in the hearts of all true Christians (iii. 19-21).

PART II.—Practical (iv. to the end).

1. The Apostle urges upon his readers the importance of a Christian life, and of endeavouring to keep the unity of the Spirit in the bond of peace; reminding them that there is but one body, one Spirit, one Lord, one faith, one baptism, one God and Father of all (iv. 1-6).

2. Each has his measure of the gift of Christ; some being appointed apostles, some evangelists, some pastors and teachers, until all come to the unity of the faith, and unto perfection in Christ Jesus (iv. 7-16).

3. Therefore, they are bidden not to walk, like unbelievers, with darkened understanding, but to put on the new man, created in righteousness and true holiness (iv. 16-24).

4. And in testimony thereof, to be truthful, forgiving, gentle, honest, industrious, charitable; eschewing all bitterness, wrath, malice, and evil-speaking; showing mutual kindness and forbearance; and walking in love, after Christ's example (iv. 25-32—v. 1, 2).

5. Continuing his counsel, the Apostle warns them to flee fornication, and filthy and unseasonable conversation; the darkness of heathenism having passed, they are to live as in the light, to walk circumspectly, to avoid excess in wine, to rejoice in spiritual songs and psalms, and give thanks unto God the Father in the name of Jesus Christ (v. 3-21).

6. The Apostle proceeds to a particular exhortation that wives should obey their husbands (v. 22-24), and husbands love their wives, even as their own bodies (v. 25-33); that children should honour their parents, and servants obey their masters (vi. 1-9).

7. The Apostle concludes with a comparison of life to a battle, in which the Christian, if he would withstand the wiles of the devil, must put on the whole armour of God, praying always with all prayer and supplication in the Spirit, and in their prayers neither forgetting all the saints nor Paul himself, that, though an ambassador "in bonds," he may speak boldly as he ought to speak (vi. 9-20).

8. With a commendation of Tychicus as "a faithful minister," and with the usual benediction, the Apostle concludes (vi. 21-24).

Epistle to Philemon.

[Philemon (Φιλήμων) is supposed to have been a native of, or, at all events, a resident in, Colossæ; first, because Onesimus, on whose behalf Paul, as we shall see, addressed him, was a Colossian (Col. iv. 9); and, second, because Archippus, whom St. Paul addresses conjointly with Philemon (Philemon 1, 2), was also a Colossian (Col. iv. 17). According to tradition, his house at Colossæ was extant in the fifth century. It is said that he became Bishop of Colossæ, and was martyred in the reign of Nero.

That he was a man of substance is evident, for he is described as ruling a large household, and dispensing a lavish hospitality not only towards his friends, but to the saints in general. He had been converted to Christianity by St. Paul himself (Philemon 19), though under what circumstances the Apostle and disciple came into contact, we can only conjecture. If St. Paul visited Colossæ on his way through Phrygia (Acts xvi. 6), the difficulty would vanish; but from Col. ii. 1 it may be doubted whether he ever passed through that city. We may perhaps conclude that he was at Ephesus during St. Paul's long sojourn there in A.D. 54-57, having been attracted thither by the fame of his preaching, and that he was then rescued from the thraldom of heathenism.

Among his servants, or slaves, was Onesimus, who contrived to effect his escape and fly to Rome, where, among a population counted by millions, he might reasonably hope to avoid detection. Some commentators assert that he fled because he had robbed his master;* but there does not seem the slightest foundation for such a charge.

At Rome he saw and heard the Apostle, of whom he had probably heard in his master's household. He became a Christian (Philemon 10), and attached himself to St. Paul as a faithful and indefatigable attendant, making himself useful in a variety of ways. Paul would fain have kept him by his side, but he felt that Onesimus ought to return to his master and earn his forgiveness. With generous self-denial, he therefore sent him back to Colossæ, charging Philemon to receive him "no longer as a servant," but as something more than a servant—as "a brother beloved" (Philemon 16).

Here the narrative ends, so far as the apostolic records are concerned; but the traditions of the Church represent that Onesimus was set free,† and afterwards ordained Bishop of Beræa in Macedonia, that he a second time visited Rome, and perished in the Neronian persecution.]

1. Paul begins his letter with a salutation to Philemon, to Apphia and Archippus, and to the Church in Philemon's household (1–3).

2. He expresses the joy with which he has heard of Philemon's hospitality towards the saints (4–7);

3. And having consolation in his love, he therefore asks as a favour what otherwise as an apostle he might have commanded (8, 9)—

4. Namely, that he will receive back into his house his former servant Onesimus, whom he himself would gladly have retained, if he could have done so with Philemon's consent (10–15).

---

* It cannot be said that verses 18 and 19 will justly bear such an interpretation.

† Of this there can be little doubt, and hence it was, as Dr. Wordsworth (Bishop of Lincoln) remarks, that by Christianizing the master, the gospel enfranchised the slave. "It did not legislate about mere names and forms, but it went to the root of the evil: it spoke to the heart of man. Where the heart of the master was filled with Divine grace and warmed with the love of Christ, the rest would soon follow. The lips would speak kind words, the hands would do liberal things. Every Onesimus would be treated by every Philemon as a beloved brother in Christ."—"St. Paul's Epistles," p. 328.

5. But Philemon is to receive him, not as a servant, but as a brother beloved; and if he had in any wise wronged his master, the wrong was to be put to Paul's account (16–19).

6. In conclusion, the Apostle expresses his confidence that Philemon will obey him in this matter, and anticipating his early release from his bonds, desires him to "prepare a lodging" in Colossæ (20–22).

7. With the usual salutations and benediction, the epistle closes (23–25).

Epistle to the Philippians.

[This epistle, says Professor Lightfoot,* must be ascribed to the close personal relations existing between the Apostle and his converts. It was not written, like the Epistle to the Galatians, to counteract doctrinal errors, or, like the First to the Corinthians, to correct irregularities of practice. It enforces no direct lessons of Church government, though it makes casual allusion to Church officers. It lays down no dogmatic system, though incidentally it refers to the majesty and the humiliation of Christ, and to the contrast of law and grace. It is the spontaneous utterance of Christian love and gratitude, called forth by a recent token which the Philippians had given of their loyal affection. As the pure expression of personal feeling, not directly evoked by doctrinal or practical errors, it closely resembles the Apostle's letter to another leading Church of Macedonia, which likewise held a large place in his affections—the First Epistle to the Thessalonians.

To all ages of the Church, continues our authority—to our own especially—this epistle reads a great lesson. While we are expending our strength on theological definitions or ecclesiastical rules, it recalls us from these distractions to the very heart and centre of the gospel—the life of Christ, and the life in Christ. Here is the meeting-point of all our differences, the healing of all our feuds, the true life alike of individuals and sects and churches : here doctrine and practice are wedded together; for here is the "creed of creeds" involved in and arising out of the work of works.†]

* Professor Lightfoot, "On the Epistle to the Philippians," pp. 65, 72.

† "There is a great distinctness, a great individuality, in the tone and style of his description and of his exhortation. It is quite unlike that in which the

PART I.—Personal (i. and ii.).

1. According to the usual custom, the epistle opens with a salutation "to all the saints at Philippi, with the bishops and deacons" (i. 1, 2).

2. The Apostle gives thanks to God for the converts he has made, and prays that their love of Christ may continue to increase (i. 3-11).

3. He enters upon an explanation of his personal position, and describes the success of his preaching, not only among the soldiers of the imperial guard, but in a far wider circle: this success had stimulated most of the brethren with boldness, so that they preached the word of God without fear (i. 12-14).

4. After an allusion to some false preachers, he solemnly declares his earnest hope that Christ may ever be magnified in his body, whether by his life or by his death. To live, he says, is Christ; to die is gain (i. 15-26).

5. Thence he is led to exhort them to unity, and to fortitude under persecution; and he encourages them to persevere in a lowly spirit by the high and glorious pattern of our Lord's humility (i. 27-30; ii. 5-11).

6. How that example should be realized by men, he proceeds to show (ii. 12-16);

7. And next he enters upon an explanation of his intentions: he will shortly send Timotheus unto them; he refers to the illness and recovery of Epaphroditus, whom he will also send to Philippi (ii. 17-30).

PART II.—Doctrinal (iii. to end).

1. The Apostle warns the brethren to beware of the Judaizing teachers, and with reference to the law, shows that he, "an Hebrew of the Hebrews," would have much more reason than they to trust in its efficacy (iii. 1-6).

2. But that, nevertheless, he counts it as "dung," so that he may gain Christ and His righteousness (iii. 6-11).

Apostle writes to the Romans, the Corinthians, the Galatians, or the Ephesians. It is quite evident that he feels towards the Philippians a very peculiar affection. They had been singularly thoughtful, singularly affectionate towards him."—Dr. Vaughan, "Lectures on the Philippians," p. 7.

3. He bids them to be of the same mind as he is, to avoid those who are enemies of the cross of Christ, and to remember that their faith is in the Saviour (iii. 12–21).

4. Therefore he exhorts them to abandon all discussions (iv. 1–4), to rejoice in the Lord, to abstain from worldly care, to pursue all things that are just, true, honest, and of good report (iv. 5–9).

5. He thanks them for their alms, received through Epaphroditus, and praises their thoughtful liberality (iv. 10–20).

6. The epistle concludes with the usual salutations and benediction (iv. 20–23).

Epistle to the Hebrews.

["The origin and history of the Epistle to the Hebrews [*] was a subject of controversy even in the second century. There is no portion of the New Testament whose authorship is so disputed, nor any of which the inspiration is more indisputable. The early Church could not determine whether it was written by Barnabas, by Luke, by Clement, or by Paul. Since the Reformation, still greater diversity of opinion has prevailed. Luther assigned it to Apollos, Calvin to a disciple of the Apostle. The Church of Rome now maintains by its infallibility the Pauline authorship of the epistle, which in the second, third, and fourth centuries the same Church, with the same infallibility, denied. But notwithstanding these doubts concerning the origin of this canonical book, its inspired authority is beyond all doubt. It is certain, from internal evidence, that it was written by a cotemporary of the Apostles, and before the destruction of Jerusalem; that its writer was the friend of Timotheus (Heb. xiii. 23); and that he was the teacher (Heb. xiii. 19) of one of the apostolic churches. Moreover, the epistle was received by the Oriental Church as canonical from the first. Every sound reasoner must agree with St. Jerome, that it matters nothing whether it were written by Luke, by Barnabas, or by Paul, since it is allowed to be the production of the apostolic age, and has been read in the public service of the Church from the earliest times. Those, therefore, who

---

[*] The titles of all the epistles are of later date than the epistles themselves. The present was first known merely as πρὸς Ἑβραίους, and not as Παύλου πρὸς Ἑβραίους.

conclude with Calvin that it was not written by St. Paul, must also join with him in thinking the question of its authorship a question of little moment, and in 'embracing it without controversy as one of the apostolical epistles.'"*—Conybeare and Howson, ii. 508, 509.†]

1. The Apostle explains the final revelation of God in the person of His Son, who is higher than the angels (i. 1-14).

2. For which reason believers ought to give the greater heed to His word. If every infraction of the Mosaic law was punished, how would *they* escape who neglected the salvation offered by Christ? (ii. 1-9).

3. Certainly, Jesus had undergone the humiliation of death, but this was needful; in order that by His sufferings He might be consecrated as our High Priest, and having Himself endured sorrow, might be able to succour us when we are tried (ii. 10-18).

4. The Apostle next proceeds to enlarge on the infinite superiority of Christ to Moses (iii. 1-6); and,

5. To warn his readers against apostatizing from the gospel, setting forth the doom that thereby they would assuredly provoke (iii. 15-19; iv. 1-13).

6. What needed they of any high priest but Christ, who could be touched with a feeling of their infirmities, and was named by God a High Priest "after the order of Melchisedec"? (iv. 14-16; v. 1-10).

7. The Jewish Christians are next reproached for their lack of understanding (v. 11-14; vi. 1, 2);

8. Are again warned of the consequences of apostasy (vi. 3-9);

9. And affectionately reminded of the blessings awaiting those who through faith and steadfast endurance inherit the promises (vi. 9-12).

10. What these promises are the Apostle shows (vi. 13-20).

11. In two important circumstances—eternal duration and efficacy

---

* The truth seems to be, that whoever wrote this epistle embodied the views and thoughts of St. Paul, if not his exact language; but in many places the phraseology seems to us evidently Pauline. We venture to agree with Dr. Davidson, Mr. Bullock, and others, that St. Paul's collaborateur was St. Luke.

† *See* Rev. C. Forster's "Apostolical Authority of the Epistle to the Hebrews," and B. F. Westcott "On the Canon of the New Testament."

—Christ's priesthood (typified by the priesthood of Melchisedec) surpasses the Levitical priesthood; and Christ as a High Priest all other high priests, being "holy, harmless, undefiled, separate from sinners, and ascended above the heavens" (vii. 1-28).

12. The Apostle now proceeds to sum up his arguments: the Mosaic law, which his readers have shown a disposition to overestimate, was nothing more than an imperfect foreshadowing, with its temple, priests, and sacrifices, of the better covenant, purer priesthood, and all-availing atonement of Christ. This point is elaborated with many striking illustrations, and with abundant reference to the Jewish ritual, at considerable length (viii., ix., x. 1-18).

13. The brethren are therefore called upon to avail themselves of the new covenant, and to hold fast the confession of their hope without wavering (x. 19-24).

14. Various exhortations follow, and a warning against despising the blood of the Saviour (x. 25-31).

15. They are not to let fear conquer their faith; and what faith *is*, the Apostle defines in impressive language as "the substance [or foundation] of things hoped for, the evidence of things not seen." Its operation is illustrated by numerous examples (xi.).

16. They are exhorted to imitate these examples, looking onward unto Jesus, the foremost leader and the finisher of their faith, and regarding whatever chastisements may fall upon them as full of hope, inasmuch as they yield "the fruit of righteousness in peace" (xii. 1-13).

17. They are cautioned against indulgence in sensual sin (xii. 13-18);

18. For in proportion to the superiority of the gospel over the law,—a superiority like that of the heavenly over the earthly Mount Zion,—will be the punishment of those who despise it. For God is a consuming fire (xii. 18-29).

19. In conclusion, the Apostle admonishes the brethren to the performance of certain moral duties,—brotherly love, hospitality, conjugal purity, contentment, obedience to their spiritual leaders, and steadfast adherence to the faith (xiii. 1-17).

20. He desires their prayers, and gives them his own (xiii. 18-22).

21. The epistle closes with the information that Timotheus has been set at liberty, and with the usual salutations and benediction (xiii. 23-25).

It is possible that this epistle was written in A.D. 63, the year in which Paul's long captivity may be supposed to have terminated. For the best modern authorities* are agreed that about this time the Apostle was summoned before the imperial tribunal, and the charges against him falling to the ground, was acquitted and released. Much as he must have rejoiced at his escape from the weariness of captivity, he must not the less have felt happy in the knowledge that his captivity had not proved unfruitful, but that while he remained in bonds the Christian Church had largely increased its numbers. Not, indeed, from among the great and powerful, whom the voice of a Jewish prisoner could hardly reach—though one of high birth and rank, Pomponia Græcina, the wife of Plautius, the conqueror of Britain, was probably a convert; but from the middle and lower classes of society, the soldiers of the Prætorian Guàrd, the successful tradesmen, the skilled artizans, and the confidential retainers of noble houses. The members of the Roman Church, says Professor Lightfoot,† saluted in St. Paul's epistle could assuredly boast no aristocratic descent, whether from the proud patrician or the not less proud plebeian families. They bear "upstart names," mostly Greek, sometimes borrowed from natural objects, sometimes adopted from a Pagan hero or divinity, sometimes descriptive of personal qualities or advantages, occasionally the surnames

---

* Cf. Alford, Conybeare and Howson, Lewin, Wieseler, and Davies.
† Lightfoot "On the Philippians," pp. 20, 21.

of some noble family to which they were perhaps attached as slaves or freedmen,* but in very few cases bearing the stamp of high Roman antiquity. Of Rome it was not less true than of Corinth, that "not many wise after the flesh, not many powerful, not many high-born" were called (1 Cor. i. 26).

According to the general testimony of the Early Church, the Apostle, after obtaining his freedom, visited Asia Minor, and fulfilled the strong desire to which he had given expression in his epistles (Philemon 22; Phil. ii. 24) of examining the condition of the Churches planted by his labours. It is probable that he made Ephesus his centre, and thence, at different times, proceeded to Colossæ, Laodicea, Hierapolis, and other towns. An obscure passage in Clement's First Epistle has been understood as bearing witness to St. Paul's journeying as far westward as Spain. Chrysostom and Jerome seem to allude to the same expedition, which we know was long meditated by the Apostle (Rom. xv. 24, 28), and which occupied, it is said, nearly two years (A.D. 64–66). But the evidence is of the vaguest description.

Supposing the Spanish journey to have actually taken place, and Paul in A.D. 66 to have returned to Ephesus, we may conclude that about the end of that year, or early in 67, he addressed his Epistles to Timothy (the First) and Titus. They are wholly different in character from his former writings, and are rather to be looked upon as pastoral letters, containing directions for the government of Christian Churches, than as doctrinal expositions

---

* As examples of these different classes of names, take Stachys; Hermes, Nereus; Epænetus, Ampliatus, Urbanus; Julia, Claudia (2 Tim. iv. 21).

dealing with the fundamental truths of Christianity. Having gone on a journey into Macedonia, he was unable personally to deal with the distractions of the Christian community at Ephesus, caused by the efforts of heretical teachers; and therefore he despatched a letter of instructions to Timotheus, whom he had left behind him as his deputy.

Under these circumstances, as we believe, was written the First Epistle to Timotheus, or Timothy.

From Macedonia the Apostle returned to Ephesus, and thence sailed to Crete in company with Titus, to visit the Churches which had been founded in that island by the exertions of private Christians. He made but a brief sojourn, again returning to Ephesus, with the view of proceeding to Nicopolis,* in Epirus, before the winter (Titus iii. 12). In reply apparently to a communication from Titus, which had reference to the difficulties he experienced in organizing the Cretan Churches,† St. Paul, previous to setting out on his journey, addressed him a pastoral letter. Of this, and of the First Epistle to Timothy, we subjoin our usual analytical summaries :—

First Epistle to Timothy.

[In the Pastoral Epistles—that is, the two Epistles to Timotheus, and the Epistle to Titus—we find a change of thought and style, which shows that they were written late in St. Paul's life, and probably when he was weakened by old age, suffering, constant labour, and confinement. From internal evidence we are led to fix their dates between A.D. 66 and A.D. 68 (the year of St. Paul's martyrdom); and, as we have indicated, there are good grounds for believ-

---

* There were several places of this name, but the only one of any importance was in Epirus.—*See* Bishop Christopher Wordsworth's "Greece," pp. 229-232.
† Conybeare and Howson, ii. 476.

ing that the First Epistle to Timothy, and the Epistle to Titus, were written just before Paul's last imprisonment, and the Second Epistle to Timothy during his imprisonment, and shortly before his death.

Schleiermacher, Baur, De Wette, and Dr. Davidson contend that the Pastoral Epistles were not written by Paul. After a careful consideration of their objections, we cannot adopt their view. There is not a shadow of an argument to support the plea that they were forged; such a forgery could not have escaped detection; and it is in truth sufficient to state that they were universally accepted as genuine by the Early Church. In the Muratorian Canon, as well as in the Peshito Version, they are included among the Pauline Epistles. No doubts as to their authenticity are expressed by Eusebius, Tertullian, or Irenæus. Their other objections are not less easily disposed of, as will be seen by any candid reader who carefully examines the answers given by Bishop Christopher Wordsworth, Dean Alford, Professor Plumptre, and Conybeare and Howson.

In reference to Timotheus, it may here be added that he probably soothed the last sufferings of his great teacher by his presence and affectionate ministrations. Tradition states that he afterwards acted as Bishop of Ephesus, and was murdered by the mob on the occasion of a great festival to Diana (the καταγώγιον), in their rage at his denunciations of its profligacy and license. He seems to have inspired a warm affection in all with whom he came in contact; and it is pleasant to remember that his name is associated (2 Tim. iv. 21) with those of a Roman noble, Pudens,—the daughter of a British king, Claudia,—and a future Bishop of Rome, Linus.*]

1. The Apostle commences in the usual form (i. 1, 2), and then proceeds to remind Timotheus of the duty he had been charged to fulfil at Ephesus,—namely, to oppose the false teachers, and encourage the brethren in the true faith. The law, he points out, is not meant to fetter the righteous, but the disobedient; and such too is the spirit of the gospel. He praises God that he has been made its preacher, and then expresses his confidence in the fidelity of Timotheus, in contrast to the errors of Hymenæus and Alexander, whom he had solemnly excommunicated (i. 3–20).

---

* Alford, Excursus in "Greek Testament," iii. 104.

2. He lays down rules for the due performance of public worship, and explains the proper place and work of woman (ii.).

3. The qualifications of office-bearers in the Church are described,—bishops, deacons, and deaconesses being particularized (iii. 1–13).

4. The Apostle here interpolates—(perhaps the awkwardness of the passage is due to his amanuensis)—a reference to an intended visit to Timotheus, and a kind of enthusiastic ejaculation on the "mystery of godliness" (iii. 14–16).

5. He returns to the false teachers already spoken of, and controverts their teaching (iv. 1–6).

6. Whence he is led to point out the qualities of a true Christian life, with a personal but affectionate application to Timotheus himself (iv. 6–16).

7. For his better guidance he enunciates a variety of wise and prudent maxims, and lays particular stress on the due selection of widows for the office of female elders. That Timotheus may be "a proper censor of others, he is directed to be free himself from inordinate enjoyments; but without countenancing asceticism." He adds a remark "about different ways of discovering the true character of men"* (v.)

8. Finally, he refers to the duty of Christian servants; cautions Timotheus to avoid heretics; proclaims godliness to be the only true gain; and concludes with a warm, earnest, and tender appeal to his beloved disciple to fight the good fight of faith, and lay hold on eternal life (vi.).

Epistle to Titus.

[Titus is nowhere mentioned in the Acts; and the only notices that occur of him are to be found in the Epistle to the Galatians, the Second Epistle to the Corinthians, the Epistle to Titus himself, and the Second Epistle to Timothy. He was a Gentile proselyte; perhaps a native of Antioch, since he would seem to have been one of those brethren who accompanied Paul and Barnabas from Antioch to Jerusalem (compare Acts xv. 2, and Gal. ii. 1, 3). He was afterwards entrusted with a mission to Corinth† (2 Cor. ii. 13), and

---

* Dr. Davidson, "Introd. to New Testament," ii. 143.
† To carry, as Macknight and Stanley suggest, the First Epistle.

directed to meet St. Paul at Troas; which he failed to do, but overtook his master in Macedonia (2 Cor. vii. 6, 7, 13-15). He was then sent back to Corinth, as bearer of the Second Epistle, and accompanied by Tychicus and Trophimus; and specially enjoined to urge forward the collection which was being made for the poor Christians of Judea (2 Cor. viii. 6, 17, 23).

Years elapse before we again hear of Titus. Between St. Paul's first and second imprisonment, he and the Apostle visited Crete (Titus i. 5). He remained there to organize the Church throughout the island, and to restrain the ill-doing of the Judaizers. After the arrival of Artemas and Tychicus (iii. 12), we may conjecture that, his work being done, he joined Paul at Necopolis, and accompanied him to Rome on the occasion of his second imprisonment.

Tradition professes to finish his biography by making him Bishop of Crete for the remainder of his life; and the modern capital, Candia, claims the honour of being his burial-place. In the fragment by Zenas, quoted by Falkener, he is said to have been Bishop of Gortyna, whose ruined church retains the name of "Saint Titus."*]

1. The epistle opens with the usual salutation (i. 1-4).
2. The Apostle explains the duties which he requires of Titus; namely, the organization of the Cretan Church by the appointment of presbyters, whose qualifications are described (i. 5-9).
3. There are many false teachers, who must be sternly reproved; their character is painted in strong colours (i. 10-16).
4. In opposition to their erroneous doctrines, Titus is directed to impress on his flock the necessity of a pure and holy life—on the older men, the older women, the younger men, and the slaves—setting them in himself a good example† (ii. 1-12);
5. In which he and they may be encouraged by the glorious hope of Christ's Second Coming, and His Atonement (ii. 13-15).

* *See* Professor Birks, "Horæ Apostolicæ," appendix to his edition of Paley's "Horæ Paulinæ," p. 299, *et seq*.

† It is noticeable that in the Pastoral Epistles St. Paul exhibits a greater tenderness and regard for domestic duties than in his earlier ones. Age and suffering have tempered the fiery heart, and the stern Apostle becomes more of the humble and considerate Christian pastor.

6. Further instructions are given in practical duties; obedience to lawful rulers being enjoined,* and a general spirit of forbearance; and these duties being based on our sense of past sin, and our regeneration in the Holy Ghost (iii. 1–7).

7. Foolish speculations are to be avoided, and heretics, who will not amend, are to be excommunicated (iii. 9–11).

8. The epistle concludes with reference to various personal matters; Titus is to join the Apostle at Nicopolis; after he has expedited Zenas and Apollos on a certain journey, and Artemas or Tychicus may be expected in Crete (iii. 12–14).

9. Salutation and benediction (iii. 15).

Nicopolis, the "city of victory," was the principal centre of a large and important province, and for this reason may have been chosen by Paul as his winter residence. It was founded by Augustus as an enduring memorial of his great victory at Actium, and occupied the site of the camp which his army had occupied previous to the battle. Its original extent and importance are attested by the extent and importance of its ruins. A long and lofty wall still spans the now desolate plain; to the north, on the hill's green summit, rises the shattered *scena* of a theatre; and to the west the broken but extended line of an aqueduct connects the far-off mountains and their secret reservoirs with the fallen city.

Paul, however, was not permitted to pass the winter at Nicopolis. As the year 68 opened, he was again arrested, on the testimony perhaps of some informer, and hurried away to Rome, *viâ* Apollonia and Brundusium. On his arrival at Rome, he was subjected to a

---

* St. Paul himself had no doubt insisted on the duty of obedience to the civil magistrate when he was in Crete. The Jews throughout the Empire were much disposed to insubordination at this period.

far severer imprisonment than had formerly been his lot; he was not only chained, but treated as "a malefactor." "It was dangerous and difficult to seek his prison (2 Tim. i. 16); so perilous to show any public sympathy with him, that no Christian ventures to stand by his side in the court of justice (2 Tim. iv. 16). And as the final stage of his trial approaches, he looks forward to death as his certain sentence" (2 Tim. iv. 6-8).

The cause of these altered conditions is easily explained. At the epoch of his first imprisonment the Christians were an obscure and almost unknown body. But the conflagration of Rome in A.D. 64 drew attention to their increasing numbers and peculiar tenets, which enabled Nero, in order to avert from himself the public wrath, to charge it upon this new and remarkable sect—a sect which despised the Roman gods, shrank from the Roman temples, never offered oblations or sacrifices at Roman altars, and might well be suspected, therefore, of the most atrocious crimes.* Thence originated the Neronian persecution; after which event the Imperial Government began to recognize the Christians as a dangerous, and, perhaps, a traitorous body—all the more dangerous from their very gravity, reserve, and silence.

St. Paul was one of the most prominent leaders of this suspected faction, and having a second time fallen into the hands of the Roman authorities, would necessarily undergo the most rigorous severity. He enjoyed, nevertheless, the melancholy pleasure of occasional correspondence with his friends, and thus was enabled to communicate to Timothy the yearning which he, aged, worn,

* Tacitus, "Annales," xv. 44.

and weary, felt for the society of his beloved disciple. He was prepared to die; he felt himself supported by the God in whom he trusted; but before he passed away and was at peace, he would fain see once more his young fellow-worker. This feeling was in his heart when he wrote that deeply pathetic and impressive letter, known as the Second Epistle to Timothy (A.D. 68).

Second Epistle to Timothy.

[For the reader, who doubtlessly accepts this epistle as the authentic work of St. Paul, it will have a peculiar interest as, in all probability, the last letter he wrote. It breathes a remarkable spirit of true affection, and in its noble resignation to the will of God is worthy of the great Apostle of the Gentiles. His confident hope, moreover, that "a crown of righteousness" was laid up for him, is the natural sequence of the firm faith which had supported him in perils by land and perils by sea.

There is something, to us, peculiarly affecting in every line of this tender and earnest letter—penned, as we believe it to have been, while its writer stood within the very shadow of death, and waited for the summons which should lead him to the martyr's grave. Who but St. Paul *could* have written it? Is it not the fitting complement of his Apostolic Epistles—milder and gentler than those in which he lashed the sins of the heathen and the follies of the Judaizers—but not less emphatic in its testimony to the fulness of the love of Christ? As, in the First Epistle to the Thessalonians, we see the Apostle, in his vigorous manhood, bold, resolute, uncompromising, and enthusiastic; here we see him, aged and broken, but not less firm in his hope and faith—milder, less vigorous, more subdued—but still Paul, the saint, the confessor, the Christian warrior, filled with a love and devotedness to his Master which no man has ever equalled.]

1. The salutation (i. 1, 2).
2. He recalls the sacred lineage of Timothy (i. 3–6);

3. And thence exhorts him to steadfastness in the faith as taught by the Apostle (i. 6-15).

4. He refers to certain of the brethren (i. 15-18), and again exhorts his disciple to serve the Lord in all simplicity and truth (ii. 1-17).

5. After a reference to the false teachers, Hymenæus and Philetus (ii. 17, 18), he enlarges upon the truths of the gospel, and describes what a servant of the Lord should be in life and conduct (ii. 19-26).

6. Filled with a spirit of prophecy, he dilates upon the perilous times to come (iii. 1-5);

7. And describes the enemies of the truth who will seek to lead the brethren into temptation (iii. 6-9).

8. After alluding to his own life, he cautions Timotheus against falling into false doctrines, and recommends him to continue his study of the Holy Scriptures, which alone can make him wise unto salvation (iii. 10-15).

9. Commending the Holy Scriptures as given by inspiration of God (iii. 16, 17), he charges Timotheus to preach them "in season and out of season," and though others should go astray, to do his duty with all care and diligence (iv. 1-5).

10. As for himself, his time is come, and he is ready (iv. 6-8).

11. Before his death he longs to see his disciple, especially as Demas has forsaken him; while Crescens is away in Galatia, Tychicus at Ephesus, and Titus in Dalmatia. Only Luke remains with him (iv. 9-12).

12. He gives him directions in reference to his cloak, book, and parchments; cautions him against Alexander the coppersmith; and repeats his expressions of confidence in the Lord (iv. 13-18).

13. The epistle concludes with the usual salutations and benediction (iv. 19-22).

We cannot certainly say whether Timothy was able to obey the summons of the Apostle, but who will not hope that he was by his side in his last sufferings, was present to receive his latest words?

There is every reason to believe that St. Paul's trial followed very quickly upon his imprisonment; and that it was not protracted over many weeks. Its issue, in truth, could not be for a moment doubtful, and it resulted, as St. Paul anticipated, in a sentence of capital punishment. Happily, as a Roman citizen, he could not be subjected to the shameful and terrible death by which so many of his brethren had suffered. His fate was the more merciful one of decapitation. The place where he perished, according to St. Jerome and the general tradition of the Church, lies outside the city walls, on the road to Ostia. It is commemorated by the cenotaph of Caius Cestius, which, rising above the tombs of the Protestant cemetery, remains a monument unconsciously erected by a pagan to the memory of a martyr;—a monument, if any were needed, to the memory of the greatest teacher the Christian Church has seen,—the heart of fire--the fearless, yet tender spirit—the subtle, versatile, and penetrating intellect—the loving, devoted, and enthusiastic soul, —PAUL, THE APOSTLE AND SERVANT OF JESUS CHRIST.

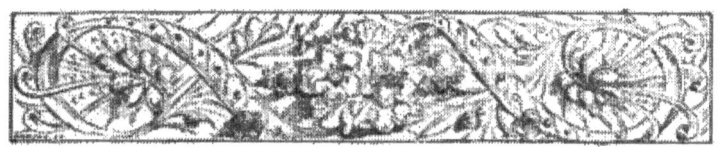

CHAPTER VIII.

THE CHARACTER OF ST. PAUL.

His Earnestness—His Faith—His Tolerant and Charitable Spirit—His Zeal tempered by Prudence—His Contempt of Earth—His Yearning after Heaven.

WHEN we come to consider the character of the great Apostle whose career we have briefly traced in the preceding pages, we see that foremost among the high qualities which distinguished him, and fitted him for the work he had to do, was his earnestness. His was no slothful, apathetic, easy spirit, willing to make the best, if possible, of both worlds. He was a true soldier of the Church militant; and his fervid soul loved the keenness of the fight and the tumult of the fray while fighting under its Master's banner. Reference has been made by more than one commentator to the numerous images which the Apostle in his writings has borrowed from the gladiatorial arena and the battle-field, from military scenes and the warrior's life. The Christian is constantly exhorted to "fight the good fight," to "run the race" set before him, to "put on" the whole armour of God,—the sword of the Spirit, the helmet of salvation, and the shield of faith. · He is to press toward the mark,—the goal, or *meta*, of the arena,—for the prize of the high calling of God in Christ Jesus. It is evident that such illustrations as these came naturally to the Apostle's mind,—that they were in accord with his eager, zealous, impetuous disposition. There was nothing feminine, except his lovingness, in the Apostle of the Gentiles ; he was a man to the heart's core. Like a warhorse, he scented the battle from afar off, and responded gladly to the summons of the trumpet ; that is, if it rang out an inspiring, invigorating strain, strong and strenuous and fervent, and neither trembled nor paused when the eddies of the strife surged up around.

If there be one lesson more than another which we may and should learn from the work and example of the great Missionary-Apostle, it is the value of earnestness. *This* was the secret of his universal success ; at Corinth, at Ephesus, at Antioch, at Rome. *This* it was which carried him triumphant through his perils by land and perils by sea ; which supported him in all his sufferings and all his trials ; which maintained the calmness of his mien when he stood in the regal presence of Agrippa ; which gained him an immediate mastery over the barbarians of Melita ; which drew to his side a host of loving, faithful followers in heathen cities and strange lands. It burns steadfastly in every line of his matchless epistles. And whether he addressed the Jewish Sanhedrim, or the philosophic Athenians, or the Christian Church, *this* it was which exalted and inspired his eloquence, which overcame the defects of his bodily presence.

Holy tenacity of purpose, says Dean Howson,* is what the Christian needs in this human life of cloud and conflict; and of this holy tenacity the Apostle Paul is an eminent example. In all his actions we see very visibly illustrated the most heroic perseverance under discouragement—the steady struggling onward through hours of weakness—the rising above all shocks of doubt and fear—the eye fixed on the coming light in the midst of darkness and perplexity,—the hard work continued notwithstanding opposition, distrust, disappointment, failing health—and all this made harder by the bitter consciousness of sin, and by inward temptations which the Apostle needed all his trust in God to conquer. Such activity, such diligence, such entire abnegation of all social and domestic pleasures, such single-minded devotion to a lofty aim, had never been seen before. They were possible only to a follower of Christ, only to an Apostle, only to St. Paul.†

A French writer very justly and very finely says that, "a model of all Christian virtues, St. Paul possessed them all in a supereminent degree. Their combination formed that grandeur of character which no obstacle could bend, which no persecution could discourage, which counted sufferings and death for nothing."‡ In charging the Apostles with the duties of their high and holy mission, their Divine Master said to them—"Ye are the light of the world......Let your light so shine before men, that they may see your good works, and glorify your

---

* Dean Howson, "The Character of St. Paul," pp. 257, 258.
† Stanley, "On the Epistles to the Corinthians," p. 562.
‡ Vidal, "Saint Paul: sa Vie et ses Œuvres," ii. 397.

Father which is in heaven" (Matt. v. 14, 16). That is, they were not only to lead the Christian Church, but to set before its members the beauty of their example, the pattern of their own pure and blameless lives. In like manner, every Christian, if he lives according to the will and way of Christ, shines, a burning and a shining light, in the world's darkness (Phil. ii. 15). Much more forcibly was this the case with St. Paul. He has been likened to a vase filled with perfume, whose sweet breath purifies the air: he was enriched with graces, and high qualities, and virtues, and rare intellectual gifts, not to concentrate them in himself, but to diffuse their influence all around him. From this precious vessel overflowed truth, the knowledge of divine things, a burning charity, devotion to the Church, self-sacrifice, love of the cross!

There is an eloquent passage in St. Chrysostom which may here be quoted:*— The eye delights in the spectacle of the glorious radiance of the heavens, and though unable to endure its brilliancy, yet its ardent desire to see the intensity of that radiance stimulates it to fix its gaze upon the source whence it proceeds. I am sensible of a similar feeling, says St. Chrysostom, when I contemplate the glory of St. Paul. My eyes are dazzled by it; my soul is overwhelmed by his apostolic grandeur; and yet I long to look upon it. His luminous virtues shine like so many rays of sunlight. I struggle against them in order that I may reach their fountain. I maintain a contest with a splendour I am unable to bear, while I feel myself attracted towards it.

* St. Chrysost., Hom. viii., "In Praise of St. Paul."

The earnestness of which we have spoken suggested the Apostle's activity. He could not rest while there was work to be done; and so long as the heathen world lay in the bondage of darkness, the work was urgent and immense. So he hastened from city to city, from island to island; now at Antioch, now at Ephesus; now at Troas, now at Corinth: to trace his journeys is to trace a line through a very considerable portion of the civilized world. He not only journeyed, but he preached and taught; and not only taught, but wrote. Upon him rested the burden of all the Churches; and yet he undertook, in addition, the task of fixing the dogmas and formulating the theology of the infant Church. Working in the name of his Master, he gave to that Church the direction which it has continued to preserve for eighteen centuries. What a wonderful energy was in the man! What a capacity to labour, and strive, and endure! How great must have been his hopefulness, to have supported him through all his years of toil!

It is astonishing, says Adolphe Monod,* what a man may accomplish,—a single man, alone, almost unaided. The marvellous activity of the Apostle gave him a kind of ubiquitousness throughout the Roman Empire, over the vast extent of which the name of ST. PAUL everywhere projects its mighty shadow. "What are we," exclaims Monod, " the preachers or missionaries of to-day, in the presence of such a man (for he is but a man, a simple man,—truly, it needs an effort not to forget this fact)? Should we not deem his history incredible, if it were related in any but the sacred Scriptures? You

* Adolphe Monod, " Saint Paul: Cinq Discours," pp. 24–27.

can best estimate the prodigiousness of his work by considering the change that would have taken place in the history of the world if St. Paul had not been born. You or we the less in the world, and the effect would scarcely be visible beyond the circle of a few friends, of a very limited public, of, at most, a generation or two. But no St. Paul!—who can calculate the immense results in the maxims, the manners, the literature, the history, the entire development of the human race, beginning with our own ancient Europe, which might apply to itself unreservedly the words written by the Apostle to the Thessalonians:—'What is our hope, or joy, or crown of rejoicing? *Thou*, thou thyself, art our glory and our joy' (1 Thess. ii. 19, 20). No St. Paul!—take care, stand aside, or you will be crushed under the ruins of the social edifice of eighteen centuries, crumbling upon its foundations. No St. Paul!—sweep away all the churches which have sprung up by hundreds in his footsteps; rear again those temples and those idols which he overthrew, not, indeed, with his own hands, for such was not the apostolic manner, but by the virtue of his eloquent speech; crush the life out of those fertile germs of regeneration for the individual, for the family, for society, which he planted from place to place; plunge Europe again, plunge the Roman Empire, into the barbarism of a civilization 'without God and without hope.' ......But, ah, of whom am I speaking? Is it of the Son of God? No; only of His humble messenger; but of a messenger who was inspired by His grace, and who has shown us what can be accomplished, notwithstanding an infirm physical frame and a hesitating tongue, by a man, a simple man, when he wills only what God wills."

Another notable feature in the character of St. Paul was his personal piety, his holiness. He lived only for Christ, and Christ lived in him. He seems to have consecrated all his thoughts, all his feelings, all his aspirations, all his sympathies, all his time, to the service of his Master. He had no ambition beyond *that*. He lived in an age of unrest and action, when genius was not slow in coming to the front; and he possessed powers which might have won him fame as an orator, or distinction as a writer; but the prizes of this world had no attraction for him. He was a Hebrew of the Hebrews, and deeply sensible, we may well believe, of the glories of his race; and with the advantages of his birth and culture, and his natural gifts, he could easily have attained to a position of renown and influence among his people, have been recognized as their leader, and have headed them in a struggle to recover their ancient liberties. But he was something higher than a patriot; he was something more than a Jew. No human passions obtained the mastery over that earnest soul, which was sanctified by an all-absorbing love for the Son of God. The great deep currents of life passed by him unnoticed. He had no thought for the history of his time, —for the emperors, and generals, and statesmen who wielded the destinies of the Roman Empire. He could see nothing but the wickedness of an impenitent world, and the judgment that would surely overtake it. "Of the times and the seasons, brethren," he says, "ye have no need that I write unto you. For yourselves know perfectly that the day of the Lord so cometh as a thief in the night" (1 Thess. v. 1, 2).

So perfect was the sanctity of the great Apostle, that he knew he might justly set himself as an exemplar for all who, like him, accepted the service of the Lord. He speaks of himself as "always bearing about in the body the dying of the Lord Jesus, that the life also of Jesus might be made manifest in our body" (2 Cor. iv. 10). His holiness was from no merit of his own. In one sense, he was the very chief of sinners; but, in another, he was strong in the strength vouchsafed unto him, and therefore was entitled to bid the Christian Church follow in his footsteps, and live according to his example. "I am not a whit behind the very chiefest apostles" (2 Cor. xi. 5), he says; and knowing that this is no empty boast, he can also say: "Brethren, be followers together of me, and mark them which walk, so as ye have us for an ensample" (Phil. iii. 17).

It has been well remarked that the Apostle, in thus placing himself before the Church as a model, was animated by no vulgar pride or sinful egotism. He knew that he was an earthen vessel, but he also knew that the vessel had been set apart for a special purpose. The early Christians, in casting off the fetters of Paganism or Judaism, did not arrive all at once, by a sudden leap, at Christian perfection; they climbed gradually towards that height of holiness which is unattainable by humanity, except when purified and strengthened through Christ. Who, says Vidal, could guide these neophytes in their upward march? Who could support and develop these tender plants? Apart from the teaching of the faith, they needed an accessible model, a living model ever present before their eyes, to the end that they might measure it, imitate it, and reproduce it in their own lives.* Where was this model to be found? Evidently in the Apostle who had brought them to the feet of the Master. In the ordinary course of life, the father gives himself as a pattern to his children. And St. Paul was, if we may use the expression, so perfect an image of Jesus, his Lord, that he could say, without exaggeration: "I live; yet not I, but Jesus Christ lives in me." Well therefore might he propose himself for their imitation; a finished model, he vividly reflected the features of the Saviour, not in all their original splendour, but softened and veiled by the shadow which His humanity projected upon them.† In studying this model, which did not overpass the conditions of human nature, which owed everything to the grace of God and to the influence of the life and teaching of Christ, the Christian became convinced that holiness was not impossible of attainment. Had they said among themselves that St. Paul was a master, and a great master, while they were but humble apprentices, he would have replied that the distance which separated him from them was infinitely less than that which separated him from Jesus Christ, and yet he imitated *Him*, and reproduced Him in his life, so far as was possible to weak humanity: to the divine grandeur of the Master no human creature, indeed, could hope to attain; but they might, it was

---

* Vidal, "Saint Paul: sa Vie et ses Œuvres," ii. 399.
† Ibid., ii. 400, 401.

certain, equal the apostolic copy. Not, in truth, that the Apostle proposes to be always a model: when he spoke to the faithful, to them who were perfect, he preached "not the wisdom of this world, but the wisdom of God in a mystery, even the hidden wisdom, which God ordained before the world unto our glory" (1 Cor. ii. 6, 7); to these he proposed that they should be "followers of God, as dear children" (Eph. v. 1). Before the children of God he effaced himself, and directed their wistful gaze towards their heavenly Father. Far from him the presumption of interposing between God and the creature, like a cloud between earth and the glory of the sun.

St. Paul, moreover, offered himself to the imitation of his brethren from the point of view of the mercy which he had obtained from God. "This is a faithful saying, and worthy of all acceptation, that Christ Jesus came into the world to save sinners; of whom I am chief" (1 Tim. i. 15). Here was a source of consolation for the sufferer; of hope for the depressed; of strength for the feeble. I, Paul, the persecutor, the blasphemer, the chief of sinners; I, who looked on exultant when Stephen fell under the cruel blows of a fanatical multitude; *I* have tasted of the Divine compassion: then why are ye afraid? Those heathens, "suckled in a creed outworn," those Jews, long fettered by the traditions of the Law, who from the depth of corruption and impiety had been received into the holy circle of the Church, so keenly felt the burden of their sins, were so painfully conscious of their imperfections, that they scarcely dared to approach their God. How shall such as we presume to enter the

Holy of Holies? How can we raise our feeble eyes towards the splendour of the Sun of Righteousness? Then the Apostle stepped forward, and encouraged them by his example: "*I* have obtained mercy,"—not to myself alone, but to the end that Christ might first set forth in me the wonderfulness of His patience, the strength and might of His longsuffering, so as to confirm the faith of those who believe in Him, to the end that they may obtain everlasting life. And listening to these words, the sinner took heart of hope, and the weak cast aside their fears.

As St. Augustine remarks: * "If Saul has been saved, why should I despair? If so desperate a disease has been healed by so great a Physician, ought I not to desire that He should lay His hands on my wounds? Ought I not to hasten to humble myself at His feet?......It was that men might speak thus that Saul the persecutor became Paul the Apostle."

Like a skilful painter, remarks Vidal,† St. Paul has traced in himself, with the vivid colouring of his virtues, so perfect an image of the Saviour, that, in this imitation, he has surpassed the saints both of the Old and New Testament. Or, to speak more correctly, it is Jesus Christ who paints Himself in St. Paul; has reflected Himself in him through His divine grace. All men alike possess an organized body and a soul; but all have not, like St. Paul, a will firmly fixed in the love of Jesus Christ,—fixed with such a steadfastness of purpose that

---

* St. Augustine, Sermon ix., "De Verb. Apost."
† The following paragraph is suggested by some remarks of the French historian.

he can defy every creature to tear him from that love! His soul, sunk at first in sin and ignorance, blasphemed its Lord; but as soon as He who orders all things for His glory had renewed in that soul His divine image, immediately the will of St. Paul was bent upon holy living and holy dying, and he could exclaim: "I am persuaded, that neither death, nor life, nor angels, nor principalities, nor powers, nor things present, nor things to come, nor height, nor depth, nor any other creature, shall be able to separate us from the love of God, which is in Christ Jesus our Lord" (Rom. viii. 38, 39).

St. John Chrysostom, in a comparison of St. Paul with other "men of God," shows that he surpassed them all in the grandeur and perfection of his virtues. Abel offered to God "the firstlings of his flock and the fat thereof;" Paul made a daily offering of himself. "For thy sake we are killed all the day long; we are accounted as sheep for the slaughter" (Rom. viii. 36). In speaking to the Corinthian Church of the constant risk of death to which he exposed himself in order to save souls, "I die daily," he writes (1 Cor. xv. 31); "I stand in jeopardy every hour." And not content with the offering of himself, he urges upon his brethren a like self-sacrifice: "I beseech you, by the mercies of God, that ye present your bodies a living sacrifice, holy, acceptable unto God, which is your reasonable service" (Rom. xii. 1). Could he have offered to his Master the whole universe, he would have done so; and in this design he traversed the seas, he travelled through Europe and Asia, the East and the West, everywhere proclaiming the life and death of

Christ, everywhere calling upon men to throw down their sins at the foot of the Cross!

"I feel in my heart a fire and a love for this great Apostle," says St. Chrysostom,* "which I am unable to express. When I contemplate that beautiful soul, I am ravished with ecstasy; the more I reflect upon his rare qualities, the more I am transported out of myself; and I cannot sufficiently admire that a single man should have thus reunited in himself all the virtues of Christendom, and have possessed each in perfection !......I know not if he is a terrestrial angel or a celestial man; but this I know, that he is the Temple of the Holy Ghost, and that Jesus Christ speaks by his mouth. His zeal is incomparable, his charity is infinite, or, rather, he himself is *all* charity; his care for the Church of God surpasses the natural vigilance of the shepherd; his courage approaches heroism; his fervent love for God resembles that of the seraphim."

We turn now to contemplate another side of St. Paul's character,—the loving, tender, sympathetic side. Monod justly remarks that the ideas of grandeur and energy which we are led, by a cursory perusal of the narrative of his career, to associate with the name of the Apostle, may easily induce us to forget another feature of his character revealed by a more careful and attentive study. "By a rare privilege of nature, shall I say? or of grace, St. Paul, uniting the most contrary qualities and tempering strength by meekness, bore one of the most feeling hearts that ever beat under heaven : I say not only a warm heart, but a

---

St. Chrysostom, "Homilies," ii. and xxii.

heart capable of tender attachment and vivid emotion, a heart prone to tears; so that his greatness had nothing haughty in it, his energy nothing repellent."* This beautiful femininity of St. Paul's nature, in which again he resembled Him who wept at the grave of Lazarus, is strikingly illustrated in his address to the elders at Miletus (Acts xx. 19; 31; 36, 37): Ye know, he says, how I have served the Lord with many tears......Remember, that for the space of three years I ceased not to warn you, day and night, with tears......And kneeling down, he prayed with them, and they all wept sorely, for the thought was present both to the Apostle and the brethren that they should see each other no more.

St. Paul's whole ministry, says Dean Howson,† was a ministry of tears. His apostleship and his suffering could not be separated. We see this truth very plainly set forth in the history in the Acts of the Apostles, or in his own short summary in the eleventh chapter of his Second Epistle to the Corinthians. Even at the time of his conversion, Ananias was commanded to speak to him of "the great things he should *suffer* for the name of Christ" (Acts ix. 16). At Miletus we find him looking forward to " bonds and affliction in every city " (Acts xx. 23). But this suffering was not wholly external; its bitterness lay not in chains and captivity, hunger and thirst, perils by sea and perils by land, but in the depth of his passionate desire to see men won to eternal life. He looked out upon a world lying in the darkness of the shadow, and his spirit groaned within him. He wept tears of

* A. Monod, "St. Paul: Cinq Discours," p. 59.
† Dean Howson, "The Character of St. Paul," pp. 73, 74.

solicitude and painful anxiety. Hence Monod is justified in saying that in the Apostle's tears he finds "a complete course of Christian dogma and Christian morality." * Or, better still, you may find in them, Truth instead of Dogma, and instead of Morality, Charity: "Truth, seen so clearly, that it enables him to foretell your future wretchedness if you reject it; Charity, felt so keenly, that he longs for your salvation almost as much as for his own." And so we see that his suffering proceeded in a great measure from the vitality and profundity of his faith. And so intense was his charity, so ample his love, so infinite his tenderness, that he had no peace while men refused to listen to the truths he felt constrained to preach.

It is impossible to read the Epistles of St. Paul without being struck by the breadth of his sympathies and the warmth of his affections. In the midst of all his labours and all his trials, he can think of the humblest member of the Christian household. He is anxious for the temporal and spiritual welfare of his friends. He has a deep, strong love for all the brethren in Christ. He is constantly sending tenderly thoughtful messages to those whom he has known in the course of his journeyings. He seems to forget none. His large heart has ample room for the truest friendship. When he has employed an amanuensis to write one of his pastoral epistles, he cannot refrain from appending a kindly word of greeting "with his own hands." He sends wise messages of counsel and warning: at one time to Archippus (Col. iv. 17), at another to Philemon.

* Monod, "St. Paul," pp. 60, 61.

It is desirable that the reader should dwell, for a moment, on certain defects in the Apostle's character which, but for his holiness and entire devotion to his Master, might possibly have converted him into a weakly sentimentalist: we say possibly, for it is to be remembered that he possessed a strength of will, which might of itself have rescued him from so complete a degradation.

Well, then, we think there is little doubt that the Apostle suffered, as Dean Howson points out, from "depression of spirits;" a depression so marked and so oppressive that it would seem almost to have approached to "melancholia." "In all St. Paul's life there is no more marked indication of a particular state of mind (as there is no stronger and yet more delicate link of unity between the Acts and the Epistles) than the desponding, foreboding state of mind (associated indeed with the utmost tenacity of purpose) which comes to view in the latter part of the Third Missionary Journey. To see this, we have only to read in succession the allusions which occur in the Second Epistle to the Corinthians—and then his earnest request for intercessory prayer at the end of his Epistle to the Romans—then his affecting words at Miletus—and then what took place at Tyre and afterwards at Cæsarea (Rom. xv. 30, 31; Acts xx. 23, 25; xxi. 5, 6, 12, 13) on the way to Jerusalem."

This depression may have arisen to some extent from mental causes or peculiarities of the nervous organization, but we suspect it was closely connected with the Apostle's physical weakness. For that he had no frame of iron, no superabundant muscular energy, is very evident. He did what he did, and endured what he did, through the heroism of his resolution and the intensity of his zeal; he was not supported or assisted by corporal strength; the mind, that "fiery particle," triumphed over the hindrance of the body. We do not mean to represent him as a confirmed invalid—the whole history of his life confutes and renders impossible such a supposition—but we believe that he was liable to frequent and sudden failures of health; and if these occurred at moments when the Apostle most felt the need of energy,—when he was engaged in any great enterprise,—this alone would account for his tendency to self-humiliation and anxious "self-searchings" and "upbraidings."

According to tradition, St. Paul was a man of short stature, with a bald head, full large eyebrows, clear gray eyes, an aquiline nose, and Greek oval face.* Though he was mean and weak in presence, we can well believe that there was a light of intellect on his brow, and a glorious gleam of earnestness in his eyes, which could not fail to impress upon those with whom he came in contact that they had to deal with "a king of men." He is described as being rude and even contemptible in speech; and it is allowable to suppose that some defect of utterance or

* We owe this description of the person of St. Paul to Malela, or John of Antioch, who lived towards the end of the sixth century, and probably wrote from traditions long prevalent in the city where Paul had resided for no inconsiderable period. His exact words are:—Paul was short of stature, bald at the crown, with grayish hair on his head and chin, an aquiline nose and blue eyes, the eyebrows closely knit, the complexion fair and ruddy, a graceful beard, a benignant expression, of sound judgment, and gentle, winning, and courteous address. (Παυλος ετι περιων τη ηλικια κονδοειδης φαλαρκος μιξοπολιος την καραν και το γενειον, ευρινος, υπογλαυκος, συνοφρυς, λευκοχλους, ανθρωποπροσωπος, ευπωγων υπογελωντα εχων τον χαρακτηρα, φρονιμος, ηθικος, ευομιλος, γλυκυς, υπο πνευματος Αγιου ενθουσιαζομενος και ιαμενος.—Chronog. x.)

want of fluency was the "thorn in the flesh" to which he so pathetically alludes.*

* Much discussion has taken place as to the true nature of the "thorn in the flesh" (2 Cor. xii. 1) from which the Apostle suffered; but the best authorities seem agreed that it was an ophthalmic disease. His eyes, says Lewin,*a* were so affected by ophthalmia, a state of constant inflammation, as not only to injure the vision, but also to render him a distressing object to every beholder. In support of this hypothesis, the following passage is quoted from the Epistle to the Galatians:—"Ye know how on account of bodily weakness I preached the gospel unto you the first time, and my temptation which was in my flesh ye despised not, nor spit me out, but received me as if I had been an angel of God, even as Jesus Christ. Where is then the blessedness ye spake of? for I bear ye witness that, had it been possible, *ye would have plucked out your own eyes, and have given them to me*" (iv. 13–15). But the emphatic clauses which we have italicized refer to a popular proverb, and are by no means to be taken as a literal assertion of ocular disease.*b* They do not afford sufficient ground for building a theory upon them. Another passage is quoted from the same epistle:—"Henceforth let no man trouble me, for it is I who bear on my body the marks [τὰ στίγματα] of Jesus;" that is, the scars he had received in the course of his noble testimony to the truth of the gospel, which proved him to be the servant of Christ, even as the brands, or "stigmata," burned into the flesh of slaves, indicated them to be the property of certain masters. We can find in this verse (Gal. vi. 17) no allusion whatever to physical infirmity, nor do we see any in a third passage in the same epistle (vi. 11) which is frequently brought forward:—"See in how large letters [in what large sprawling characters] I write unto you with my own hand." One who wrote so little as did the Apostle,—who was continually preaching and teaching, and engaged in manual labour when not occupied by his apostolic duties,—could scarcely have been an accomplished penman. To sum up: the word "thorn" in 2 Corinthians xii. 7 (σκόλοψ τῇ σαρκί) may also be translated "a stake" or "sharp-pointed staff," and hence cannot be understood as conveying the idea of a prickly pain, such as results from some forms of ophthalmia. Unquestionably it refers to a physical infirmity, but it is at least as probable that this was a nervous affliction, or a bodily malady which put the Apostle to shame in the public presence, as a disease of the eyes, which, however troublesome and injurious, would rather excite compassion than encourage contempt. Disorders in the eyes, says Alford, however sad in their consequences, are not usually of a very painful or distressing nature in themselves. The conclusion at which the unprejudiced critic arrives is, that the *true* nature of the Apostle's "thorn in the flesh" cannot be safely predicated. Enough for us to know that he suffered, and in suffering found strength.

a Lewin, "Life and Epistles of St. Paul," I. 213.
b Jowett, "Epistles of St. Paul," I. 290, *et seq*.

The circumstances to which we have adverted will account for, and excuse, what Dean Howson considers another weakness or defect in the Apostle's character, though, for our own part, we regard it as the fitting complement of his loving and tender nature, his "craving for personal sympathy."

We might gather this, says the Dean,* in the very earliest of his letters, from the tone in which he speaks of being left at Athens "alone," and prays that he may be directed to the Thessalonians so as to "see their face again" (1 Thess. iii. 1; 10, 11). But it is more distinctly visible in the way in which he clings to individuals. It may justly be said of the Apostle, that he never forgot a friend. Friendship seems to have been a necessity to him, the very breath of his life, the very strength of his soul. We know how deep an affection he felt for Titus, and how ill he could bear to be parted from him:—"I had no rest in my spirit," he says, "because I found not Titus my brother" (2 Cor. ii. 14). He grieved at his separation from Onesimus (Philemon 11-14):—"I beseech thee for my son Onesimus, whom I have sent again, but would fain have retained with me." And for the companionship of Timotheus he expresses a deep longing (2 Tim. iv. 9, 10, 21): "Do thy diligence to come unto me...... Do thy diligence to come before winter." These pathetic touches beautifully soften the Apostle's rugged, heroic character, and serve to connect him, as it were, with our common humanity. Sometimes when we look upon him, we see him so transfigured by the splendour of his ardent faith and noble constancy, that we are in danger of elevat-

* Dean Howson, "Character of St. Paul," pp. 99, 100.

ing him upon a pedestal which belongs only to his Master; and we need to be reminded by his occasional weaknesses that, in spite of the grandeur of his mission and the wonderfulness of his work, he was, after all, a man even as we are.

A peculiarity of St. Paul's character, which must not pass unnoticed, springing as it did from his abundant lovingness and Christian generosity, was the extent of his sympathy with others, and his large and liberal consideration for their feelings, opinions, and even prejudices. On this point we cannot do better than quote John Henry Newman :—*

"St. Paul," he says, "was one of those saints who are versed in human knowledge, who are busy in human society, who understand the human heart, who can throw themselves into the minds of other men; and all this in consequence of natural gifts and secular education. While they themselves stand secure in the blessedness of purity and peace, they can follow in imagination the ten thousand aberrations of pride, passion, and remorse. They have the thoughts, feelings, frames of mind, attractions, sympathies, antipathies of other men, so far as these are not sinful: only they have these properties of human nature purified, sanctified, and exalted.

"In St. Paul the fulness of divine gifts does not tend to destroy what is human in him, but to spiritualize and perfect it. The common nature of the whole race of Adam spoke in him, acted in him, with an energetical pressure, with a sort of bodily fulness, always under the

* Dr. Newman, "Sermons on Various Occasions," pp. 106, 108, 109.

sovereign command of divine grace, but losing none of its real freedom and power because of its subordination. And the consequence is that, having the nature of man so strong within him, he is able to enter into human nature, and to sympathize with it, with a gift peculiarly his own."

Again, Dr. Newman very finely says:—

"He who had the constant contemplation of his Lord and Saviour was nevertheless as susceptible of the affections of human nature and the influences of the external world, as if he were a stranger to that contemplation. He who had rest and peace in the love of Christ, was not satisfied without the love of man. He whose supreme reward was the approbation of God, looked out for the approval of his brethren." He loved them not only "for Jesus' sake," to use his own expression, but for their own sake also. He lived in them; he felt with them and for them; he was anxious about them; he gave them help, and in turn he looked for comfort from them. His mind was like some instrument of music, harp or viol, the strings of which vibrate, though untouched, with the notes which other instruments give forth.

We come next to consider another very eminent virtue in the Apostle's character,—his profound and simple *faith*.

"Faith," remarks a French writer, "has a certain divine air, which distinguishes the children of God from the children of this world." This difference manifests itself more particularly in their different works. While the faithful, confident in their inheritance of the promises of Christ, raise their thoughts above things mutable and uncertain to fix them on the hopes of immortality and heavenly bliss, the "children of the world" are given over to worldly desires, worldly pursuits, worldly pleasures, until both mind and heart are utterly steeped in worldliness. They live only in the present; in the future they seem to have no share and no hope. Of what avail is human life, if not elevated and purified by faith? Faith lends strength to the intellect and vigour to the mind. It is the talisman of liberty which frees the soul from its shackles; the eternal lamp which illuminates the darkness of human reason; the anchor to which the wavering mind holds fast when tossed to and fro on the wide sea of speculation. *Without* faith, we can do nothing; *with* faith, we may rise, as on angels' wings, to the very gate of heaven. *Without* faith, we can undertake nothing good or great in the cause of God or man; *with* faith, we can go forth exultant, to battle with oppression and wrong and error. Every difficulty vanishes, every shadow departs, before the warrior who carries on his arm the shield of faith.

There can be no doubt about the earnestness of St. Paul's faith; we recognize it in the definition which shows his sense of its true nature, its real grandeur, its mighty influence. "Faith," he says (Heb. xi. 1, 3), speaking either by himself or through another, "is the substance or foundation of things hoped for; the evidence of things not seen. Through faith we understand that the worlds were framed by the word of God, so that things which are seen were not made of things which do appear." And this faith, by which patriarchs and prophets and martyrs accomplished such great and glorious deeds, comes from on high: Jesus, he says, is "the author and finisher of our faith" (Heb. xii. 2). The Apostle acted what he taught. He ran with patience the race set before him,—through faith. Through faith the drooping hand was raised, and the feeble knee was strengthened. Through faith he served God acceptably, with reverence and godly fear. Through faith he bore the heavy burden of "bonds and imprisonment." His life, it has been well said, was nothing else than his heroic faith transmuted into action. He believed; and as he believed, he lived.*

Not less remarkable than the Apostle's faith was his unfailing charity. His intense love of God was naturally supplemented by his earnest love of man, and his large generosity led him to look compassionately upon the errors and follies of humanity. He never condoned the sin, but he could readily forgive the sinner. With the sufferer his sympathy was active and permanent; his heart overflowed with feelings of pity and tenderness. His, indeed, was the exalted charity which he himself so eloquently praised; the charity that beareth all things,

* "Faith, in its origin, is a ray of the light and wisdom of God, which falls upon the soul imprisoned in the body, and enlightens it upon the true happiness, the mysteries of the spiritual life, and its future destinies. This pouring forth of faith is regarded as an *intellectual* creation. In the first creation, God made man in his own image; in the second, he renews that image in its fairest and holiest proportions. *Sponsabo te mihi in fide.* God allies himself with man through faith: it strengthens the human spirit, which, naturally feeble, vacillates too often between error and truth. Confirmed in the truth, it rises to the knowledge of the divine mysteries, and penetrates into the invisible. A divine and loftier manifestation of reason, it prevails over the natural reason. A submission of the mind and understanding to the will of God, it is the satisfaction of the injuries which Idolatry offers to His Supreme Majesty. Familiar with all mysteries, it enters into the infinite as into its natural sphere; it comprehends, as it were, in its vast bosom the limitless ocean of the divine perfections."—Vidal.

believeth all things, hopeth all things, endureth all things. It was a living and a practical charity; a charity not only of the hand but of the heart; a charity which not only relieved the poor and needy, but put the best interpretation upon motives, and judged its neighbour with a gentle judgment. *All* the virtues were, for the Apostle of the Gentiles, summed up in this one transcendent, comprehensive virtue of Charity. They formed, it has been remarked, a perfect combination of the most precious spices, which, heated by the glow and fervour of charity, diffused abroad a living and healing odour. The charity of St. Paul was no commonplace manifestation of liberality; it went deeper and further; it included the sublimest patience and the loftiest benignity. It suffered long; it did not vaunt itself; it was not easily provoked; it thought no evil. It delighted in taking upon itself the cross that others should have carried:—" I rejoice in my sufferings for you," he writes to the Colossians (i. 24), " and am filling up the deficiencies τὰ [ὑστερήματα] of the afflictions of Christ in my flesh on behalf of his body, which is the church."

When lingering in captivity, depressed by his separation from his friends, and grievously afflicted in mind and body, he neither feels the injury, nor is tormented by the pain; he can think only of the salvation of his brethren.

From this abundance of his love and charity proceeded his great zeal. He was fain that all men should enjoy the blessings which he himself enjoyed, and partake, as he partook, of the mercies of his Lord and Master. He could not rest, day or night, for his ardent desire to make known the truths of the gospel. He says, with touching simplicity: "I will very gladly spend and be spent for you." That his brethren, his kinsmen, might be brought to the foot of the Cross, he was ready to endure unto the end: "I could wish," he writes to the Romans (ix. 3, 4), "that I myself were accursed from Christ for my brethren, my kinsmen according to the flesh." And this Pauline fervour to secure the salvation of souls and the glory of Christ knew no measure of decay. The sacred fire burned incessantly; he was as active at Rome as at Ephesus or Antioch.

"Like a soldier who, assailed by the whole world," says St. Chrysostom,* " in the midst of a host of enemies set in battle array against him, should receive not a single wound, Paul, finding himself alone in the midst of the barbarian and Gentile peoples of all the earth, remained invincible; and, like a spark of fire which falls among withered herbage or dried-up straw, and changes into its nature everything it consumes, so the Apostle, diffusing everywhere the influence of his zeal, kindled in the hearts of all nations the love of truth. He was, as it were, an impetuous torrent, which opened a passage in all directions and overthrew all obstacles. Figure to yourself a vigorous athlete, now contending in the wrestling-match, now in the race, now in the combat; figure to yourself an intrepid soldier, fighting at once upon land and sea, in the open plain and in front of the walled city,—and you will have some idea of St. Paul, plunging simultaneously into every phase of conflict. Weak as

---

* St. Chrysostom, Homilies: "In Praise of St. Paul."

was his body, it strengthened the entire world; and the mere sound of his voice scattered his enemies in flight.

"The trumpets of the Israelites did not overthrow the walls of Jericho with as much swiftness as Paul cast down the strongholds of evil spirits, and subjected to the empire of Truth those who had previously fought under the banner of Falsehood. After having captured and brought together a legion of captives, he armed them and arrayed them as a new body of combatants, with whose help he soon achieved fresh victories. David, by a single blow of a stone, felled Goliath to the ground; but compare this exploit with the exploits of St. Paul, and you will find that David's deed was but the deed of a child, and will recognize between the king and the apostle as great a difference as between a shepherd and the commander of an army. Paul did not discomfit Goliath with a blow of a stone, but with his words alone he put to flight a whole host of devils; he was like a roaring lion, breathing nothing but flames. He opened a way for himself into all parts of the world, and no one could stand before him; he visited sometimes one people, sometimes another. He traversed all regions, swifter than the wind, ruling the earth as if it were but one house or a single vessel; rescuing from the waves those who were on the point of being engulfed, supporting the passengers in their troubles, encouraging the crew, taking up his position at the helm without losing sight of the prow, handling the ropes, unfurling the sails, plying the oars, with eyes fixed upon heaven, discharging the duties both of seaman and pilot, busy at all parts of the ship, enduring all things in order to deliver others from their ills."

Yet this restless, burning zeal was constrained by prudence and directed by tact. St. Paul read the character of men with wonderful sagacity, and according to their character made his approaches. He adapted himself to the nature of his work; was one thing in the presence of Festus, and another in the presence of Felix; dealt differently with the Ephesians and the Corinthians, with the Church in Galatia and the Church at Philippi. His zeal never outran his discretion; his enthusiasm never overpassed the bounds of moderation. He was no heedless fanatic, making light of obstacles, and deluded by ideal projects; in all things he was thoroughly practical, and if he could destroy, he could also build up. There is a rich mine of common sense and worldly prevision in the Pauline epistles, and one acknowledges that the zeal of their writer was that of the wise, thoughtful, foreseeing general, rather than that of the knight-adventurer, who cares more for the display of his own gallantry than the success of his cause.

This attempt at a survey of the principal points of a many-sided character must close with a brief reference to the exceeding humility of the Apostle, which we shall embody in the eloquent language of a French commentator.

Humility, which is pre-eminently the Christian virtue, that penitence of the heart and spirit taught by Jesus Christ, that foundation of the whole spiritual edifice, was a virtue unknown even by name to the heathen philosophers. These were men wise in themselves, and through themselves; rivals of the gods in intellect and wisdom: how then could they understand that virtue which effaces man before God, and renders him so much the stronger as he confesses his weakness and infirmity with the greater sincerity and deeper conviction? That virtue of so rigorous a justice, which renders to God all it has received from Him, and of so surpassing a truthfulness, since without God man is nothing, and can accomplish nothing. Ah, how much it costs human pride to make that avowal! What a struggle before it can obtain the victory over itself! But in St. Paul this virtue was deeply based. A perfect imitator of Jesus Christ, when he speaks of his Lord's lowly-mindedness, he makes of it a picture so vivid, so forcible, that it casts a reflection of its brightness upon his own character and life and teaching. Undoubtedly he followed his Master at a distance, but he followed Him into the depths of His humiliation.

But, by its external forms, humility can lend its mask to hypocrisy, and beguile the eyes of men; how, then, shall we discover the truth? By a self-control which manifests its truthfulness or falseness; this self-control is patience: false humility, or pride disguised by the thin veil of a pretended humility, is necessarily impatient. Contradict it, or refuse to pay it homage, it allows the mask to drop, and abandons itself to a sometimes excessive transport. *True* humility is meek and long-suffering, and bears its neighbour's burden without complaint or denial. Humility and Patience are the daughters of Charity. He who loves God with all his heart suffers all things in order to please Him. To please God, he shrinks not from the severest trial. He submits himself to every cross with no other anxiety than to work out his Master's glory. "I," said St. Paul (1 Cor. xv. 9), "I am the least of the apostles, that am not worthy to be called an apostle, because I persecuted the church of God." "This is a faithful saying, and worthy of all acceptation, that Christ Jesus came into the world to save sinners; of whom I am chief" (1 Tim. i. 15). "I thank Christ Jesus our Lord, who hath enabled me, for that he counted me faithful, putting me into the ministry; who was before a blasphemer, and a persecutor, and injurious; but I obtained mercy, because I did it ignorantly in unbelief" (1 Tim. i. 12, 13). When St. Paul held this language in the face of the Church and the world, he was bending under the weight of the success of his apostolic work; all the faithful admired and exalted him, on account of his great labours and the numerous converts he had added to the Church. The triumphs of his apostolate were unequalled; but the more dazzling the glory of his mission, the more it was calculated to awaken pride, the more keenly did he feel the necessity of taking refuge in humility, and of veiling himself from the eyes even of men, by opposing to it the remembrance of his life before his conversion.*

That other Christian virtue which raises man to a level with the angels, bodily purity, shone brightly in St. Paul, so that one of the fathers might well exclaim: "From his infancy this *spiritual man* worshipped the spirit and subdued the flesh. From the height of his sublime medi-

* Vidal, "St. Paul: sa Vie et ses Œuvres," pp. 424-426.

tations he could not descend to the vulgar pleasures of the world. His heart and soul were so absorbed by his devotion to the Master he loved, that he could give no thought to the meretricious occupations of a luxurious life. He was temperate in all things; pure in all things; and secure from temptation, because he kept the body in subjection."

Such, then, was St. Paul the Apostle; and being such, we can desire no more glorious example of the influence of the religion of Christ in exalting, strengthening, purifying, and inspiring man.

APPENDIX.

I.

Writings Attributed to St. Paul.

GOD, in giving to the Church her great Apostle, willed that he should leave for her edification an admirable exposition of Christian doctrine; a complete arsenal in which the Christian should find all the weapons necessary for repelling the attacks of his enemies, and successfully combating every heresy. In addition to the speeches which St. Luke has recorded in the "Acts of the Apostles," St. Paul has left behind him fourteen wonderful epistles; masterpieces of logic, commentary, exhortation, elucidation, encouragement, argument, impassioned eloquence. To these, in the preceding pages, we have devoted a few elucidatory lines. We have now to speak of certain writings attributed to the Apostle, but not accepted as his by the Church or by scholastic criticism.

Human curiosity, observes Vidal,* insatiable in its nature, always in quest of novelty, is unable to rest satisfied with the realities of life. When it has completely exhausted the earth, it carries its presumptuous investigations towards the unknown. The celestial regions unexplored by men has a peculiarly powerful attraction for it, and there, in truth, it can give free course to the most extravagant

* Vidal, "St. Paul: sa Vie et ses Œuvres," p. 476.

imaginations. Nothing arrests it; fantastic pictures, vain shadows, unreal phantoms,—it feeds upon all; for it is certain to find a considerable number of minds disposed to welcome them. Every century presents the same spectacle of intellectual unrest and feverish mental activity. The Cainites,[*] a sect of heretics who allowed their vagrant curiosity to wander far afield, laid before their adepts a book explaining, as they pretended, the ineffable mysteries seen and heard by St. Paul when he was carried up to "the third heaven." They asserted that the Apostle had written a treatise entitled 'Ἀναβατικόν, or "The Ascension," and declared that in its pages he had interpreted what he himself has spoken of as incommunicable.

The following passage from Epiphanius may interest the reader:—[†] "The Cainites," he says, "invented, under the name of the Apostle Paul, another treatise filled with profound corruption, which the Gnostics made use of; they called it "The Ascension of St. Paul." It was suggested by what the Apostle says in his Second Epistle to the Corinthians (xii. 4, 13),—that he had been carried up to the third heaven, and that he had heard the secret words which it is not permitted to man to reveal. Here, said they, here are those secret words. Now, they taught all these things, and others like them, to the end that the ill might be honoured and the good repudiated. For they think that the virtue (or 'principle') of Cain was very strong, and that of Abel very weak. And they affirm that these virtues, being united in Eve, she gave birth to both of them. The one was Abel, and the other Cain. Nay, more, Adam and Eve derived their origin from these same virtues or angels. The children which they afterwards brought into the world, namely, Cain and Abel, fell into variance; and he who had been engendered by the stronger virtue slew the child of the weaker and inferior virtue."[*]

In this way the Cainite heresy proposed to unveil ineffable mysteries, and to initiate its disciples into secrets hidden from all the rest of the world. But it is just this pretension to make known the unknown, and to reveal the invisible, which has ever had a charm for credulous curiosity. And in vain was the apostolic warning

---

[*] This sect arose about A.D. 130.
[†] Epiphanius, Hæres. xxxviii. 1.

against all such fictitious revelations,—against all who pretended to be the depositaries of supernatural knowledge. Men willingly became the dupes of their own vague aspirations after the powers and influences of the unseen world.

St. Augustine sternly refutes the wild fancies and empty promises of the leaders of the Cainite sect:—*

Certain would-be spiritualists, he says, have arrived at a knowledge of things of which it is not permitted that man should speak. They have fabricated the Apocalypse of St. Paul, which the Church rejects,—a book filled with innumerable fables. They assert that it is the revelation of his reception to the third heaven, and of the secret words which man is forbidden to utter. The audacity of these men would have been more tolerable had the Apostle said he understood the things which it is not lawful to make known to men; but having said, "Of which it is not permitted man to speak," who then are those who dare impudently and unhappily to discuss them?

Towards the end of the fourth century another "Apocalypse" of St. Paul, apparently written by the same shameless fabricator, got abroad. It was unknown to the ancient fathers of the Church, though it gained some repute among certain credulous and ignorant monks. It was discovered, so ran the story, in the time of the Emperor Theodosius, through a divine revelation, in the house formerly occupied by St. Paul, at Tarsus in Cilicia; the precious manuscript was inclosed in a marble coffer, buried underground. Sozomen, after relating these details, adds:—"When I made inquiries about the incident, a Cilician priest attached to the Church of Tarsus told me it was utterly false. His gray hairs bore witness to his advanced age. He said that nothing of the kind had ever been found at Tarsus, and he suspected that the story had been invented by heretics."†

We learn that Theophylactus, in his "Commentary on the Epistle to the Corinthians," alludes to the "Apocalypse" of St. Paul as apocryphal. Mark, the Alexandrian patriarch, who lived early in

---

* St. Augustine, Tract xcviii. In Joannem.
† Sozomen, "Hist. Eccles.," lib. vii., c. 19.

the third century, mentions the "Visions of St. Paul" as a book popular in Egypt, and inquires of Theodore Balzamon whether it is lawful to read it. The latter replied that Christians must mistrust all writings forged by heretics, however respectable the names attributed to them by the forgers. Though labelled "honey," they are more bitter than wormwood.

Nicephorus Homologetes, or "the Confessor," who lived in the third century, classes the "Apocalypse" of St. Paul with the books of Esdras and Zozimus, and various supposititious "Acta Martyrorum," among the books which Christians are to reject as not authentic.

Assemanni, in the *Bibliothèque Orientale*, refers to an Arabic manuscript in the Vatican library, which contains an Apocalypse ascribed to St. Paul. Theodores, the grammarian, a Greek author, attributes it to the heresiarch Paul of Samosata.

With this "Apocalypse" of St. Paul the reader must not confound a work composed in the Middle Ages, which narrates the descent of St. Paul into Hades and Purgatory, whither he is conducted by St. Michael. It is probable that this Provençal romance was known to Dante.* It was written by the troubadour Adam de Roi.

* We may here bring together the passages in the "Divina Commedia" in which Dante refers to St. Paul. In Canto ii. of the "Inferno" he alludes to his vision of the third heaven :—

"In after-times
The chosen vessel also travelled there,
To bring us back assurance in that faith
Which is the entrance to Salvation's way."

In Canto xxix. of the "Purgatorio" the poet describes him as

"Bearing a sword, whose glitterance and keen edge,
E'en as I viewed it with the flood between,
Appalled me."

The sword is the emblem of St. Paul, in allusion, probably, to the keenness of his style.

In Canto xxi. of the "Paradiso" we read :—

"Cephas came:
He came who was the Holy Spirit's vessel,
Barefoot and lean."

In Canto xxviii. he represents Dionysius the Areopagite as having learned

Predicationis Sancti Pauli.—This production would seem to have been known at a very early period in the history of the Church, and it is quoted by St. Clement of Alexandria. It is mentioned also in a treatise on "the Non-renewal of the Baptism of Heretics," discovered by Sirmond among the manuscripts of the Church of St. Reney at Rheims. Cave, in his "Literary History of Ecclesiastical Writers," speaks of a manuscript of the Vatican as pointing to the African monk Ursinus, who lived in the fifth century, as the author of this work. Some authorities attribute it to the disciples of Simon Magus.

what he professed to know about the angelic hierarchy from St. Paul's "Apocalypse."

"He had learned
Both this and much besides of these our orbs,
From an eye-witness to heaven's mysteries."

This Dionysius was the Athenian convert of St. Paul, to whom reference is made in Acts xvii. 34:—"Howbeit, certain men clave unto him, and believed; among the which was Dionysius the Areopagite." Dante places him among the theologians in the Heaven of the Sun. (Canto x. 115):—

"Near by behold the lustre of that taper,
Which in the flesh below looked most within
The angelic nature and its ministry."

The book, *De Hierarchia Cœlesti*, in which he was supposed to have recorded the knowledge gained from St. Paul, does not appear to have been known until the sixth century.

"The author of this and other extraordinary treatises," says Dean Milman,[*] "which, from their obscure and doubtful parentage, now perhaps hardly maintain their fame for imaginative richness, for the occasional beauty of their language, and their deep piety,—those treatises which, widely popular in the West, almost created the angel-worship of the popular creed, and were also the parents of Mystic Theology and of the higher Scholasticism,—this poet-theologian was a Greek. The writings which bear the venerable name of Dionysius the Areopagite, the proselyte of St. Paul, first appear under a suspicious and suspected form, as authorities cited by the heterodox Severians in a conference at Constantinople. The orthodox stood aghast; how was it that writings of the holy convert of St. Paul had never been heard of before? that Cyril of Alexandria, that Athanasius himself, were ignorant of their existence? But these writings were in themselves of too great power, too captivating, too congenial to the monastic mind, not to find bold defenders. Bearing this venerable name in their

[*] Dean Milman, "History of Latin Christianity," viii. 189, 190.

The Manichæans composed the "Acts" of St. Peter and St. Paul, and a similar enterprise was undertaken by the Ebionites.*

The Priscillianists, a sect founded about A.D. 380 by a noble Spaniard, named Priscillian, compiled a book which they called "Memoirs of the Apostles," containing numerous details relative to the life of St. Paul. It included an *Itinerarium*, or journal of the travels of this saint and of the other apostles. Nor is St. Paul forgotten in the "Apostolic History" of Abdias.

The majority of these books are lost, having perished with the sects who invented and propagated them. But for the references and quotations occurring in the ecclesiastical writers, they would be wholly unknown.

Some of the early Christian authorities praise the "Acts," or Περίοδοι, of Paul and Thekla, which are founded on a legend of the conversion of the latter at Iconium.† According to Tertullian, they were fabricated by a priest in Asia, who was justly punished for the attempted imposition by degradation from the ministry.

The ancients set a considerable value on the reputed letters from Seneca to St Paul and from St. Paul to Seneca. It is almost unnecessary to say that they are wholly apocryphal. Their sole foundation is the fact that the Apostle was the contemporary of the Philosopher, and that the former lay "in bonds" in Rome when

front, and leaving behind them in the East, if at first a doubtful, a growing faith in their authenticity, they appeared in the West as a precious gift from the Byzantine Emperor to the Emperor Louis the Pious. France in that age was not likely to throw cold and jealous doubts on writings which bore the hallowed name of that great saint, whom she had already boasted to have left his primal bishopric of Albino to convert her forefathers, whom Paris already held to be her tutelar patron, the rich and powerful Abbey of St. Denys to be her founder. There was living in the West, by happy coincidence, the one man who at that period, by his knowledge of Greek, by the congenial speculativeness of his mind, by the vigour and richness of his imagination, was qualified to translate into Latin the mysterious doctrines of the Areopagite, both as to the angelic world and the subtile theology. John Erigena hastened to make known in the West the 'Celestial Hierarchy,' the treatise 'on the Name of God,' and the brief chapters on the 'Mystic Philosophy.'"

* Epiphanius, "Adversus Hæresios," 47.
† See *ante*, pp. 56, 57.

the latter was a favourite guest at the palace of the Roman Emperor. It is very improbable that Seneca was one of the readers or the hearers of St. Paul, though he may have learned something of the "new doctrines" taught by the Christians. Seneca, says Dr. Farrar,* would have stood aghast at the very notion of his receiving the lessons, still more of his adopting the religion, of a poor, accused, and wandering Jew. The haughty, wealthy, eloquent, prosperous, powerful philosopher would have smiled at the notion that any future ages would suspect him of borrowing any of his polished and epigrammatic lessons of philosophic morals or religion from one whom, if he heard of him, he would have regarded as a poor wretch, half fanatic and half barbarian.

The sect of the Paulicianists, founded by an Armenian named Constantine about A.D. 660, accepted as authentic an "Epistle to the Laodiceans," attributed to St. Paul. The internal evidence of style and thought shows, however, that it was never written by the Apostle. The forgery was undoubtedly suggested by Colossians iv. 16—"And when this epistle is read among you, cause it to be read also in the Church of the Laodiceans, and do ye likewise read the letter *to* † the Laodiceans." Of this epistle no satisfactory account can be given. Wieseler's theory,‡ that it was identical with what we now call the "Epistle to Philemon" is not accepted by our most trustworthy Biblical critics. Nor does there seem any foundation for the suggestion of Paley and Ussher, that the Letter to the Ephesians was a circular letter addressed to Laodicea and other Churches, as well as to Ephesus. At all events, the so-called *Epistola ad Laodicenses* is a forgery, and a very bad one. It now exists only in Latin MSS., and its contents are awkwardly compiled from the Epistles to the Ephesians and Galatians.§

There is no reason to believe that the Apostle ever visited Laodicea.

---

* Dr. Farrar, "Seekers after God," pp. 170, 171.

† In the English version, "from." But such is not the exact meaning of the Greek, Τὴν ἐκ Λαοδικείας. See Alford (iii. 246), and others,—especially Meyer.

‡ Wieseler, "Apostel. Zeitalter," p. 450.

§ Jones, "On the Canon," ii. 35, *et. sqq.*

II.

Chronology of the Life of St. Paul.

[From Vidal, ii. 485, 486.]

A.D.
34. Martyrdom of Stephen.
35. Conversion of St. Paul.—Damascus.

> [Death of Tiberius, after a reign of twenty-two years, seven months, seven days. He is succeeded by Caius Caligula.]

36. The Apostle withdraws to Arabia.
37. His return to Damascus.

> [Embassy of the Jews to Caligula.]

38. His first journey to Jerusalem.—Retires to Tarsus.
39. Preaches in Syria and Cilicia.
40. Continues his labours as a preacher.

> [Caligula is slain by Chaereas, after a reign of three years, ten months, eight days. Succeeded by Claudius.]

41. Barnabas seeks St. Paul at Tarsus, and conducts him to Antioch.
42. St. Peter at Rome. (?)
43. The faithful at Antioch assume the name of "Christians."
44. Second journey of St. Paul to Jerusalem.—He is accompanied by Barnabas.
45. Return to Antioch: his vision, his ordination, his First Apostolic or Missionary Journey with Barnabas.—Visits Cyprus.
46. Visits Pamphylia, Antioch in Pisidia, Iconium, Lycaonia, Lystra: the heathens take Paul and Barnabas for gods.—Derbe.—Returns to Antioch, through Pisidia, Pamphylia, Attaleia.—The Apostle makes known to the believers that God has opened to the Gentiles "the door of the faith."
47. The Church at Antioch is disturbed by Judaizers.—St. Paul and Barnabas are deputed to go to Jerusalem.—Council of Jerusalem; its decree.—The Apostle returns to Antioch.
48. Second Missionary Journey of St. Paul, with Silas.—He traverses Syria and Cilicia.—Barnabas returns to Cyprus with St.

Mark.—St. Paul visits Derbe, Lystra, where he takes Timothy as a co-operator.—He traverses Phrygia and Galatia, leaves Mysia and Bithynia, and comes to Troas.—In the last-named town he is joined by St. Luke.—The angel of Macedonia appears to him, and implores his assistance.—He embarks for that country.—At Philippi he converts Lydia, and cures a man possessed with an evil spirit.—After being scourged, he is cast into prison.—He converts the jailer, and baptizes him and his family.

49. St. Paul goes to Thessalonica by way of Amphipolis and Apollonia.—Persecuted by the Jews, he takes refuge at Berœa.

50. He quits Berœa as a fugitive, and repairs to Athens.—He disputes in the Agora with the philosophers.—His speech at the Areopagus.

[Death of Herod-Agrippa I. Agrippa II. king of Chalcis.]

51. From Athens he goes to Corinth, where he meets with Aquila and Priscilla.

52. His preaching.—Crispus converted; Gallio and Sosthenes.

[In connection with a religious commotion occasioned, as Tacitus tells us, by the followers of *Chrestus*, Claudius expels the Jews from Rome, and, with them, the Christians.]

53. St. Paul writes from Corinth his *First Epistle to the Thessalonians*, and soon afterwards his *Second*.—Departure from Corinth.—He embarks at the port of Cenchræa, and visits Ephesus.—From that town he repairs to Antioch, and afterwards to Cæsarea.—His Fourth Journey to Jerusalem.

[Felix, procurator of Judæa.]

54. Afterwards he traverses Galatia and Phrygia. — Apollos preaches at Ephesus.—Instructed by Aquila and Priscilla, the great missionary goes to Corinth.—Return of St. Paul to Ephesus.

[Claudius dies of poison, after a reign of thirteen years, eight months, and twenty days. Nero succeeds him.]

55. Children of Sceva, magicians.

56. St. Paul writes his *Epistle to the Galatians* and *First Epistle to the Corinthians.*—Popular outbreak caused by the silversmith Demetrius and his workmen.

57. He visits Macedonia.—From Philippi he writes his *Second Epistle to the Corinthians.*

58. He visits Corinth.—Writes his *Epistle to the Romans.* After collecting the alms of the faithful, he quits that province and arrives at Troas. He preaches at nightfall, and resuscitates Eutychus. He goes to Assos, then to Mytilene; finally to Miletus, where he assembles the presbyters and elders of Ephesus, and addresses to them a pathetic discourse.—Visits Coos, Rhodes, Tyre, Ptolemais, Cæsarea.—Fifth Journey to Jerusalem. His arrest in the Temple. Lysias transfers him to Cæsarea. Is brought before Felix.—Festus succeeds Felix. St. Paul speaks in the presence of Agrippa and Bernice. His appeal to Cæsar. He embarks for Italy.—Tempest; shipwreck on the island of Melita.

59. Leaves Melita.—Visits Syracuse, Reggio, Pozzuoli.—Arrives at Rome.

60. In his "hired house" he teaches all who come to him.

61. Makes several converts in the household of Cæsar. Writes his *Epistles to Philemon, the Colossians,* and *the Philippians.* His release. Writes (?) the *Epistle to the Hebrews.*

62. Visits Crete and Judæa.

63. Asia and Macedonia.—Writes his *First Epistle to Timothy* and *Epistle to Titus.*

64. His journey to Spain.

65. His return to Rome. Is cast into the Mamertine Prison. Makes various converts. Writes his *Epistle to the Ephesians* and his *Second Epistle to Timothy.*

66. Martyrdom of St. Paul.

III.

The Creed of St. Paul.*

1. That Jesus Christ was the Son of God.
   [Heb. i. 2, 5; Gal. iv. 4; Heb. v. 5.]

* Lewin, "Life and Epistles of St. Paul," ii. 1008-1010.

2. That He was made much better than the angels, and that by Him all things were made.

[Heb. i. 3, 4; Col. i. 16; Eph. iii. 9.]

3. That He was God blessed for ever.

[Rom. ix. 5; 1 Tim. iii. 16; Phil. ii. 6; Col. i. 15; 2 Cor. iv. 4.]

4. That "being in the form of God, and thinking it not robbery to be equal with God, yet He made Himself of no reputation," and came into the world to save sinners.

[Phil. ii. 6; 1 Tim. i. 15.]

5. That He took our nature upon Him, and became man.

[Rom. v. 15, 19; 1 Tim. ii. 5.]

6. That He was born of the seed of Abraham, after the flesh.

[Heb. ii. 16.]

7. That He was of the tribe of Judah, and of the family of David.

[Heb. vii. 14; Rom. i. 3.]

8. That He went about preaching the tidings of salvation, which were confirmed by His apostles with signs, and wonders, and divers miracles.

[Heb. ii. 3.]

9. That He chose twelve apostles, among whom were Peter and James and John, and some of His own brethren.

[1 Cor. xv. 19; ix. 5; Gal. i. 18, 19; ii. 9, 11, 12, 14.]

10. That He glorified not Himself, but was glorified by the Father.

[Heb. v. 5.]

11. That His life was one of sorrow and suffering.

[Heb. v. 8.]

12. That at last He was betrayed.

[Rom. iv. 25.]

13. That on the night of His betrayal He instituted the Eucharist.

[1 Cor. xi. 23–26.]

14. That His death was a crime committed by the Jews, and more particularly by their rulers.

1 Thess. ii. 15; 1 Cor. ii. 8.]

15. That before Pontius Pilate He bore testimony to the truth of His teaching.

[1 Tim. vi. 13.]

16. That in order to accomplish the salvation of man, and as a ransom for the sins of the world, He suffered death upon the cross.
>[Gal. iii. 13; Col. i. 14; Titus ii. 14; Heb. v. 9; Eph. v. 2; and in many other places.]

17. That His crucifixion took place outside the gates of Jerusalem.
>[Heb. xiii. 12.]

18. That He was buried.
>[1 Cor. xv. 4.]

19. And on the third day rose again from the dead.
>[1 Cor. xv. 4; 1 Thess. i. 10; 1 Thess. iv. 14.]

20. That He was then seen by Peter.
>[1 Cor. xv. 4.]

21. Afterwards by the Twelve Apostles.
>[1 Cor. xv. 5.]

22. Then by above five hundred brethren at once.
>[1 Cor. xv. 6.]

23. Then by James.
>[1 Cor. xv. 7.]

24. That He ascended into heaven.
>[Eph. iv. 8; 1 Tim. iii. 16; Heb. iv. 14; vi. 20; ix. 24.]

25. That He revealed Himself to St. Paul.

26. That to His disciples He communicated the gift of the Holy Spirit.
>[Rom. v. 5; 1 Cor. ii. 13; 1 Cor. xiv.; 2 Cor. v. 5; Eph. iv. 8; Titus iii. 6.]

27. That He sits at the right hand of God.
>[Rom. viii. 34; Eph. i. 20; Col. iii. 1; Heb. i. 3; viii. 1; x. 12.]

28. That in heaven He acts as our High Priest and Intercessor.
>[Rom. viii. 34; Heb. ii. 17; iii. 1; v. 10; ix. 24.]

29. That He is the Head of the Church.
>[Eph. v. 23.]

30. That in Him we are saved by grace through faith.
>[Eph. ii. 8.]

31. That all believers in Christ are united in one body.
>[1 Cor. x. 17; xii. 25.]

32. That Christ will appear again.
> [1 Cor. iv. 5; Col. iii. 4; 1 Thess. iv. 15; 2 Thess. ii. 1.]

33. And that He cometh to judge the quick and the dead.
> [Rom. xiv. 10; 2 Cor. v. 10; 2 Tim. iv. 1.]

34. And that eternal happiness is reserved for the children of God.
> [1 Cor. ii. 9; and elsewhere.]

Such are the leading truths set forth by the Apostle in his teaching; it was for the advocacy of these he lived, and it was in defence of these he died (1 Cor. iv. 9–13).

IV.

Authorities.

[The following list does not profess to enumerate *all* the writers whom we have consulted in the preparation of the foregoing pages, or *all* the authorities of credit and character who have discussed the various questions connected with the Life and Work of St. Paul. But it may be useful to the young student, as indicating the direction in which he should prosecute his inquiries, and naming the principal books it is important he should not neglect.]

Alford, Dean, *The Greek Testament, with a Critical and Exegetical Commentary*, 4 vols. (ed. 1871).

Arnold, Matthew, *St. Paul and Protestantism* (ed. 1870).

Baur, *Paulus der Apostel Jesu Christi* (ed. Stuttgart, 1845).

Besser, *Paulus* (English edition, 1865).

Bungener, *Saint Paul: sa Vie, son Œuvre, et ses Epîtres* (ed. 1867; English edition, 1870).

Conybeare, Dr., and Dean Howson, *Life and Travels of St. Paul* (ed. 1852 and 1870).

Cotterill, H., Bishop of Edinburgh, *The Genesis of the Church* (ed. 1871).

Davidson, Dr., *Introduction to the New Testament* (ed. 1868).

Davies, Rev. J. L., M.A., art. "Paul" in Dr. Smith's *Dictionary of the Bible* (ed. 1863).

Ellicott, Dr., Bishop of Gloucester and Bristol, *Commentaries on*

St. Paul's Epistle to the Ephesians (ed. 1864); *the Philippians and Colossians* (ed. 1865); *the Thessalonians* (ed. 1866); *and the Galatians* (ed. 1867).

Ewald, G. H. von, *Sendschreiben des Apostels Paulus* (v. y.).
Farrar, Dr., *Seekers after God* (ed. "Sunday Library," n. d.).
Howson, Dean, *Character of St. Paul* (ed. 1873).
Jowett, Professor, *Commentary on the Epistles of St. Paul to the Thessalonians, Galatians, and Romans* (ed. 1855).
Leathes, Professor Stanley, *Witness of St. Paul to Christ* (edit. "Boyle Lectures" for 1870).
Lewin, T., *Life and Writings of St. Paul*.
Lightfoot, Professor, *Commentary on the Galatians* (ed. 1869), and *Commentary on the Philippians* (ed. 1870).
Lyttleton, Lord, *Conversion of St. Paul* (edit. by Professor Rogers, 1868).
Macduff, Dr., *Footsteps of St. Paul*.
Merivale, Dean, *Conversion of the Roman Empire* (ed. 1865).
Meyer, *Critical and Exegetical Commentary on the New Testament* (an English translation is in course of publication by Messrs. Clark of Edinburgh, 1873–4).
Milman, Dean, *History of Christianity* (ed. 1867).
Monod, Adolphe, *Saint Paul: Cinq Discours* (ed. 1859).
Neander, J. A. W., *Pflanzung und Leitung der Christlichen Kirche durch die Apostel* (ed. 1842)
Newman, Dr. J. H., *Sermons on Various Occasions* (ed. 1837).
Paley, Dr., *Horæ Paulinæ* (edit. by Professor Birks, with appendix by the latter, entitled "Horæ Apostolicæ," 1870).
Pressensé, E. de, *Discours Religieux* (ed. 1859).
Robertson, F. W., *Expository Lectures on St. Paul's Epistles to the Corinthians* (new ed., 1868).
Smith, James, *Voyage and Shipwreck of St. Paul* (ed. 1866).
Stanley, Dean, *Epistles of St. Paul to the Corinthians* (ed. 1865).
Stier, *Reden der Apostel* ("Words of the Apostles," English translation, by Venables, ed. 1869).
Tate, *Continuous History of St. Paul* (n. d.).
Vaughan, Dr., *The Church in the First Days*, 1st, 2nd, and 3rd series (ed. 1865); *Sermons on St. Paul's Epistle to the Romans*

(ed. 1870); *Sermons on St. Paul's Epistle to the Philippians* (ed. 1872).

Vidal, M., *St. Paul: sa Vie et ses Œuvres* (ed. 1863).

Westcott, B. F., *History of the Canon of the New Testament* (ed. 1870).

De Wette, *Einleitung; and Exegetisches Handbuch.*

Whately, Archbishop, *Lectures on the Character of Our Lord's Apostles* (ed. 1850).

Wieseler, *Chronologie des Apostolichen Zeitalters* (ed. 1848).

Wordsworth, Chas., Bishop of St. Andrews, *Outlines of the Christian Ministry* (ed. 1872).

Wordsworth, Chris., Bishop of Lincoln, *Commentary on the New Testament* (v. y.).

www.ingramcontent.com/pod-product-compliance
Lightning Source LLC
Chambersburg PA
CBHW030731230426
43667CB00007B/667